THE CROWNED HART

CONTEMPORARY IRISH STUDIES

Series Editor Peter Shirlow
School of Environmental Studies, University of Ulster, Coleraine

THE CROWNED HARP
Policing Northern Ireland

Graham Ellison and Jim Smyth

Pluto Press

LONDON • STERLING, VIRGINIA

First published 2000 by Pluto Press
345 Archway Road, London N6 5AA
and 22883 Quicksilver Drive, Sterling, VA 20166-2012, USA

British Library Cataloguing in Publication Data
A catalogue record for this book is available from the British Library

ISBN 0 7453 1398 1 hbk

Library of Congress Cataloging-in-Publication Data
Ellison, Graham.
    The crowned harp : policing Northern Ireland / Graham Ellison
    and Jim Smyth.
        p. cm. — (Contemporary Irish studies)
    Includes bibliographical references and index.
ISBN 0–7453–1398–1 (hbk)
    1. Royal Ulster Constabulary. 2. Police—Northern Ireland.
I. Smyth, Jim. II. Title. III. Series.
HV8197.5.A2 E55 2000
363.2'09416—dc21   99–089714
                                                                  CIP

Designed and produced for Pluto Press by
Chase Production Services, Chadlington, OX7 3LN
Typeset from disk by Marina Typesetting, Minsk, Belarus
Printed in the European Union by TJ International, Padstow

For our parents

Contents

Preface

This book was written at a time when the immobility of politics in Northern Ireland seemed to be shifting in reaction to both internal and external pressures. For many participants and commentators, the political negotiations were about building trust between the parties involved and understanding the fears, concerns and aspirations of the other. While the two communities have constructed, over the years, a pragmatic system for dealing with everyday social intercourse, this same *modus vivendi* was based upon a pact of silence as far as cultural, national and political issues were concerned. The failure to address the roots of division between the two communities was constitutive of the nature of state and society in Northern Ireland. Thirty years of internal war intensified already deeply etched fissures and suspicions – those institutions and agencies designed to manage the conflict reinforced and 'normalised' the idea that the conflict could be simply reduced to one of defeating terrorism.

The focus of this book is one such institution: the Royal Ulster Constabulary (RUC). The policing of Ireland has been a preoccupation of the British state since the beginning of the nineteenth century and the methods, organisation and practice of policing reflect and refract the changing focus of policy towards Ireland. The RUC has been the main agent of state control since the establishment of Northern Ireland in 1922 and is seen by many Protestants as an essential bulwark against the threat posed by Irish nationalism. To understand the central importance of the RUC, one must confront both the particular nature of policing in Ireland and the way in which the police embodied the fears and aspirations of Protestants as well as confirming the worst suspicions of Catholics. Irish society has always been divided on ethnic lines and division has historically coalesced around questions of identity and nationality. The traditional role of the police in Ireland, embracing the country as a whole from the early nineteenth century until Partition and then the new state of Northern Ireland, has been to police division and enforce the domination of one ethnic group over another. This book attempts to trace the central role of policing as a means of social control and the policing of division. We do not see Northern Ireland as a unique society but one which, with all its historical and social idiosyncrasies, exemplifies the problems facing societies which are, apart from the perennial problems of class differences, also divided on lines of culture, ethnicity and nationality. Our approach combines a number of methodologies, as we are convinced that no single approach can appreciate the complexities of a divided society. The social sciences are particularly susceptible to theoretical tunnel vision and we have tried to avoid this by a theoretical and methodological pluralism that hopefully does not come to grief on the reefs of eclecticism.

There is no such thing as a neutral book on Northern Ireland. Whether overtly or covertly, a position must be taken on the central constitutional and national questions that embody division. While we reject the notion that Northern Ireland, prior to the outbreak of serious unrest in 1969, was a 'normal' society in any sense of the word, particular criticism must be directed at the policies of successive British administrations since 1969. By presenting the problem as law and order, the British state deployed vast resources to convince the world that the problem was simply a security one and cynically invoked paranoid fears of a global terrorist threat. The militarisation of the conflict invoked a scenario where victory for one party could only mean total defeat for the other. In particular, the use of the RUC as the frontline force against republicanism deepened division. Thirty years of direct British involvement in Northern Ireland are an object lesson in how *not* to deal with the problems of a divided society and we hope lessons can be learned that will be of use elsewhere.

Our sources for this book have been eclectic and manifold. We have made extensive use of historical sources and have, when such sources have been found wanting, carried out our own research. Graham Ellison's interviews with serving and retired police officers give an unrivalled insight into the mindset of RUC officers and this research is deployed throughout the book. While we have not had any special access to official sources or documents, conversations with serving and former members of the security forces sometimes pointed us in interesting directions. The same is true of contacts and conversations with members of loyalist and republican organisations. Both authors come from a social science background but whether this was a hindrance or a help we will leave the reader to decide.

Without the many people who talked to us this book would never have seen the light of day. Some, such as members and ex-members of the RUC and USC, republicans and loyalists have strongly held opinions on policing. Listening to many ordinary people, some unwittingly caught up in the maelstrom of violence, confronted us with some of the human tragedies of the last thirty years. Most would not wish to be named but we are grateful to them all. Ciaran Acton, Aogan Mulcahy and Mike Brogden read parts of the work in progress. Graham Ellison would like to thank Tony Jefferson and his colleagues at Keele University for their help and support. The staffs of the National Library in Dublin, the Linenhall Library and the Central Library in Belfast were generous with their time and assistance.

We apologise to all those who suffered from our bouts of ill humour during the book's production.

Introduction

The idea that the conflict in Northern Ireland is an atavistic throwback to the religious wars of the seventeenth century no longer dominates interpretations of the problem. From being viewed as an anachronistic society out of step with the rest of Europe, Northern Ireland is increasingly attracting attention as an example of a conflict situation in which culture and ethnicity play a significant role. Dealing with the question of cultural and ethnic diversity is becoming a global problem and one that is increasingly preoccupying the countries of the European Community. The murderous conflict in the former Yugoslavia and the ongoing war in Chechnya have global implications and consequences. The flow of refugees and displaced populations lapping at the door of Fortress Europe, is adding new ethnic groups to those, like the Turks and North Africans, who helped reconstruct the continent after the Second World War.

Much has changed since the conflict in Northern Ireland ignited over thirty years ago. The empires of the nineteenth century have finally departed the stage of history and globalisation has eroded the economic, cultural and political power of nation states. The collapse of old certainties has fuelled the rise of right-wing political parties in many European countries and this virulent and unfortunate trend has latterly spread to Austria, Switzerland and Sweden. Set against these developments is an increasing emphasis on diversity, minority rights and the implementation of human rights legislation and a recognition that the traditional homogeneity of the nation state is no longer viable. If there is one lesson to be learned from the conflict in Northern Ireland, it is that the suppression of identity and the denial of rights to minorities is not a solution. A more complex lesson is that minorities must also respect the rights of majorities and not turn themselves into mirror images of their putative oppressors.

Successive British administrations, often held in thrall to Unionism, have obstinately confused consequence with cause, and dismissed legitimate demands and aspirations with the conflations of the rhetoric of terrorism. In pursuit of a military solution to a political problem, the British state drew on a tradition of policing in Ireland which has its roots in the early nineteenth century. This tradition, embodied in the RUC after 1922, has been militaristic, unaccountable and divisive. Prior to 1969, the RUC was deployed to uphold the rule of an exclusive ethnic regime without regard for the inevitable consequences. Perhaps confused by the experience of the long retreat from empire, the response of the British state to escalating conflict slid into a familiar groove as the conflict was increasingly militarised. The deployment of a professional army, hardened in colonial wars, was a terrible mistake and confirmed the worst suspicions of nationalists. Both sides to the conflict became consumed by the dream of a military victory over the other and, as the dream turned to nightmare, war became for many a way of life. As with all modern wars, the victims have been the innocent, the children, women and men who happened to be in the wrong place at the wrong time. As far as the Stormont state was concerned, and after 1971 the British state, the solution lay in repression and the agents of repression: first the British Army, and after 1974 the RUC and the locally recruited Ulster Defence Regiment, were deployed not just against the IRA but against the Catholic population as a whole.

If those who forget history are condemned to repeat it, the amnesia of those who made policy in Northern Ireland for over twenty years is frightening. The legacy of policing and repression in nineteenth-century Ireland was there for all to see: when eventually confronted by the armed movement it helped to create, the Royal Irish Constabulary melted away like snow on a ditch, unable to stem the tide of Irish nationalism.

Multiethnic empires and states tend to be ramshackle rather than efficient, careful to consolidate the power of the centre with judicious concessions to minorities. Few states insisted on such ethnic exclusivity as Northern Ireland after 1922 and the deployment of such a comprehensive apparatus of repression and control of political, cultural and economic life was unique to any so called democracy. Of course, the Unionist regime could never have achieved this without the sanction of its erstwhile masters in London. When Stormont was eventually forced to cede its authority to a reluctant British government, the latter showed no inclination to learn from history but instead embarked upon a long war in a not-so-distant province. The poverty of ideas was a characteristic of both parties to the conflict and it sometimes appeared as if the pursuit of war was a way of waiting for history to catch up.

Perhaps history has now, at last, caught up. The collapse of empires and the erosion of the nation state are two sides of the same coin. Unionists can no longer depend on the unswerving loyalty of British governments and the dream of a united Ireland makes little sense as the Irish Republic transforms itself into an offshore platform for multinational capital and picks at the scabs of endemic corruption. Wars have their own logic: easy to start and hard to stop. The tenacious belief that there could be a security solution to a society as deeply divided as Northern Ireland was sustained by the activities of a massive security apparatus blind to the futility of its own perverse logic. It is perhaps to the credit of the IRA that they were the first to realise that a military victory was a dangerous chimera which, even if it were possible, offered no solution.

The focus of this book is the policing of Northern Ireland after partition in 1922. The first chapter looks at the emergence of a dense apparatus of control in nineteenth-century Ireland that set the parameters for the next century. Without the extensive apparatus of coercion and control constructed after 1922, the Stormont regime could not have survived: policing was central to the very existence of the state and Protestant hegemony. If there were peaceful years during the early decades of the state's existence, it was the peace of a graveyard, where expressions of minority culture and identity were seen as a threat and ruthlessly suppressed. The decision to replace the British Army by the predominantly Protestant RUC after 1974 was a fateful one further compounded by the transformation of the police into a fully-fledged counter-insurgency force.

This decision confirmed, in the eyes of nationalists, that the police were simply the agent of British policy and a proxy for continued Unionist domination. For Protestants, the RUC was 'their' police, protecting them from the depredations of the IRA. The police themselves took to their task with a will, safe in the belief that their activities would not be seriously questioned and that they would not be called to account for their actions. The book traces the twists and turns of security policy as the RUC and their political masters fruitlessly sought *the* tactic that would eventually crush the IRA. When internment

without trial failed to stem the violence, an elaborate policy
of 'Ulsterisation' was embarked upon giving the RUC the lead
role in the counter-insurgency campaign. The use of special
non-jury courts was intended to reinforce the image of normality and sustain the myth that the conflict was caused by a
small band of ruthless terrorists who enjoyed little or no support.

In the two decades after 1969, political initiatives were subordinated to increasingly desperate attempts to crush the IRA:
internment was followed by normalisation and criminalisation;
interrogation centres were opened to feed the new Diplock
courts with confessions extracted from suspects. Special units
were deployed in undercover operations, initially by the British Army and later by the RUC. The introduction of computers
allowed the development of a unprecedented level of surveillance of whole populations who were gradually corralled into
electronic prisons. The priority given to security policy was
not simply a response to IRA violence. It was a policy which
failed to confront the nature of the society created under nearly
seventy years of Unionist rule, a society which was politically,
culturally and economically exclusionist not only on class
lines, but on grounds of religion and culture.

The conflict in Northern Ireland is, broadly speaking, about
ethnicity, identity and culture. Although deeply differentiated
and fractured on class lines, with widespread inequalities in
education, employment and wealth distribution, socio-economic
inequalities are refracted through the prism of ethnicity.
Indeed, the policies pursued by successive Unionist regimes
after partition tended to reverse the (partially successful) attempts of Britain in the late nineteenth century to integrate
Ireland more firmly in the orbit of empire. Paradoxically, the
exclusion and marginalisation of the Catholic population
forced the development of a particular sense of identity and
cultural distinctiveness, while failing to unify the Protestant
community in more than a superficial manner. When the question of reforming the Unionist state was posed by the Civil
Rights Movement in the 1960s, it was Unionism that began
the long process of disintegration. The primary role of the RUC,
in the period prior to 1969, was to police cultural and ethnic
practices and to suppress any concrete expression of Catholic
grievance. It is a further paradox that the very practice of policing during this period – discussed in Chapters Two and Three
– helped produce communities that were self-contained and

cohesive in the face of a hostile state. In many ways it was Unionism which created the particular identity of the Catholic community in Northern Ireland, a community that showed extraordinary resilience in the face of a counter-insurgency campaign that was directed as much against ordinary people as the IRA. Although religion remains the main criterion of differentiation between the two communities, Catholicism is no longer a strategic component in the identity of Northern Catholics.

The inability of the state to deal with the demands of the Civil Rights Movement – discussed in Chapter Four – was a result of an inability to understand the changing social composition of the Catholic bloc and the novelty of its demands. Of all the institutions of the state, the RUC had the least comprehension of what was going on. Its advice to the Unionist and British governments was predicated on the reduction of everything to a republican conspiracy to destroy the state, a mindset that soon came to be shared by the British Army. The opportunity to grasp the nettle of policing was passed over in favour of an intensification of repression and the placing of the RUC in the forefront of this misguided policy. Chapters Five and Six examine the development and consolidation of the security apparatus from the mid-1970s onwards. Once again, the single-mindedness of security policy was to have unintended consequences. The attempt to impose a normal prison regime on republican prisoners led directly to the hunger strikes of 1980–81 and had the effect of forcing Sinn Féin to try its hand at electoral politics and abandon the dogma of abstentionism. The electoral success of Sinn Féin had two important consequences: it shook the Dublin government out of its political torpor regarding the North, and it gave the lie to the assertion that republicanism had no significant support. The hunger strikes led to the deployment of the RUC in a front-line role in nationalist areas. An index of the turmoil of the period is that over 30,000 plastic bullets were fired, and the alienation of a new generation of Catholics from the police was assured.

The retreat from communal conflict remained painfully slow despite the insertion of politics into the equation. A security solution remained the first priority of the Conservative government during the 1980s, and although the conflict may have been contained during that decade it was at a terrible cost in human suffering. Tactics were deployed that discredited both sides of the conflict. Chapters Seven and Eight look at two of the most controversial tactics deployed by the security forces during this decade: undercover operations and collusion with loyalist death squads.

By the end of the 1980s, the RUC had become what amounted to a third community in Northern Ireland. Police officers were startlingly well-paid, equipped with a vast panoply of powers and equipment and seemingly accountable to no one. Officers lived in comfortable middle-class ghettos around Belfast and few had any contact with many of the areas they policed except through the gun ports of armoured jeeps. There is at least a probable connection between the social isolation and elitism of the RUC and their apparent willingness to use whatever means they saw as necessary to defeat the IRA.

The cessation of the IRA campaign after the cease-fire in 1994 put the RUC in the awkward position of having to justify its practices in new terms. In Chapter Nine, the use of survey evidence to demonstrate the acceptability of the RUC to the Catholic community in particular is examined in the context of the publication of the Patten report on policing (Patten Report, 1999). Both the Police Authority for Northern Ireland (PANI) and the Chief Constable continue to make use of the results of public attitude surveys to dilute calls for a transformation of policing in Northern Ireland. We argue that such survey evidence is at best ambiguous and at worst misleading and in itself should not be used for the basis of policy decisions.

Unionist and RUC opposition to reform, since the publication of the Patten Report, has tended to focus on recommendations that the symbols of policing be changed. Suggestions that the insignia, name and other trappings be depoliticised have ignited a furious reaction and tell us much about the importance of symbols in a divided society. All societies use the power of symbols to express the reality of power and powerlessness, but most can do so in a relatively non-contentious manner. A monopoly over the public use of symbols has been a feature of Unionist rule and has been a component part of the creation and maintenance of division (Cairns, 1999).

The Patten Report is the most comprehensive analysis of policing ever undertaken in Ireland or the UK. Drawing on the results of extensive consultation, and an examination of

policing in other countries, the report offers a model of policing which aims to transcend the inherent difficulties of
policing a divided society. Whether intentionally or otherwise, the report has repercussions and implications far beyond
the narrow confines of Northern Ireland. In societies that are
increasingly diverse and differentiated on grounds of colour,
ethnicity, religion and a multitude of other characteristics,
policing has become a much more sensitive and contentious
issue. No longer can the police attempt to subjugate the lower
orders to the manners and ways of their social betters; they
must operate with consent and be made accountable. This is
the precise thrust of the Patten document: policing can only
operate properly by consent allied with strong structures to
ensure accountability. The practice of policing in Northern
Ireland has been lacking in both these areas and if the last
eighty years are an example of how things should not be done,
the opportunity is now available to show the rest of the world
how they should be done.

1 Policing Nineteenth-century Ireland: Setting the Parameters

Policing Class Society

Modern police forces emerged as institutions essentially dedicated to the surveillance of target populations. To use Ignatieff's phrase, capitalism created a 'society of strangers' (Ignatieff, 1978), where traditional mechanisms of social control no longer worked, leading the state to embark on a long process of the bureaucratisation and centralisation of social control. Yet the system of penality into which the police are embedded is not simply about repression, but also has the function of shaping, constructing and legitimising cultural meanings and practices (Garland, 1990). Many institutions of nineteenth-century Europe had a didactic role in the transformation from a pre-capitalist to an industrial economy: the churches, the education system and the ever denser institutional control of deviant populations through the agency of hospitals, orphanages, workhouses and asylums. The police, although formally part of the system of penality, performed a broader function as an adjunct to other institutions of social control in attempting to transform and remould moral and political understandings. In the last analysis, of course, the police had recourse to legitimate coercion when all else failed.

Pre-capitalist societies depended on a process of indirect control of populations mediated by the patronage of local elites and local customs. This was consolidated by what Foucault (1979) terms 'exemplary punishments' conducted in the full public gaze. The English 'Bloody Code' of capital punishment, for instance, contained over two hundred offences which brought a sentence of public execution, although most such offences were so narrowly defined that prosecutions were rare and pardons common (Emsley, 1997, p. 251). There were an astonishing number of trivial capital crimes. People could be hanged for damaging Westminster Bridge, for damaging trees, for stealing five shillings and for 'taking away a maid or a widow for the sake of her fortune' (Reith, 1938, p. 231) Between the last quarter of the seventeenth century and the middle of the nineteenth century, the criminal law was extensively reformed in England and elsewhere in Europe to the extent that, with the exception of murder and treason, transportation and prison sentences replaced capital punishment. The public symbolism of execution as a spectacle that manifested itself in England through the procession of the condemned through the streets of London to Tyburn (Foucault, 1979; Lindbaugh, 1975) was discontinued in 1783 and public executions were abolished in the 1860s. Similarly, physical punishment as a public ritual had all but disappeared by this time.

Behind these changes in the nature of punishment lay profound shifts in the nature of social and economic relations. Bourgeois society rests upon twin pillars: formal and legal equality on one hand, and deep-seated economic and social inequalities on the other. This essentially contradictory reality brought with it new conflicts and locations of resistance. In the mobile and increasingly urbanised society of industrial capitalism, new definitions and categories of crime were introduced to protect and consolidate the new order. An expanding nexus of social relations based upon possessive individualism (Macpherson, 1964) had, by the beginning of the nineteenth century, successfully infiltrated the fabric of English society bringing with it a new matrix of criminal offences. The destruction of rural custom and the enclosure of common land criminalised many aspects of traditional rural life and the new urban working class was the subject of extensive new legislation to curb their militancy and consolidate the factory system.

Foucault's analysis of the changing nature of punishment and power vividly charts this shift in the *modus operandi* of social control, of which policing is a central part. Social control becomes increasingly bureaucratised. Dandeker (1990, p. 111) for instance, points to four important changes central to this process:

1 A revolution in punishment took place, with prisons replacing public physical punishment.
2 New bureaucratic structures were created for the processing of deviant populations.
3 The police became the agent of the rational discipline of society.

4 Supervision, surveillance and control became the watchword of the new professions.

The consolidation of the modern state developed an apparatus of surveillance and control, which reached deeper than
ever before into society. The police became the agent for the
rational disciplining of society. Supervision, surveillance and
control became the watchword of the new professions. But
the new structure of power was never as ubiquitous and total
as commentators such as Foucault and Dandeker seem to
imply. The stability of bourgeois society may rest ultimately
on the threat of repression, but its everyday existence depends
upon legitimacy and complicity. The legitimacy of the modern state rests on a number of pillars but central is the acceptance
of a set of property relations. By the early nineteenth century,
the precepts of possessive individualism were well entrenched
as the basis of the power of the bourgeoisie and formed the
basis of cultural and economic stability. This precarious stability was not achieved without struggle, as E.P. Thompson so
often reminded us (Thompson, 1963, 1975, 1980). Complicity is a more elusive and slippery concept but without it no
state or powerful institution can survive (Donzelot, 1980).
The Catholic Church in nineteenth-century Ireland could
only impose its brand of repressive sexual politics because a
predominantly peasant society survived on late marriages
and the strict control of women's bodies to ensure that ille-
gitimacy would not upset the smooth workings of inheritance
(Smyth, 1995). Equally, the police depend upon complicity
for their very survival. A significant section of the population, embracing all sections of the class structure, are
generally united in their condemnation of certain crimes and
willing to assist the police in their efforts to apprehend per-
petrators.

Moral sanctions condemning crimes such as rape, murder
and personal assault pre-dated capitalist society and cut
across class lines. The reality of a more mobile and impersonal society made such offences more difficult to sanction
without the presence of a uniformed and bureaucratic police
force. The state, via the agency of the police, took over the
role of policing and punishing those already beyond the pale.
The respectable working class clearly demarcated itself from
the criminal class, particularly as the working class was,
and still is, the main victim of property crime. The police

depended upon both the legitimacy of the new economic and political order and the complicity of the population in the control of the criminal classes. In general, the penal system reinforced both the power and authority of the state as well as propagating a particular version of morality and legitimate social relations. The police, during the nineteenth century, became part of an institutional discourse aimed at the reorganisation of society.

A certain ambiguity characterised the attitude of many working people towards the new system of policing. While they resented the strict enforcement of property rights on the part of landowners and others, they were also prepared to invoke the law to enforce their own meagre property rights. E.P. Thompson writes in a similar vein: 'What was often at issue was not property, supported by law, against no-property; it was alternative definitions of property rights: for the landowner, enclosure; for the cottager, common rights; for the forest officialdom, "preserved grounds" for the deer; for the forester, the right to take turfs' (Thompson, 1975, p. 261).

The introduction of the 'policed society' in the nineteenth century had complex roots. At one level, the new urban propertied classes felt a need to protect themselves from the threat of revolution and the reality of riot, and at a more prosaic level there was a need to consolidate and police new property and class relations. As the historian of London, William Robson, has pointed out, the preservation of property counted for more than 'any other aspect of local government whatsoever' (Robson 1939, p. 50).

The police also played a significant part in suppressing what were seen as anti-social forms of behaviour and recreation among the working classes. Popular 'rough' sports and recreations were suppressed in an attempt to undermine collective forms of association as well as altering patterns of behaviour (Phillips 1983; Storch 1975, 1976). The police were one of the agencies who transmitted the message that certain cultural practices would no longer be tolerated. Opposition to new forms of policing did not only come from below. The rural gentry were opposed to the erosion of their traditional powers consolidated under the eighteenth-century system of law which suited them in so far as it granted informal control over their own semi-autonomous areas (Hay, 1975).

Was Ireland Different?

The question arises, in what way was Ireland different, if at all, from other countries in Europe in the way in which the police, in particular, were used both as an agent of social control and an arbiter of cultural change? By the middle of the eighteenth century, Ireland was a relatively peaceful society if only because the wars of the previous century had destroyed and driven into exile the leadership of the old Gaelic order. Levels of crime were lower than in countries such as France and England, and travellers in seventeenth- and eighteenth-century Ireland were quick to note this: '... yet the robberies, felonies, burglaries etc. usually committed in this Kingdom are not so numerous but there are commonly sentenced to die in a monthly session at the Old Bailey more than in a half year's circuit of Ireland' (quoted in Connolly 1992, p. 218).

Agrarian unrest – after the Hougher disturbances of 1711–12,[1] when the extension of large-scale stock raising in the western counties led to the slaughter of thousands of cattle by discontented cottiers – was sporadic and low-key in a country which was enjoying an unprecedented level of prosperity, particularly after the middle of the century. Although this stability was a precarious one – based as it was on the monopoly of power and privilege in the hands of a small Protestant class – a temporary balance between rulers and ruled had been reached whereby conflict was contained and to some extent controlled by custom and compromise.

Rural unrest in Ireland began to re-emerge after 1760 but the actions of the multifarious groups, such as Whiteboys, Oakboys, Hearts of Steel and other rural secret societies (see Clark and Donnelly, 1983), were not aimed at the destruction of landlordism, nor did the secret societies make demands of an overtly political nature. Rural secret societies during this period were concerned with changes that eroded traditional practices and challenged customary rights and in this sense appear little different to the rural agitation in England described by E.P. Thompson. The increasing intrusion of commodity relations into rural life and the introduction of new agricultural practices led to protest. The enclosure of common land, speculation on leases, the extension of rents and tithes were the most common causes for complaint as impersonal economic forces inserted themselves into a society based upon patronage and deference. Such popular and widespread protest was novel even if it did not, as in later decades, lead to widespread bloodshed. But it was clear that the moral economy (Bartlett, 1983) of seventeenth-century Ireland was disintegrating, and not just because of impersonal economic forces such as the undeniable effect of a rapidly rising population which was putting pressure on the system of rents and leases. External events, such as the revolutionary struggles in France and America, had an influence in Ireland greater than in other non-involved countries. The Whig historian, W.E.H. Lecky, in his *History of Ireland in the Eighteenth Century*, writes of the influence of the French Revolution on Ireland:

> The ideas of an English country peasant seldom extended beyond his country town, and the continent to him was almost as unknown as the world beyond the grave. But tens of thousands of young Irishmen had passed from the wretched cabins of the South and the West to the great armies of the Continent where the Catholic was not looked upon as a slave, and where Irish talent found a welcome and a home and vague, distorted images of events that were happening in France – of the abolition of tithes, of the revolution in landed property, of the offer of French assistance to all suffering nations – soon began to penetrate the cottier's cabin and mingle with the cottier's dreams (Lecky, 1972, p. 272).

It is perhaps here that the crucial distinguishing feature of protest in Ireland can be seen. Historical grievances, buried but not forgotten, offered an inadequate framework for protest given the destruction of the old Irish order, but the grievances remained, ready to be reformulated and emerge once more onto the stage of history.

The rapid collapse of the moral order which had held Ireland together in the first part of the eighteenth century was also accelerated by suggestions that Catholics be granted greater rights – a suggestion that was not immediately rejected by the British government (Connolly 1992, p. 249) – but which increased the paranoia and fears of conservative Protestants, already unsettled by the emergence of rural unrest. Another component in the new constellation of social forces was the expansion of a new, increasingly self-confident and prosperous Catholic middle class irritated at their continued exclusion from political power and their subjection to repressive legislation.

Literacy levels were rising in the population, and radical texts and newspapers were challenging the basis of the Protestant ascendancy in Ireland. Newspapers such as the *Northern Star* brought mainstream radical European thinking to a wide, if English-speaking audience (Elliott, 1989, pp. 168–9). However, as Lecky pointed out, radical ideas in Ireland were not confined to the English-speaking urban middle classes, but had also infected the Irish rural poor, who were showing a new ability to combine grievances with the formation of politically motivated organisations. The Protestant establishment, ever fearful because of its numeric inferiority, became increasingly twitchy and frightened.

Thomas Bartlett sees the events surrounding the attempted introduction of the Militia Act in 1793 as a turning point in the collapse of the moral economy of eighteenth-century Ireland (Bartlett, 1984). Dublin Castle, the nerve-centre of the British administration in Ireland, viewed the establishment of a militia as essential to policing, particularly if the British Army units normally garrisoned there were to be used abroad in the war against France. Despite reassurances to the contrary, the militia raised during the American war had been sent overseas, which was one cause of discontent. Men were compulsorily selected for Militia service by ballot in local areas and parishes – the complex informal practices of deferment, and evasion of service, also fuelled the subsequent unrest. The initial focus of resistance rapidly expanded to include demands for liberty and equality and the issuing of death threats to men of landed property (Elliott, 1989, p. 221). The failure of the British government to gain the support of the Catholic gentry by instituting reforms was crucial and, as Elliott notes: 'The government had been within easy reach of gaining the support of the Catholic leaders and with them their considerable powers of control over the lower orders. Instead they were unable to deliver on promises and their influence disintegrated' (Elliott, 1989, p. 222).

With the collapse of the traditional order and the inability of either the Catholic or Protestant gentry to control the Catholic rural poor, the stage was set for a direct confrontation between the populace and the British Army as a new spiral of secret crime, organised outrage and military repression emerged (Bartlett, 1983, p. 218). The rebellion of 1798 shocked the British government for a number of reasons: its egalitarian republican ideology, the participation of Presbyterians on the side of the United Irishmen and the intervention of France. More lives were lost in the course of the rebellion –

about 30,000 – than during the French Revolution. The British government, after the slaughter of 1798 and the Act of Union, directed its attention to establishing law and order in Ireland. The old order was irretrievably lost and with it the culture of deference and compromise, leaving the military as the blunt weapon of social control. The lessons of Ireland were not lost on the future leaders of imperial expansion, such as General Sir Charles James Napier, who conquered the Scinde (now Pakistan): 'Rendering the civil power dependent upon the military for protection in ordinary cases is of all evils the greatest. I speak from nearly 50 years experience. I saw it in Ireland in 1798, and again in 1803. I saw it in the Ionian Islands. I saw it in the Northern District. I saw it in Scinde' (cited in Palmer, 1988, p. 534).

The lessons of 1798 were twofold: Ireland could not be allowed to go its own way and threaten the ideological cohesion of the burgeoning British Empire, and, more subtle forms of control and cultural transformation must be found.

Order and Control: the Policing Solution

Any analysis of the development of policing in Ireland immediately confronts a number of apparent anomalies. The absence of an industrial revolution and the widespread survival of a rural and pre-capitalist economy seem difficult to reconcile with the early development of a centralised, armed and bureaucratic police force. It was this type of force that was proposed for Ireland in the mid-eighteenth century, and by 1786, the Dublin Metropolitan Police was in existence (it was not until 1829 that a similar force was established in London). The first serious attempt to rationalise policing in rural Ireland was made in 1814 when Robert Peel pushed an Act through Parliament to allow the appointment of paid magistrates and officers (the 'Peace Preservation Force') in designated 'disturbed' areas.

Peel, whose long career in British politics was inextricably linked to the Irish question, saw the problem of order as a first priority when he came to Ireland in 1806. He was aware that the disturbed state of Ireland was in large measure attributable to its economic and political circumstances, but he showed little inclination to try and rectify this other than by opting for a security solution. The rationale for a law and order approach was, in the words of Peel: '"The Irishman's natural predilection for outrage and a lawless life which I believe nothing can control", combined with the very nature of the Irish character: "you have no idea of the moral depravation of the lower orders"' (cited in Foster, 1988, p. 294).

But apart from this, rather familiar, assessment of the Irish psyche, Peel faced other problems. The great upheaval of 1798 had been suppressed only with great difficulty and a measure of luck. The central problem of the country, that is, disaffection with the political and economic order, remained, and at times of agricultural depression and falling agricultural prices, opposition to the given order was not restricted to the rural poor, but moved up the social scale to involve larger farmers. Opposition, as in the rural disturbances of 1813–16, 1821–24 and the 1830s, focused on issues that had distinct political resonance: the question of tithes, eviction and land tenure (Clark and Donnelly, 1983). In contrast, levels of 'normal' crime were low. Foreign visitors were still wont to comment on the ability of travellers to move unmolested through disturbed areas. Lewis comments that, 'the object of crime in Ireland is not personal gain, but are preventative and exemplary crimes intended to influence the conduct of persons in respect of some future action' (Lewis 1836, p. 54). A contemporary commentator, Charles Townshend, agrees: 'Much of Irish violence and intimidation in the 19th century was directed not by "extremists" in any useful sense of the term, but by representatives of the community whose object was to maintain, not destroy, social order' (Townshend, 1983, p. 9).

The rationale for the introduction of bureaucratic policing in Ireland arose from the lack of legitimacy of the colonial order, and the inability of informal methods of social control to master the situation. If legitimacy was a problem, complicity was equally absent. The authorities were totally mystified by the activities of rural secret societies. Even when arrested and charged, people maintained a wall of silence. The authorities depended, almost exclusively, on the reports from the Anglo-Irish gentry that flooded into the castle and drove Peel to despair. Ignorance, indifference and paranoia dictated the attitudes of the Anglo-Irish.

Both the Catholic poor and the middle classes were alienated from the state. The emergence of agrarian secret societies in the early nineteenth century reflected both the weakness of the central state and the legacy of 1798. The state in the early nineteenth century had little effective power, apart from the use of the army, outside the few urban centres. The Dublin Castle administration was, however, convinced that no uprising could take place without outside help. The Irish peasant bands, which sporadically dominated large areas of the south and west of the country in the first three decades of the nineteenth century, lacked both discipline and arms, rendering them incapable of winning set-piece battles against regular forces.

The use of the military to impose internal order was a far from ideal solution and beset with problems. The military establishment was against the use of soldiers in a policing role and the London government was intent, for internal political and financial reasons, to reduce the numbers of soldiers garrisoned in Ireland. It was also recognised that the military was, at best, a blunt instrument. Both the military establishment and Dublin Castle officials were acutely aware of the problem of using the army in a public order role. Apart from anything else was the prosaic problem succinctly described by Norman Gash: 'The problem of obtaining an adequate military force was one that exercised the minds of Irish officers. In time of war the troops were wanted elsewhere, in peace the taxpayer did not want them at all' (Gash, 1961, p. 186).

Apart from the regular army, the main agent of repression was the Yeomanry. This was an exclusively Protestant and 'Orange' force, used to terrorise the Catholic population with a deserved reputation for 'ill discipline and brutality' (Crossman, 1996, p. 51). Incidents of beatings, burnings and murder were common, as in Shercock, Co. Cavan, in 1814, where a force of Yeomanry killed 13 people and wounded scores of others in an unprovoked attack (Clark and Donnelly, 1983, pp. 129–35). The attitude of the Castle towards the Yeomanry was ambiguous. Though he was not prepared to countenance their disbandment, Peel was privately critical of them, as in a letter of 1815:

> Admitting that the Yeomanry are generally speaking unfit for those very duties in the performance of which their main utility would consist, namely in relieving the army from the maintenance of internal order and the collection of revenue, I am not quite prepared to come to your conclusion that it would be the wisest measure to disband the whole force. (cited in Parker, 1891, p. 174)

In rejecting a suggestion from the officer commanding the British Army in Ireland, Peel was probably sharing the attitude of a later correspondent, who in writing to the Chief Secretary, Goldbourn, commented: 'I know that the Yeomanry are unpopular, but so is everything that is constitutional and loyal. They saved the nation in 1798 and the disaffected dread them more than they do the regulars because they are well aquainted with their character and know their haunts' (Clark and Donnelly 1983, p. 128).[2]

The Catholic population had a more jaundiced view of this force as put by Daniel O'Connell[3] in the House of Commons in 1831: 'He could not tell the House with what disgust and abhorrence, exciting to resistance, the Yeomanry Corps were held by the people of Ireland'.[4]

Although the Yeomanry faded away over the first half of the nineteenth century, its spectre was to return to haunt the politics of Northern Ireland in the form of the Ulster Special Constabulary (USC) and later the Ulster Defence Regiment (UDR). It is one of those ironies of history that almost immediately after the establishment of the Specials in 1920, a constabulary lodge was founded, known as the Sir Robert Peel Memorial Loyal Orange Lodge, whereas under the original regulations of the Royal Irish Constabulary (RIC), membership of the Orange Order was forbidden. In 1936 a report of the Commission of the National Council of Civil Liberties (NCCL) commented, 'In practice membership of the "B" Specials is confined to members professing the Protestant faith who are also members of the Orange Order – that is, supporters of the Unionist Party' (Gallagher, 1957, p. 179).

Policing and Legitimacy in Nineteenth-century Ireland

The problem which faced the British authorities in Ireland in the nineteenth century was complicated. Although many influential Anglo-Irish figures opposed any move towards replacing the military with an alternative force (and were particularly opposed to any tinkering with the Yeomanry), the Castle was acutely aware of the problems of using both these forces for internal policing. The authorities were equally aware that only a continental-style model of policing, centralised, militarised and heavily armed, would be adequate to impose order on the recalcitrant Irish and that any such move could provoke widespread opposition both in Ireland and England. Since the Anglo-Irish were the only allies of the Castle in the country-side outside the North East, caution was the order of the day. It was important not to alienate the gentry by emasculating their monopoly over the local enforcement of the law. How-ever, it was equally necessary to modernise the apparatus of surveillance, control and punishment given the chronic lack of legitimacy enjoyed by a system of land ownership which condemned the native population to grinding poverty.

In the eyes of the Castle, the country could not afford the luxury of a police system in tune with the rights of free-born Englishmen, given the unsettled nature of the country and the reluctance of London to embark upon significant reform of the land system. There were isolated figures within the establishment who clearly saw that the problem lay elsewhere than in the nature of the Irish character, but such voices went unheeded. Charles Grant, who succeeded Peel as Chief Sec-retary in 1818, was convinced that unrest and disorder could only be contained if the state made significant political con-cessions – particularly Catholic emancipation – to reduce the disaffection and alienation of the population. However, Grant was seen to be leaning too far towards the Catholic cause during the disturbances of 1821 and he was swiftly removed (Crossman, 1996, pp. 25ff).

The Irish countryside between 1800 and 1823 was ravaged by agrarian disturbances, with only five relatively tranquil years during this period. During the Napoleonic Wars, the British Army establishment in Ireland was between 40,000 and 50,000 of which 20,000 were Militia. By the end of the war in 1813, the number had fallen to 35,000, of which a mere 11,000 were regular troops. The Castle estimated that at least 40,000 were needed to police the country. Since the Militia and Yeomanry were seen as being of little value in a policing role, Peel had an ideal opportunity to realise his ambition to establish a police force in Ireland as an alternative to the use of the mili-tary. The new force, called the Peace Preservation Force, was brought into being by Act of Parliament in 1814. In the event, the Peace Preservation Force was a compromise between a fully-fledged centralised police force and the extensive use of the military in a policing role.

The compromise was necessary because of deep-seated opposition to a centralised police force. In London the leader of the House of Commons, Castlereagh, opposed the measure and the Prime Minister, Liverpool, criticised the bill as being 'not English' (Broeker, 1970, p. 60). In this they were expressing the perceptions of a powerful landed class, in both Ireland and England (but especially in the latter) who were loath to see their control of local law and order removed. Liverpool was hinting at the fact that centralised models of policing were associated with France and, of course, no good could come from there. Emsley writes:

> In England the idea of an uniformed body of policemen patrolling the streets to prevent crime and disorder was anathema. Such a force smacked of the absolutism of continental states. The fact that these models were French, in itself, was sufficient to make most eighteenth century English gentlemen conceive a police force as something inimical to English liberty. (Emsley, 1997, p. 217)

Peel himself, when appointed Home Secretary in 1822, chaired a committee in that year which concluded that a continental-style police force in England would be 'odious and repulsive ... it would be a plan which would make every servant of every house a spy on the actions of his master, and all classes of society spies on each other' (quoted in Hall, 1999, p. 660).

However, given the unsettled state of Ireland, such concerns had to be put aside – the Peace Preservation Act of 1814 was the first attempt to deal with the problem of policing rural Ireland, but it enjoyed only mixed success. Increasingly, the inability of the Peace Preservation Force – a sort of riot squad sent into disturbed areas to restore order – to fulfil its function became apparent. The appearance of the Peace Preservation Force in disturbed areas was resented both by the native population and the gentry, who saw it as often upsetting the delicate local balance of power. Dissatisfaction with the force led to the establishment in 1822 of the County Constabulary as a permanent, national police force that existed alongside the Peace Preservation Force until their amalgamation in 1836 as the Irish Constabulary (IC). Prior to its amalgamation, the Peace Preservation Force had a complement of 2,336 men, 16 per cent of whom were Catholic.

The Irish Constabulary was, in the opinion of its first Inspector General, more akin to a light infantry regiment than a 'normal' police force. The force was under military-type discipline and drill was a central part of training and practice. Control was centralised in Dublin Castle; the force was heavily armed and, effectively, garrisoned in barracks scattered strategically across the country. In both organisation and practice, the IC was a military force rather than one dedicated to civil regulation.

In the years before the famine, the police force's main function was to attempt to control agrarian disorders, to disrupt popular practices and to police evictions. Along with their important intelligence-gathering function, the police imposed public order and had little aptitude or inclination towards the more regular police functions of investigating and preventing non-political crime. The police force established in 1822 swiftly became the direct interface between state and people. The state had found an effective organisational form for the enforcement of policy, and a means of keeping the tensions and contradictions of British rule under some sort of control. There may have been some ambiguity towards the police on the part of the Catholic middle classes, but in general the police were despised and hated by the native population (Palmer, 1988). After his election to the House of Commons, Daniel O'Connell exerted himself to discover the number of people killed by the police, remarking in the House: 'The effects of the establishment (of the police) has been, that whenever the people resist the police they are put to death by them. In England, resisting the police was a misdemeanour but in Ireland it was punished with death.'[5] Returning to the same topic two years later, though admittedly in a somewhat hyperbolic fashion, O'Connell said: 'It appeared that four times more men fell at the hands of the police than by the hand of the executioner. Thus four times more men were shot to punish rioters than to punish all other crimes. The land was red with blood spilt by police.'[6]

The official figures for the number of deaths at the hands of the constabulary between 1823 and 1830 was 84 killed and 122 seriously injured. These figures probably underestimated the actual numbers, since it was a common practice among the people to spirit away the bodies of people killed in encounters with the constabulary for secret burial (Crossman, 1996, p. 44, Bartlett, 1983, p. 207). The extent and intensity of rural unrest in nineteenth-century Ireland defined the role of the police as that of enforcing deeply unpopular laws and left little room for the practice of normal policing. As O'Farrell (1975, p. 168) points out, although a number of explicit armed challenges to British rule during the century were unsuccessful, these events represented the tip of the iceberg in a country where English conceptions of order were, at an everyday level, imposed by force and force alone. Commenting on the situation in the middle of the century, O'Farrell writes:

> In the 1850s Irish agrarian relations were at a level resembling guerrilla warfare. Landlords and land agents carried arms as a matter of course: the peasants killed them when they could. In 1882 a force of a hundred armed men was thought necessary to undertake the seizure of cattle from one tenant in arrears: there were 3,432 agrarian outrages in that year alone. (1975, p. 168)

British policy in nineteenth-century Ireland had set itself a dual agenda. The suppression of agrarian and political unrest was a priority, but an important part of the agenda was cultural transformation, that is, a modernisation and Anglicisation of Irish society as well as the eradication of 'wild shamrock manners'. Although many shared the despair of Peel that the Irish could ever be civilised, the task had to be undertaken, and the police were central to both these objectives. If punishment is a social institution which helps define the nature of society (Garland, 1990, p. 287), British policy in Ireland activated the police force as a central institution in this endeavour by using them to condense an array of cultural meanings and social and property relations. Not only did the Irish Constabulary carry out a repressive function through evictions, combating agrarian unrest and armed uprisings, it also policed popular practices such as pattern days, fairs, wakes and other cultural practices of the lower orders. By its garrisoned presence across the country, it consolidated the use of English as the publicly-used language of native Irish speakers and, along with the Catholic Church, helped spread the virtues of Victorian values. The Constabulary also became a career of choice for the sons of Catholic small farmers, and the numbers of Catholics in the force increased to almost 80 per cent in the course of the century. The importance of the police to the authorities was reflected in manpower staffing Levels. In 1836, the number of police officers per head of population was three times that of England and Wales and still twice the level of the United Kingdom in 1897.

Yet the general population cannot have been unaware that the primary function of the Constabulary was a repressive one and the transformation of the force into the Royal Irish

Constabulary in 1867 after their role in defeating the Fenian uprising was indicative. The prefix 'Royal', intended as an honour, cannot but have profoundly irritated the ever-increasing section of the population who saw themselves as nationalists and the substitution of the harp for shamrock on the official insignia might well have been regarded as an arrogant appropriation of Irish symbolism. Since the rebellion of 1798, the harp had stood for Irish cultural self-expression and a link to the pre-colonial past; its cultural importance grew in the course of the following century. As Leersen writes:

> The insistent use of harp imagery should also be placed against the importance of the sense of orality in early nineteenth-century verse ... harp symbolism thus feeds into the theme (popularized most effectively by Moore) of a struggle against muteness and cultural amnesia, which adds an ideological sounding board to the vogue for songs and ballads as the authentically Irish genres of verse and poetry. (1996, p. 81)

As a contested symbol, the harp had gone through a process of appropriation and reappropriation since its first appearance in Tudor times as the official heraldic insignia of Ireland (see Cullen, 1997). The fixation of unionists, in particular, on the changes to RUC insignia in the wake of the Patten Report on policing in 1999, attests to the almost material quality attached to the appropriation of symbols in Ireland.

The parameters of policing that were set in the early decades of the nineteenth century crumbled somewhat as the century progressed. The ambiguities of policy – particularly over the relationship between the police and military (Muenger, 1991) – were instrumental in a decline in the military effectiveness of the RIC and the ability of the force to deal with internal disorder. The author of an official report on the state of defence in Ireland in 1912 wrote: 'Although the [Constabulary] force is organised on military lines for the purpose of administration, its members have only a rudimentary training in the use of firearms and it cannot be regarded as a military force in any circumstances in the event of a hostile landing in Ireland' (cited in Crossman, 1996, p. 188).

Such organisational problems – including demoralisation due to poor pay and conditions, and the increasing isolation of policemen in an increasingly nationalist Ireland – were compounded by the increasing difficulty in imposing English culture upon Ireland. Not only was the RIC to soon lose its capacity to suppress and silence political deviance, it was also failing to help impose a particular meaning and normality upon Irish society at large. The police force that Peel imposed on the citizens of London in 1829, which within thirty years had become the model for police forces in the rest of England, broadly achieved its objectives. Crime levelled off after 1840 (Gatrell, 1980) and began to decline after the middle of the century. Despite bitter opposition, the English police established itself not only as an agency of social control, but became an institution of central symbolic importance, seen as embodying the very essence of Englishness. Peel's Irish experiment was less successful. The introduction of a continental-style model was an admission that Ireland was different and while Peel protested that 'God forbid that he should mean to countenance a system of espionage' (Critchley, 1978, p. 47) with regard to policing in England, he had no such scruples about Ireland.

2 Policing After Partition: Constructing the Security Apparatus

Establishing the RUC

The Anglo-Irish Treaty, ending the hostilities between the Provisional Irish Government and the British Empire, was ratified by a small majority of seven in the Dáil on 7 January 1922. In March of the same year, the RIC was withdrawn from 19 of the 26 counties which comprised the Irish Free State and disbandment centres were established. Until 1920, the RIC was deployed in the front line against the IRA by a British government unwilling to give credence to the IRA contention that they were fighting a war. Casualties were high among the RIC. Prior to the truce in 1921, 400 policemen had been killed as opposed to 160 British soldiers (Foster, 1988, p. 497). Resignations had already reached unacceptable levels by 1920 and for the most part the police did not leave their heavily fortified barracks unless forced to do so by IRA attacks.

In the Free State, the process of disbanding the RIC, which had begun in March 1922, was effectively complete by May. In Northern Ireland, the RIC remained intact until the establishment of the RUC on 1 June, when almost 1,000 RIC men were absorbed into the new force. The final administrative measures were complete by 31 August. In any event, it is unlikely that the RIC would have been accepted either in the South or North. In the South, the force was perceived by many nationalists to represent the eyes and ears of Dublin Castle (Ellison and Smyth, 1996) and was unacceptable because of its role during the War of Independence. Indeed, many ex-RIC officers sought the protection of armed IRA guards who escorted them to the ships destined to take them to colonial forces, or to the train for Belfast, where they would enlist in the new Northern force (Palmer, 1988).[1] Equally, in Northern Ireland, unionist suspicion of the RIC was intense. Many unionists believed the RIC to be overly sympathetic to Sinn Féin. Also, it was seen by unionists as having been inept and ineffective in dealing with the IRA during the War of Independence (Hezlet, 1972).[2]

After partition, the governments in both parts of Ireland broadly adopted the RIC organisational model of policing but with crucial differences. The decision of Michael Collins and the Provisional Government that the Garda Siochana should be an unarmed force was based upon the assumption that the new police force would be accepted as a legitimate arm of the new state and, broadly speaking, this was to be the case. Although the Dublin authorities did not indulge in a fundamental reorganisation of policing, there were a number of symbolic changes. The insignia was redesigned, avoiding contentious symbols, the uniform colour was changed to blue, and a less militaristic style and cut of dress was adopted. In Northern Ireland, policing was to revert to a model akin to that which had existed in the first half of the nineteenth century. In January 1922, the new Northern Ireland Minister for Home Affairs, Dawson Bates, appointed a 15-member committee, including two Catholics, to investigate the establishment of a new force for Northern Ireland (Farrell, 1983, p. 188). The terms of reference for the committee were to consider the organisation of the new force; recruitment and conditions of service; strength; and cost (Ryder, 1989, p. 48).

The Committee reported on 28 March 1922 (the first official report of the new Northern Ireland Parliament) and proposed that the new force be called the Ulster Constabulary, with Sir Charles Wickham to be appointed as Inspector General (he was to remain in the post until 1945). A recommendation was made for approval to include 'Royal' in the title, which was later granted by George V on 29 April. The committee concluded that the new force should be based around the existing organisational structure of the RIC, and that it was to draw on RIC and USC personnel. The initial quota for the force was set at 3,000 officers, which approximated the number of RIC personnel that were previously stationed in the Six-County area, with a small increase to allow for the transfer of administrative staff from Dublin (Farrell, 1983, p. 188). Of the initial 3,000 quota, one-third was to be allocated to Catholic ex-members of the RIC, with the remainder to be filled by Catholic civilians in the event of the quota not being met. Not more than 1,000 Protestant RIC members were to be recruited, and for the USC, preference was to be given to members of the full-time 'A' Specials. However, in what can be seen as a portent of the coming nature of sectarian relations within the new Northern state, nine of the fifteen committee members signed a document complaining that too many places were allocated for Catholic recruits, and outlining their reservations about the recruitment of ex-RIC personnel (Ryder, 1989, p. 48). None the less, the Northern Ireland government accepted the Report, and the Constabulary Act, passed on 1 June 1922 brought the Royal Ulster Constabulary into being though the debate in the Northern Ireland Parliament in relation to the Police Committee suggests that many members were unhappy with these criteria.

The embryonic RUC was organised upon lines similar to that of the RIC. Like the RIC, it was to remain heavily centralised and under direct political control. The Inspector General was directly answerable to – and received instructions from – the Unionist Minister for Home Affairs in the Northern Ireland Government. Like the RIC, the RUC was devised primarily as a paramilitary force. All officers were routinely armed with a .45 Webley, had access to a rifle and bayonet, and could avail themselves of more powerful firearms and Lancia armoured cage cars, though the British government turned down Solly-Flood's proposal to equip the RUC with patrol boats, planes and tanks. The RUC, like the RIC, retained an officer corps, the lowest level of which was Head Constable – a non-commissioned officer grade. Most importantly, however, the RUC swiftly reverted to being a predominantly Protestant force, reversing a century-long trend in the RIC towards the increased inclusion of Catholic officers.

The force was divided into 'A', 'B' and 'C' classes. The first was the full-time police, 'B' the part-time force and 'C' a reserve force. This arrangement ensured that, if necessary, every able-bodied Protestant male could be uniformed and armed to defend the state. By the summer of 1922, 13 battalions of regular British Army troops augmented some 50,000 full- and part-time police which meant there was one armed member of the security forces for every thirty citizens of the new state. The departmental committee set up to examine the issue of policing had recommended that one-third of the force be Catholic, with preference given to ex-members of the RIC. The provisions of the Craig-Collins pact of February 1922 reinforced this recommendation.[3]

The fate of the pact was indicative of what was to come. A crucial clause in the pact dealt with policing. The clause specified that the 'B' Special units in mixed districts of Belfast were to be 50 per cent Catholic, that an advisory committee with Catholic members was to be set up to assist with recruiting, and that any search for arms was to be carried out by a mixed force. In addition, Catholic representation was to be guaranteed on the police recruiting committee.

The potential effect of this provision of the pact was enormous. The unionist monopoly over policing would have been challenged and, more importantly, nationalists would have had input into the religious composition of the force and the possibility of some direct control over policing. Ultimately, this may have contributed to the internal stability of the region, since Catholics may have been more inclined to accept the institutional arrangements of the new Northern state, but in the face of concerted opposition from all sides within his party, Craig crumbled. As Farrell notes, 'It seems that Craig had to choose between confronting his own forces and undermining the pact. He chose the latter' (Farrell, 1980, p. 115).

Organisation, Recruitment and Composition of the RUC

The new state of Northern Ireland was organised into a number of administrative districts for the purposes of policing. Under the Local Government (Ireland) Act 1898, Belfast and Derry had been established as County Boroughs; the County Borough of Belfast was headed by a City Commissioner and by 1927 was divided into five districts (Ryder, 1989). Outside Belfast, the basic organisational division was the County; this was divided into six or eight districts headed by a County Inspector, often assisted by a Head Constable. These districts were further divided into eight to twelve sub-districts and depending on their size came under the command of a sergeant, or in the larger towns a Head Constable (Hezlet, 1972). The 'barrack' represented the base of the organisational hierarchy. This was manned on a 24-hour basis by a station sergeant, and in the smaller towns and villages between four and six constables, often working in excess of eighty hours per week. In addition, members of the 'A' and 'B' Class Special

Constabulary mobilised for full-time barrack duties were also permanently stationed there.

In 1922, there were approximately 224 police barracks inherited from the RIC, though many of them, particularly in rural areas, were in a bad state of repair, having been a frequent target for IRA attack. In 1936, the Stormont government (Parliament Buildings at Stormont had been opened by the Prince of Wales in November 1932) allocated £800,000 for a programme of rationalisation and repair to police barracks throughout the six counties. Consequently, the number of barracks in use was reduced from the 1922 figure of 224 to 196 (Hezlet, 1972). In 1922 a Criminal Investigation Department was established on the recommendation of Major Solly-Flood, with CID officers being attached to each division. The RUC were to make use of a training camp established at Newtownards in 1920 for the training of the USC. In 1936, training was moved to the Depot in Enniskillen, Co. Fermanagh, where it remained until 1986, before transferring to Garnerville in East Belfast, after being damaged in an IRA mortar attack. Training for recruits was conducted in two stages. The first stage took place over a twenty-week period at the Depot in Enniskillen. Recruits were then attached to a police station for eighteen months, after which the probationer constable returned to the Depot for another eight weeks (Hunt Report, 1969, p. 17).

In 1922, three weeks after the formation of the force, the Minister for Home Affairs, Dawson Bates received a letter on behalf of a number of RUC officers seeking permission to attend meetings of the Orange Order. Bates passed the letter to Craig who sanctioned the formation of an Orange Lodge specifically for the RUC in January 1923. This lodge was to be called the Sir Robert Peel Memorial Loyal Orange Lodge and soon boasted a membership of 300, almost one-quarter of the force composition of 1,100 at that time. Members of the Unionist government (Ryder, 1989, p. 61) also regularly attended this lodge.

The 1922 Constabulary Act set the upper limit on RUC recruitment to 3,000 men. This stipulation remained until amended by the Constabulary Act of 1963. The 1922 Constabulary Act also made provision for one-third of the RUC to be Catholic, recruited directly from the RIC. However, the RUC was relatively slow at attaining its full complement of officers. By June 1923, the RUC had only attracted 1,100 men, which had increased to 2,130 by April, with the full 3,000 not being established until 1927. First impressions might lead us to conclude that the RUC was relatively successful in attracting Catholic recruits. For example, by 1925, 12 out of 58 officers of District Inspector rank or above were Catholics who had been recruited from the RIC. Similarly, 18 out of 64 Head Constables (28.1 per cent), and 157 out of 457 Sergeants (34.4 per cent) were Catholic in 1927. However, these figures may be misleading, since the Unionist government's attempts to attract experienced RIC officers of NCO rank or above tend to distort the picture. For example, 30.9 per cent of all NCO/Junior Officers were Catholic in 1927, but the figure for Catholic rank-and-file officers was less than half that at 13.7 per cent. In other words, Catholics tended to be well represented at NCO/Junior Officer level but rather less well represented in the rank and file. Throughout the 1930s, the proportion of Catholics in the RUC remained static and had begun to decline from the 1950s, as many founder RIC members retired after completing their thirty years' service (all figures from Farrell, 1983, pp. 266–8).

Retiring officers were invariably replaced by members of the Special Constabulary (which was itself exclusively Protestant); as a result, by 1969, the percentage of Catholic officers in the RUC had fallen to around 11 per cent (Farrell, 1983, p. 268). Indeed, recruitment from the USC persisted up until the disbandment of the force (Sir Albert Kennedy, the Inspector General of the RUC 1961–67 was an ex-'B' Special) and ex-USC personnel generally comprised between one-quarter and one-third of the total RUC membership (Farrell, 1983, p. 268). When the USC was finally disbanded in 1970, many ex-personnel enlisted in the newly established RUC Reserve force (RUCR) and the locally recruited Ulster Defence Regiment (UDR).

Powers and Responsibilities

In addition to their ordinary criminal and common law powers, the RUC had access to a wide range of 'special' powers laid down in legislation enacted by the Unionist government. On 21 March 1922, the Minister for Home Affairs announced a replacement for the Restoration of Order Act, the Civil Authorities (Special Powers) Bill. This received its Royal Assent on 7

April 1922, and gave the Minister for Home Affairs (and the RUC who were responsible for enforcing it) wide powers of arrest, search, questioning, detention, flogging and internment. The Special Powers Act effectively conveyed executive powers to the RUC, a point which was made clear by the Northern Ireland Prime Minister, James Craig, during the final reading of the Bill: 'The Civil Authority will be in general the Minster of Home Affairs but he will also have power to delegate wide executive powers to officers of the police who are under his disposal.'[4]

There was no possibility for judicial review of the RUC's behaviour. A clause contained within the Act stipulated that the Minister for Home Affairs (and agents acting on his authority) could legally 'take all such steps ... as may be necessary for preserving peace and maintaining order' (Hillyard, 1983, p. 34). This clause effectively gave retrospective legal immunity to the crown forces (that is, the RUC and USC) for 'anything done *in good faith* in the execution of their duty for the defence of Northern Ireland' [emphasis added].[5] The Special Powers Act was renewed annually until 1928, when it was renewed for a further five years and made permanent in 1933. Also, in the absence of a centralised government bureaucracy, the RUC (like the RIC) had extensive powers to perform a number of administrative tasks which allowed them to penetrate deep into the community.

From its inception, the RUC was a paramilitary force and one that played a highly political role. From its formation in 1922, the RUC was charged with implementing the Special Powers Act and other legislation (for example, the Flags and Emblems Act and the Public Order Act) designed to maintain the hegemony of the Unionist regime. While the RUC undoubtedly performed 'routine' policing duties, these were ultimately subjugated to its primary role for the suppression of nationalist dissent.

The Ulster Special Constabulary

The Ulster Special Constabulary had a slightly earlier genesis than the RUC, having been officially established by the British administration in October 1920. However, armed Protestant militias were already in existence from early 1919, with a regenerated UVF and a number of vigilante forces being established in all Six Counties. Sir Basil Brooke (later to become Viscount Brookeborough and Prime Minister of Northern Ireland) was instrumental in establishing a Citizen's Defence Force in Fivemiletown, Brookeborough, Lisnaskea, Maguiresbridge and Lisbellaw, some seven months before official permission was given for the establishment of the USC (Dane, 1970).[6] Throughout 1919 and 1920, unionists were becoming perplexed at the inability of the RIC and British Army to contain the escalating violence in the North, and were demanding the right to establish their own militia based on the UVF. The British administration in Dublin was initially reluctant to concede to unionist demands since they feared that it would exacerbate the unrest and lead to civil war (Farrell, 1983, p. 32). However, the unionists had the advantage of an increasingly divided Cabinet led by Churchill, who was swayed by Craig's insistence that insurrection in the north could be defeated by military force.

In October 1920, the newly appointed Under-Secretary in Belfast was authorised to form a Special Constabulary using powers contained in the Special Constables (Ireland) Acts 1832 and 1914. Recruitment for the officially sanctioned USC began in November 1920 and newly appointed 'A' Class Special Constables were outfitted in dyed-green army uniforms, and armed with Italian rifles left over from the First World War, although many members (particularly those from the UVF) already had their own guns. Officers were issued with revolvers (Dane, 1970, p. 4). Both Sir Basil Brooke and Sir James Craig (who was to become the first Prime Minister in the new Northern Ireland Parliament) protested to the British government that the USC were not to be regarded as a temporary force but should be retained indefinitely as an integral part of the Northern Ireland internal security apparatus (Dane, 1970, p. 10). Indeed, it was only in April 1970 that the last surviving remnant of the Ulster Special Constabulary, the 'B' Specials, was disbanded.

Originally the USC were divided into Classes 'A', 'B' and 'C', with a C1 class being formed in 1921. 'A' Specials were full-time reserve police and could be posted for duty anywhere in Northern Ireland. They were armed, equipped, uniformed and paid the same wages as the regular police. There was an upper age limit of 45. The 'B' Specials were primarily a part-time force, unpaid except for a small clothing allowance. They were expected to carry out duties in their own locality on one or two evenings per week. Initially they were distinguished by an armband in the absence of a uniform and had to supply their own weapons. However, by 1921 they were supplied with both, and from 1923 were paid for each patrol. The 'C' Specials were simply men listed as available for emergency service. They did not wear a uniform and were not provided with arms, although they were issued with a licence to obtain their own. Indeed, S.G. Tallent said in October 1925 that 'the chief object of the ['C' Specials] is to allow those who have private weapons of their own to keep them' (cited in Farrell, 1983, p. 262).

By 1921 the pre-war UVF had been organised all over the Six-Counties area, with its headquarters in Belfast under the command of Lt Colonel Crawford. According to Hezlet (1972, p. 53), this was a major embarrassment for the Unionist government who regarded Crawford's efforts as undermining recruitment for a still under-strength Special Constabulary. Consequently, the government decided to incorporate the UVF within the USC structure and authorised the formation of the C1 Special Constabulary. This was ostensibly regarded (and used) as a military unit, being organised into battalions and having a military chain of command. The C1 Special Constabulary was deployed along the border during the IRA campaign of 1921–22 and also during the Boundary Commission crisis.

Debate in the Northern Ireland Parliament suggests that unionists were distrustful of the British administration, believing that the British Army was likely to be pulled out of the North at any time. While Hezlet (1972, p. 88) does not explicitly make the connection, he notes that the projected recruitment of the C1 Class Specials was to be sixteen battalions of infantry, exactly the same as the number of British soldiers stationed in the North at the time.

The USC was organised into eight command areas: Fermanagh, Tyrone, Antrim, Down, Derry and Armagh, plus the County Boroughs of Belfast and Derry (Hunt Report, 1969, p. 40). The organisation of the USC differed between City and County forces, with the majority of Special Constables in Belfast and Derry being 'barracked' and those in the counties organised into platoons. Also, while the USC was ultimately under the control of the RIC/RUC Inspector General, the chain of command was rather more direct in Belfast and Derry. (After partition, the RIC formally operated for twelve months in Northern Ireland before being replaced by the RUC). These organisational differences also meant operational differences between the City and County forces. In Belfast, the Special Constabulary was fully integrated with – and under the direct control of – the RIC (and later the RUC) with a USC sub-district being attached to each RIC/RUC barrack. The Belfast USC was headed by a Deputy City Commandant, responsible to the City Commissioner of the RIC (RUC). In the County Borough of Derry, the USC was also integrated with the RIC/ RUC, although this was rather more loosely based than in Belfast. A City Commandant, who was responsible to the RIC/ RUC County Inspector, headed the USC in the city of Derry.

In the counties, the USC was headed by a County Commandant, with USC divisions matching as closely as possible RIC/RUC divisions. The County Commandant was solely responsible for the organisation of the USC in his particular area, although he was required to liaise with the RIC County Inspector. Each county was divided into districts under District Commandants and further into sub-districts under Sub-District Commandants. Sub-districts were broken down into platoons of around 26 Special Constables, under the command of a Head Constable and a Platoon Sergeant. Platoons were further sub-divided into Sections of between six and twelve Special Constables under the command of a Section Sergeant. In 1921, the Unionist government issued a memorandum in an attempt to clarify the duties of the USC in relation to the RIC (Hezlet, 1972, p. 30). It stated that the USC could not conduct raids, searches or patrol without RIC approval. However, while this stipulation was generally adhered to in the cities (because of the organisation of the USC in these areas), it was frequently overlooked in rural areas, where the USC were able to patrol, conduct searches and set up road checks at will. Training for the 'A' Class Special Constabulary was conducted at a training establishment at Newtownards (where they were to be later joined by the RUC) over a six-week period and also at Lurgan, in County Armagh. However, Sergeant Instructors were appointed in 1923 to offer periodic (basic) firearms and drill training to members of the 'B' Specials in each district (Hezlet, 1972). Responsibility for processing applications lay with a County Selection Board, which also functioned as a Disciplinary Board to deal with complaints and discipline. This was comprised of justices of the peace, ex-army officers and, since all applications had to be approved by the RIC/RUC in the first instance, a member of the force also. Finally, by late 1921 the 'A' Special Constabulary was given the same powers (that is, of arrest, etc.) as the regular RIC and were required to take the RIC oath of allegiance before appointment. This apparently caused consternation among the 'A' Specials – having taken the RIC oath, they were *de facto* RIC officers and technically could have been deployed to the South to reinforce the RIC there.

By 1922, and the formation of the RUC, the Special Constabulary was well established. The complement of 'A' Class Special Constables exceeded 5,000 men, who were uniformed, trained, well armed and organised throughout the Six-Counties area. The complement of 'B' Specials was also approaching 20,000, with a large number of these mobilised for full-time duty. Both 'A' Specials and those 'B' Specials mobilised full-time were stationed in 'barracks' to offer support to the fledgling RUC. In rural areas, the USC was organised into mobile platoons, patrolling in armoured cars and lorries. The introduction of wireless communication for the USC in 1922 meant that they could perform as the modern equivalent of mobile support units.

While technically one-third of places in the USC may have been set aside for Catholic recruits, the force remained an exclusively Protestant one (Farrell, 1983; Hillyard, 1983). In the early years, a number of Catholics did apply to join the 'A' Specials but generally left after a few months' service. Unionists claimed that the IRA intimidated Catholics from joining the force. However, while there may be an element of truth in this, it is also clear that there was little effort made by the Unionist government to actively encourage Catholic recruitment (Farrell, 1983). In any case, allegations of sectarian harassment and incidences of reprisals soon fostered a high degree of antipathy towards what was rapidly becoming, in both ethos and composition, an essentially Protestant and unionist militia.

Between 1921 and 1925, the complement of the Special Constabulary never fell below 30,000. This was in addition to the RIC (and later the RUC), the British Army, which had sixteen battalions of infantry stationed in the Six Counties and the ordinary 'C' Class Special Constabulary, which could include every adult Protestant male with a firearms licence (Farrell, 1983). The Unionist government was determined to keep the Special Constabulary up to strength for two reasons:

first, because of the IRA campaign between 1921 and 1922,
and second, because of the fears that the Boundary Commission was going to recommend the transfer of large areas of
land to the Irish Free State, which the Unionist government
was going to oppose at any price. In 1922, Craig declared, 'I
will never give in to any arrangement of the boundary that
leaves our Ulster area less than it is under the Government
of Ireland Act'.[7] In the event, the Boundary Commission left
the border unchanged.[8]

Having seen off the crisis posed by the Boundary Commission, the Unionist government was faced with another one.
Churchill had complained to Craig that the Westminster government could not finance the USC indefinitely and demanded
that the force be disbanded, repeating a by now historic concern of the British government about the cost of policing
Ireland, albeit a smaller part. (Between 1922 and 1925, the
USC had cost the British Exchequer £6,780,000 (Farrell,
1983, p. 253).) Craig agreed but argued that the 'B' Specials
should be retained, and stated that the Northern Ireland government would finance the force itself. Towards the end of
1925, Craig authorised Colonel Wickham to set about disbanding the A, C1 and C Class Special Constabulary, a process
that was complete by the beginning of 1926, though not without incident: the 'A' Specials mutinied in many areas of the
north, refusing to either disband or hand in their weapons
unless they were guaranteed a bonus of £200 per man. The
Unionist government adopted an unbending attitude and, with
little public support for mutiny (the general public thought
that they were overpaid anyway), it fizzled out after a couple
of days. No action was taken by the government against the
mutineers.

By the middle of 1926, it was apparent to the Unionist government that the 'B' Specials were costing three times more
than originally had been budgeted for. It was decided to scale
down the activities of the 'B' Specials, with three categories of
service advocated: full patrol, half patrol, reserve patrol. From
1927, all 'B' Specials were put in the 'reserve' category which
meant that they were required to attend parade once a year
with their equipment and uniform in good condition and intact
(Hezlet, 1972, p. 123). Despite the curtailment of the USC,
the ratio of police to population remained extremely high. In
1924, England and Wales had one police officer for 699
people, Scotland, one for 751, while in Northern Ireland there

was one police officer for every 160 inhabitants (Weitzer, 1995, p. 34).

During periods of heightened IRA activity, perceived 'crises', or more general bouts of unionist paranoia, the 'B' Specials were brought out of hibernation and mobilised to work either in mixed RUC/USC patrols or separately (Farrell, 1983, p. 268). For example, in 1932 when de Valera came to power in the south, the Unionist government mobilised 3,200 'B' Specials for active border patrol. Likewise, during a period of IRA activity in the late 1940s and during the IRA campaign of 1956–62, 1,600 'B' Specials were mobilised for full-time duty (Hezlet, 1972). In April 1966, it was decided to put the whole of the USC in the 'patrol' category for the commemoration of the fiftieth anniversary of the Easter Rising. By May 1968, the establishment of the USC was at 12,542, although by June the number had been reduced to 8,285 (Hezlet, 1972, p. 206).

Perhaps more so than the RUC, the Unionist government relied upon the Special Constabulary as its own private militia. Unlike the RUC, the Specials never made any pretence at performing 'routine' policing tasks; their sole function was for the suppression of nationalist dissent, a task for which they were used many times during their fifty-year history. Unsurprisingly, the nationalist community in Northern Ireland detested the USC (particularly the 'B' Specials), seeing them as sectarian and brutal. Indeed, Farrell outlines a number of instances where the USC were alleged to have been involved in a number of sectarian murders and murder bids (1983, pp. 298–304). In any case, members of the USC – particularly those in the 'B' Specials who were not mobilised for full-time duty – placed great store on their 'local knowledge' which extended to 'knowing' the political views of members of the Catholic community (Farrell, 1983, p. 271). However, this invariably resulted in the petty harassment of their Catholic neighbours, with even individuals known to the 'Specials' being stopped and routinely questioned about their activities. The crisis for the USC came with the civil rights campaign in the late 1960s and it was eventually, though reluctantly, disbanded in April 1970.

Institutionalising Division

The decision to abandon any attempt to make the police either representative of, or acceptable to, the nationalist community in Northern Ireland, was to have fateful consequences, but not for half a century. Unionists with long memories and a sense of history must have felt a sense of satisfaction at the course of events after partition. For, despite the efforts of the IRA and, in their eyes, the provisional government in Dublin, the status quo was maintained in the Six Counties during a period of considerable unrest after partition. The militants among the minority were quelled and held in check: the tactics of terror and repression practised by the state worked. The Civil Authorities (Special Powers) Act (1922) gave the police unprecedented powers. Many powers were transferred from the judiciary to the executive and the actions of the Home Secretary were removed from parliamentary scrutiny. The Act gave the minister the power 'to take all such steps and issue all such orders as may be necessary for the preserving of peace'. The minister had the option of delegating his powers to individual police officers. The introduction of the B Specials ensured blanket policing in nationalist areas, something which its predecessor, the Yeomanry, had never achieved. Unionists may have achieved their objective of moulding the new state in their own image, but the price was to be high. Unable, and unwilling, to establish a non-partisan police force and allow the nationalist population to participate in the running of the new state, a bitter legacy was in the making. The example of the new state in the south was instructive but ignored. After a bitter civil war – which claimed more lives than the War of Independence – the anti-treatyites under de Valera eventually succumbed to the blandishments of parliamentary democracy and turned on their erstwhile comrades in the IRA, who continued to enjoy limited support only because of the situation in Northern Ireland. Perhaps there was too much bitterness, paranoia and cultural baggage in the North to allow a *rapprochement* between the two communities but the Unionists, to their eternal shame, did not even try.

3   Policing under Stormont

Normal Policing?

In Protestant folklore, 'pre-Troubles' Northern Ireland was a mythical Eden: relatively peaceful, fairly stable, and with generally good relations prevailing between Protestants and Catholics (see, for example, McAughtry 1978, 1993; Hermon, 1997). Times may have been hard, but it was a 'great wee place altogether, if only the IRA hadn't ruined everything', to pander to the well-worn cliché (See Ulster Society, 1986; Smyth, 1989). Unfortunately, however, such a vision is not confined to Protestant folklore. The media, the British government and Unionist politicians have frequently postulated a 'return to normality' – a return to the mythical Eden of yore. A similar perspective is also manifested in academic discussions of policing in the pre-Direct Rule period. Brewer (1993) makes a distinction between the 'old' model of policing prior to 1968 and policing during 'the Troubles'. He suggests that prior to the onset of civil unrest in 1968, the RUC were able to approximate the 'liberal' model of policing found elsewhere in the United Kingdom, performing a wide range of routine and 'ordinary' policing tasks (p. 187). Such a view is also reiterated by the RUC in their official publications, and in statements from the Police Federation where they argue for the day when they can 'return to normal policing' as stated in the 1993 Northern Ireland Police Federation's Conference Report. The current paramilitary role of the RUC, according to this version of events, is an unfortunate blip in the history and development of the force.

Brewer also adopts a similar argument in relation to the precursor of the RUC, the RIC. As he suggests:

> ... policemen often provided the only source of reading and numeracy skills which the non-literate and non-numerate could draw upon when needed. So policemen often read and composed people's letters for them, did the accounts for shopkeepers, and completed various official forms for members of the public. This is a good illustration of the

benign model of policing adopted by the RIC in many parts of Ireland. (1989, p. 84)

However, while this may well be the case (see below for similar evidence from ex-RUC officers), the danger here is to confuse what the police end up doing with their intended function (Brogden, 1987). It will be argued in the following section that 'good' police – community relations, particularly with the nationalist/Catholic community could only exist in so far as they did not conflict with the RUC's principal role in stifling nationalist and republican dissent.

However, to what extent can Northern Ireland be regarded as a 'normal' society between 1922 and 1972? Equally, to what extent did the RUC perform as a 'normal' police force during this period? It will be argued here that the dominant conception of the Northern Ireland state pre-1968 and the role of the RUC within the state apparatus, is heavily infused with idealism about a mystical past. Certainly, Beckett (1972) has argued that Ireland as a whole was, between the 1920s and 1960s, at its most peaceful during recent history. However, this may apply more accurately to the South than to the North during these years. In Northern Ireland, it might be more accurate to speak about the absence of 'overt' conflict rather than the absence of conflict *per se*, given that a substantial nationalist minority was coerced into the Northern Ireland state, who neither owed nor displayed normative loyalty to it. Marenin (1996a, p. 18; 1996b, pp. 309–25) argues that in any given political structure, stability can be based on either consent or coercion. He cites the example of the Weimar Republic, where the 'police provided both effective repression (of the undesirable) and protection (the streets were safe to walk in) and were tightly controlled by the state' (1996a, p. 18). Similarly, it can be argued that in a purely objective sense both Stalinist Russia and Nazi Germany might (perversely) be described as 'peaceful' societies, for the simple reason that dissent and opposition to both regimes were ruthlessly monitored and dealt with (Broznat, 1981).

In Northern Ireland – without belittling the horrors of either Nazi Germany or Stalinist Russia – stability based on consent may have been desirable, but was in fact immaterial. 'Normality' (or more accurately the appearance of a 'normal' situation) was enforced by the formidable might of the Unionist government's security apparatus. In the early part of the

regime's history, this force could be mobilised with upwards
of 50,000 members of the USC and RUC (Ellison and Smyth,
1996, p. 174), though, as the level of violence decreased
from the 1930s, a number of Specials were transferred to
the 'reserve' category, with the potential of rapid mobilisation if required (see Farrell, 1983). This figure does not include
the Air Force, the Navy and the 16 battalions of British Army
troops already stationed in Northern Ireland, and also the 'C'
Special reserve force – whose numbers (if mobilised) could
potentially have run to a hundred thousand men. Indeed, Sir
Basil Brooke, while he was County Commandant of the USC,
boasted that he could if required, mobilise one member of the
USC for every three adult males in County Fermanagh (Dane,
1970).

The police, in common with all large organisations, engage
in presentational strategies, what Altheide and Johnson (1980)
term 'bureaucratic propaganda', to legitimate their activities.
However, for the police, these presentational strategies assume
a strategic importance given the political and public exigencies in regard to their 'impossible mandate' to control crime
(Manning, 1978). The equally problematic issue of public
order maintenance – which has historically led the police into
highly visible and damaging encounters with certain groups
within society (such as with the miners in England) – can also
challenge the carefully constructed image of legitimacy. Similarly, in divided societies such as Northern Ireland, where the
RUC are an integral part of a contested political system, there
are particular presentational difficulties.

It is, therefore, understandable that the discourse of the
RUC should hark back to a 'golden age of policing', a time
when they could operate unarmed in nationalist areas. Looking back nostalgically, one officer commented in 1980, at the
height of the hunger strikes crisis during which the RUC and
British Army fired over 30,000 plastic bullets in nationalist
areas: 'People forget what it was like. You could walk anywhere,
you could walk through Andersonstown unarmed and in uniform, with no problems. You'd go around and close the pubs
and people would buy you a pint' (*Police*, May 1980).

Similarly, another senior RUC officer recalls:

In the RUC the service ideal has always existed as part and parcel of
policing – even from the early days of the force. The service side of
things – helping people – was a major facet of policing. Even the RIC,

which pre-dated the RUC, performed a mainly service role. The service aspect was a central feature of their work, as against law enforcement which most people perceive policing to be about. (cited in Ellison, 1997 p. 145)

While such views have an obvious ethnomethodological validity, in the sense of highlighting the role of personal accounts in structuring individual subjectivities and constructions of the past (Mulcahy, 1999), they are none the less part of a broader ideological construct which views pre-Troubles Northern Ireland through rose-tinted spectacles. This ideological complacency extended to all areas of cultural life, including literature, the visual arts, and the world of academia. Unlike the South, no tradition of intellectual dissent emerged in the North. The dead hand of Unionism proved even more effective than that of the Catholic Church in encouraging conformity and apathy.

The Northern Ireland state remained under one-party dominance for over fifty years, with one Unionist Prime Minister – Sir Basil Brooke (later Viscount Brookeborough) – remaining in office for twenty years. The gerrymandering of electoral boundaries and widespread discrimination against the Catholic minority allowed Unionist hegemony to remain unchallenged (Coogan, 1995; McGarry and O'Leary, 1995).

In 1921, the Unionist government passed the Local Government (Emergency Provisions) Act which gave the Minister for Home Affairs the power to dissolve local councils with nationalist majorities and replace them with a Commissioner chosen by the Unionist government. Under the Local Government (Northern Ireland) Act and the Local Government (Franchise) Act, electoral ward districts were gerrymandered to ensure a Unionist majority and proportional representation abolished. Gallagher (1957) estimated that well over 90 per cent of local council seats in Northern Ireland remained uncontested between 1923 and the late 1950s because of the virtual impossibility of unseating the Unionist candidate (cited in Tomlinson, 1980a, p. 95–118).

The Unionist government was, of course, assisted by the security forces: the RUC and the USC were equipped with wide powers under specially enacted emergency legislation. These powers, as we have seen, were disproportionately directed at the nationalist community in Northern Ireland and rarely used against Protestants (Boyle and Hadden, 1994; Hillyard

1983, 1987). It is also difficult to argue that Northern Ireland represented a 'normal' society in so far as the state itself was formed in the absence of even a semblance of social democratic consensus and lacked the basic pillar of parliamentary democracy, a competitive party system (O'Dowd, 1980a, p. 10). In any case, the Unionist regime made little effort to encourage the normative loyalty of the Catholic minority to the new state. In fact, the opposite was often the case. In July 1933, Sir Basil Brooke, then a government minister and later Prime Minister of Northern Ireland, stated in a speech in Fermanagh:

> There were a great number of Protestants and Orangemen who employed Roman Catholics. He felt he could speak freely on this subject, as he had not a Roman Catholic about his place ... He would point out that the Roman Catholics were endeavouring to get in everywhere and were out with all their force and might to destroy the power and constitution of Ulster. There was a definite ploy to overpower the vote of Unionists in the north. He would appeal to Loyalists, therefore, wherever possible, to employ Protestant lads and lassies. (cited in Bardon, 1992, p. 538)

Cain (1979, p. 158) has noted that 'policing must be defined in terms of its key practice.' Similarly, Bowden (1978, p. 70) argues that any discussion of policing must take cognizance of the historical dimension. However, the failure to account for 'key practice' and 'history' is evident in a number of contemporary accounts on the RUC, which place considerable emphasis on the extent to which the RUC performs a wide range of 'normal' and 'routine' policing duties. While this is not to deny that the RUC (or even the RIC) performed such a role, the point remains that the RUC emerged historically, as did the RIC before it, with the primary role of counter-insurgency and political control in mind (Broeker, 1970; Ellison and Smyth, 1996; Palmer, 1988). It is this aspect to which the activity of 'normal policing' was largely subordinated. The 'key practice' then, for the RUC, has been the historical one of managing nationalist dissent and assisting in the maintenance of Unionist hegemony. In any case, the extent to which the RUC (or the RIC) performed 'routine' and 'normal' police duties is largely irrelevant in two respects. First, historical evidence suggests that all colonial forces performed a number of ordinary or routine policing tasks, which were themselves regarded as an important strategy in the legitimation of the colonial state (see Anderson and Killingray, 1991, 1992; Cain 1991, 1979). Second, to cite but one example, Anderson (1991) has demonstrated that policing in colonial Kenya eventually, after an initial coercive state, became geared towards crime prevention and crime detection. However, he notes that this was not matched by any parallel commitment towards policing by consent (pp. 183–200).

A Decentralised Power Structure

With the exception of the internal security apparatus, which was always highly centralised, the Northern Ireland state bureaucracy under the Unionist leadership remained for much of its history relatively decentralised and localised (Buckland, 1979). It was only with the advent of a more 'reformist' leadership under Terence O'Neill in 1963 that the Stormont government veered towards a more interventionist stance in relation to central government planning. Indeed, for much of the post-war period, the Unionist leadership, itself heavily recruited from the ranks of the bourgeoisie and the landed class, was committed to a strict non-interventionist and *laissez-faire* position in many areas of central government administration.[1] Policy making was often erratic and *ad hoc*, except in the field of internal security. It was more of an attempt to juggle the demands of conflicting elements in the Protestant class alliance (that is, working-class loyalists and the unionist bourgeoisie) rather than the consequence of any grand scheme or plan (see O'Dowd et al., 1980, for a discussion of policy making under the Stormont government). Reflecting this non-interventionist stance, the bulk of decision making was exercised at the level of the local state.

Local authorities had considerable power and exercised a high level of autonomy from the central state apparatus, such as it was. Until a degree of intervention, and hence centralisation, was forced on a hesitant Unionist leadership via the British Welfare State reforms of the 1940s, local authorities were solely responsible for the provision of education, housing, planning and social services (Tomlinson, 1980a, p. 98).[2]

One effect of this decentralisation was to entrust many administrative tasks to the police. As mentioned previously, the early RUC (and indeed the RIC) performed a much wider range of duties than its contemporary counterpart.[3] For example, under the Stormont regime, the RUC acted as customs agents, as registrars of births, deaths and marriages, and as livestock inspectors. Officers also conducted the census and completed tillage returns. As one ex-RUC sergeant remembers:

> I joined the force [RUC] as a raw recruit in 1936 and retired from the force in 1966. At that time you know, we had to undertake more duties than your average Constable would nowadays. There was literally no limit to the range of things we were required to do. Everything from taking a telephone message from someone's son in America, to checking that the local farmers had their Ministry [of Agriculture] paperwork complete. It was a lot better than now, at least in those days you could say that the police were part of the community. (cited in Ellison, 1997, p. 149)

In this sense, the duties and responsibilities of the RUC reflected closely those of the RIC before it:

> The duties of the constabulary are multifarious and onerous, and are becoming, every day, more and more so. In fact, whatever is to be done is expected to be performed by it. The constabulary is now the great machine by which almost every measure is worked (Mr and Mrs S.C. Hall, Ireland, London, 1841). (cited in Hawkins, 1991, p. 24)

These administrative and regulatory functions have historically been a common feature of police organisation, both in a colonial and non-colonial context (Anderson and Killingray, 1991, 1992; Brogden, 1987; Williams, 1979). Brogden (1987), for example, notes that policing in early Victorian England was equated with a form of local administration. Similarly, the nineteenth-century Parisian police were equally pervasive, performing a wide range of regulatory duties on behalf of the state:

> The lieutenant of police bore responsibility for the amelioration of city life as well as for the guarantee of public order. It was his task to protect and preserve life not only from the assassin and the armed thief, but from the entire range of its enemies: from disease and natural disaster, from accident and fire, from hunger and unwholesome food. (Williams, 1979, p. 238)

The RIC, and later the RUC became a model for colonial policing in the British Empire. The Colonial Office decreed in 1907 that the RIC Depot in Dublin would be used to train commissioned officers for colonial police service; after partition, this role was taken over by the RUC for eleven years, until training was moved to police colleges in England. From the middle of the nineteenth century onwards, the RIC was used as a model for colonial forces in places as far apart as Canada, Australia and Nigeria. The government-issued Ulster Year Book for 1956–57 took considerable pride in the role taken by the RUC in training colonial police officers: 'The police organisation in Ireland has been the model adopted by many Colonial territories, and many officers of the Colonial forces were given their initial police training either in the Royal Irish Constabulary training depot, or later, in that of the Royal Ulster Constabulary' (Ulster Year Book, 1956–57, p. 263).

Policing in Ireland not only reflected elements of a colonial model but also embodied elements of an administrative model (Hawkins, 1991). This was in keeping with the pattern established elsewhere in the Empire. For instance, Anderson and Killingray (1991, p. 9) note that in Australia and India the police quickly became one of the state's largest bureaucracies, so extensive were the duties and responsibilities they had to perform. Indeed, for the RUC the responsibility for performing many of these administrative tasks (discussed above) persisted well into the 1960s (Hermon, 1997; Ryder, 1989).

In political terms as well, it was important for the Unionist government to have a force they could rely on and trust. Farrell notes that during the formative years of the state, the Unionist leadership regarded the USC as a somewhat volatile commodity. These fears were exacerbated with the 'A' Special mutiny in December 1925, and also when some members of the Special Constabulary flirted with labour unrest during the 1926 General Strike. The RUC by contrast, were to become, 'a reliable and unquestioning instrument of government policy' (Farrell, 1983, p. 268). In the absence of a centralised and pervasive central state bureaucracy, the Unionist government initially had to rely on the RUC to rationalise its administration throughout the Six-Counties area. This factor was important, not only in a technical sense, given the minimalist nature of the central government bureaucracy, but also in a tactical sense, since it helped consolidate the position of the Unionist government in the border counties. It was in areas close to the border that hostility to the regime erupted in episodic outbreaks of violence, for example, the IRA campaign towards the end of the Second World War, and the campaign of 1956–62.

Using the police to perform administrative and regulatory functions – implying a Foucaultian notion of supervision and surveillance – was regarded in colonial situations as a useful way of 'screening' the indigenous community (Finnane, 1991). In most colonial situations, the initial and often violent consolidation of the colonial state's position through coercion later gave way to less ostensible, but no less effective measures for consolidation and control.

In Northern Ireland, from the 1930s onwards, in what was to be a period of relative stability, the Unionist government could rely on less overt forms of coercion to stifle dissent. This involved using the RUC and USC in a mainly surveillance capacity which included the routine administrative role of the RUC. Two RUC officers who served in rural areas during the 1940s and 1950s recalled their everyday surveillance role in interviews. Although the IRA was dormant during the years of the Second World War, one constable recalls that 'we were encouraged to keep an eye out … for anything that looked a bit out of the ordinary … say somebody seemed to be breaking their routine, now that would have seemed a bit odd to me' (cited in Ellison, 1997, p. 152). The administrative functions of the police could be used as a cover for political surveillance, as another officer makes clear: ' … we got a report of this bloke who seemed to be making too many trips over into Monaghan … my sergeant calls me in and says, "Call up to the house on the pretence of some paperwork and have a wee juke around"' (ibid.).

The RUC then could 'manage' political dissent at the local level without it ever erupting into a major threat to the state. Additionally, since IRA activity during this period was generally rurally based and orchestrated, the Unionist government could also rely on the USC which operated on a fairly autonomous basis in the border counties (Hezlet, 1972). An ex-platoon sergeant in County Fermanagh suggests that while officially the USC may have been employed as an auxiliary police force, they 'weren't vaguely interested in police duties' and that 'police training and police duties wasn't relevant at all' to the main task of the USC, which this officer saw as 'providing security for the country' (cited in Ellison, 1997, p. 153). The importance of the local knowledge of the terrain and its inhabitants was crucial to the role of the USC; one officer, at least, was convinced that 'The local knowledge [of the USC] was what beat the IRA as far as we were concerned.'

This emphasis on local knowledge is stressed by another USC sergeant: 'We knew absolutely everything about the area and that prevented their [the IRA's] ability to move freely within the locality' (Ellison, 1997, p. 153).

This everyday surveillance of local populations by the Specials was complemented by the RUC's performance of administrative and regulatory duties and culminated in a dense web of intelligence gathering and indirect as well as direct control of the nationalist population.

'Community policing' under the Stormont regime?

The above analysis has implications for the perception of the current conflict as outlined in official sources and in conventional mythology. There is a tendency to romanticise life in 'pre-Troubles' Northern Ireland, through the depiction of a society that was relatively stable and characterised by a high degree of normality. However, this tends to depoliticise and dehistoricise the nature of the current conflict, and in particular underdetermines the dynamics of policing within the Northern Ireland state. The perceived absence of conflict in Northern Ireland society until the late 1960s is taken as evidence that the RUC were accepted by the nationalist community. Indeed, a number of RUC officers emphasised the 'good' relationships that existed with the local community during the pre-Direct Rule period. The mindset of many police officers is aptly summed up in the words of one ex-RUC sergeant who stressed that 'there were no problems between the RUC and the Catholic community', but then went on to say that 'It was only when the Civil Rights business started that you started to get some hostility' (cited in Ellison, 1997, p. 154).

While it cannot be disputed that the RUC did perform routine duties and also that there were large areas of Northern Ireland that remained untroubled by conflict, this perception of normality overlooks two issues. First, the façade of normality was imposed by what was effectively a one-party state and enforced by the combined efforts of the USC and the RUC as opposed to normality based upon any kind of normative or social democratic consensus. Second, the primary role of the RUC was not 'community policing', but the policing of political dissent. One should be cautious about conflating the

normality of 'pre-Troubles' Northern Ireland with the ability
of the RUC to perform a 'community policing' role, since this
was contingent upon, and indeed secondary to, their principal role of controlling political dissent. Those relationships
characteristic of normal policing could only exist with the
nationalist community in so far as they did not conflict with
this goal. Even the simplest encounter could be regarded as a
potential opportunity to gather intelligence. To echo the point
made earlier, policing must be defined in terms of its 'key practice'. For the RUC, this has historically been the control of
nationalist dissent and protest, which even in periods of relative calm still remained an important aspect of their work. In
relation to this, a number of RUC officers operated with a
typology of the Catholic population as 'good' or 'bad'. In other
words, there were 'ordinary decent Catholics' who supported
the RUC and the state, and bad Catholics who supported the
IRA and who wanted to destroy the state. One police officer
distinguished between Catholics who 'were law-abiding',
'respected law and order and just wanted to get on with their
lives' and the 'politically motivated Catholic – the likes of
Sinn Féin today – who was hell bent on raising trouble' (cited
in Ellison, 1997). The intensity and closeness of surveillance
and the stereotyping of individuals and families by the police
is clear from the comments of another officer: 'You know trouble ran in the same families ... you know families that displayed
an anti-police attitude. It's the same today' (p. 155). This
typology is reflected in other accounts of policing. For example, Cain (1973) has argued that police officers operate with a
typification of the 'rough' and 'respectable' working class.

The evidence would suggest that the Northern Ireland state
existed for over fifty years in a condition of imposed normality,
where dense levels of policing and special security legislation
became the norm. It was a state where the extraordinary
became the ordinary and where the minority was held responsible for its own exclusion. What passed for normality during
the early years of the existence of the Stormont state was at-
tained through the unremitting suppression of all political
dissent, whether constitutional or otherwise, and, after the state
had consolidated its position, through less overt means. Interview data from RUC officers who served during this period
suggests that while they performed many ordinary and routine duties, the policing of dissent was none the less perceived
as a vital aspect of their role. The police, of course, shared this

role with other administrative, cultural and educational agencies, all of whom did their bit to dampen down any potential expressions of minority dissent.

After 1945: Prelude to Crisis

In his monumental *History of Ulster*, Jonathan Bardon (1992) entitles his chapter on the period after the Second World War 'The Quiet Years' and, indeed, on the surface, Northern Ireland had achieved a level of prosperity and stability absent in the previous three decades of its existence. Stormont seemed to have overcome the two great threats to its existence 'insolvency and abandonment by Westminster' (p. 587) and was about to embark upon what, on the surface at least, was the most peaceful period in the troubled history of the state. However, the tensions between the two communities did not disappear but simply became less overt. Sir Basil Brooke and his government maintained an intensive propaganda campaign against nationalism in general and the Republic in particular. The establishment of the Anti-Partition League (APL), and the higher profile on Northern Ireland adopted by the coalition government in the South, added fuel to unionist paranoia (Bardon, 1992, p. 398). The voice of unionism, the *Belfast News Letter*, hardly let a day pass without a disparaging article on events in the Republic, and no speech by a Unionist politician was complete without a sideswipe at Dublin.

It was this unrelenting triumphalism and the refusal of Brooke's government to countenance any compromise with nationalism that led to the collapse of the APL. Founded in 1945 at a meeting in Dungannon attended by all Nationalist MPs and Senators and about 500 other delegates, the League aimed to pull together under one umbrella all those opposed to partition. The Nationalist MPs abandoned abstentionism and took their seats in Stormont, and branches of the League were rapidly established all over Ireland. The new Labour government in Britain was not inclined to entertain the complaints of nationalists, and Brooke seemed unable to move beyond base triumphalism, both inside and outside Parliament. Indeed, the increasing level of anti-partition rhetoric led the Inspector General of the RUC in March 1949 to call for the establishment of a new force of a thousand special constables to counter the perceived threat:

With the ever increasing volume of propaganda against the partition of this island and the frequent threats and innuendoes that force is the only solution of the problem, it is quite possible that, contrary to the stated policy of the leaders of the government and opposition in Eire respectively, the IRA may take matters into its own hands. (cited in Hezlet, 1972, p. 155)

Towards the end of 1950 a new force, called the RUC Reserve, was established, with the objective of countering civil disturbance as well as tackling the IRA. The force was made up of three mobile platoons (150 men in total, later to be considerably expanded in size) equipped with armoured and half-tracked vehicles and infantry-style weapons, including Bren medium machine guns, grenades, 2-inch mortars, anti-tank weapons and sub-machine guns as well as the usual rifles and pistols. Equipped with its own communication and cooking facilities, the Royal Ulster Constabulary Reserve (RUCR) was steadily expanded during the next two decades to play a 'spearhead' (Ryder, 1989, p. 91) role in crushing dissent. By 1969, the unit was organised into 8 platoons with a complement of 2 District Inspectors, 9 Head Constables, 41 Sergeants, 222 Constables and 22 Special Constables. According to Farrell, the RUCR was extensively used to break up nationalist demonstrations and marches and seems to have made one of its last appearances at Burntollet Bridge on 4 January 1969, during an ambush of Peoples Democracy supporters marching from Belfast to Derry. During this encounter, loyalists and police combined in a concerted attack on the marchers (Farrell, 1980, p. 251).

Initially, the new force was deployed to break up nationalist demonstrations that were on the increase after the APL disbanded in 1951, disenchanted with its fruitless excursion into constitutional politics. Attempts by nationalists to march were inevitably banned, either as posing a threat to public order, or because the Irish tricolour was to be carried. The Minister of Home Affairs, Edmond Warnock, banned an APL parade planned in Derry for St Patrick's Day 1948, commenting in Stormont: 'So long as I am Minister of Home Affairs, I shall not permit the republican flag to be carried through Derry City ... No Surrender'.[4]

The public exposure of the tricolour became the symbolic trigger for conflict between police and nationalists during this period. Such encounters generally occured after specific events such as nationalist election victories, commemorations such as St Patrick's Day or Easter, and during various days in August when nationalist parades were held. More sporadic and unpredictable encounters regularly took place in the wake of football matches or other events. The RUC, often unbidden by its political masters, seemed determined to suppress any public expression of nationalist identity. Nationalists managed to win limited legal support for their position. In the wake of the refusal of the RUC to protect Catholic football supporters from loyalist attack in Cookstown in August 1950, the courts ruled that all citizens should expect the protection of the police on a public highway. In April of the following year, the banning of the tricolour was successfully challenged, albeit on a technicality. The attitude of the RUC towards nationalists during this period is aptly summed up in the words of a policeman who served during the 1950s:

> The thing about policing in them days [the 1950s] was that you knew who everybody was and what they were up to. I remember, I was stationed in Tempo barracks for a number of years and you soon made it your business to know all the boys – and they knew that you knew. Quite honestly, the local IRA boys couldn't so much as fart and we'd get to know about it. I would say that we knew more about the goings on in the country areas. Of course we could rely on the Specials, but the nature of our job meant that we were always seen and that we could always get good intelligence. It was good crack in them days ... like you'd maybe pull a few boys in and give them a bit of grief ... or the Specials would give them a bit of a rub over when they met them out some night. (Ellison, 1997, p. 152)

This attitude was shared by the Unionist government, which was equally determined to reserve the public highway for Protestants alone, so that they could engage in consummate displays of what Ruane and Todd (1996, p. 184) term 'ritualised offensiveness', such as Orange Order marches through nationalist areas. However, in the wake of the adverse court decisions, Stormont rushed through the Public Order Bill in July 1951. This bill further increased the draconian powers of the police. All parades and demonstrations except 'traditional' ones (that is, loyalist) would have to give 48 hours' notice, and could be banned or re-routed – without the right of appeal – if the RUC considered that a breach of the peace would ensue.

During the two decades after the Second World War, the police were engaged in two primary functions: the first was

concerned with countering the threat of a renewed IRA campaign by surveillance, harassment and the use of draconian
powers of arrest and detention. The second function was to
police the symbolic world of nationalists, not only to isolate,
but also to deny any expression to minority culture. During
this period there was, in response to the failure of constitutional and parliamentary methods to effect reforms, a gradual
escalation of nationalist street politics. As we have seen, the
flying of the Irish tricolour was generally the signal for RUC
intervention and such encounters invariably ended in violence.
For example, on St Patrick's Day 1952, the APL held a rally in
Derry City. In the wake of the rally, the crowd unfurled a tricolour, which provoked a baton charge from the RUC. Repeated
baton charges followed and street fighting between locals and
the RUC reserve continued after dark. The Public Order Act
was not the only piece of legislation directed against expressions of nationalist culture. The Public Health and Local
Government Act (1949) indirectly banned the use of Irish
street names. Section nineteen of the Act stipulated: 'When a
district council exercises the powers conferred on them ...
with respect to putting up or painting the name by which a
street is to be known, they shall not cause such a name to be
put up or painted otherwise than in English.' Further powers
were given to the police under the Flags and Emblems Act
(1954). This piece of legislation was designed to extend and
refine the Public Order Act, by making it an offence to inter-
fere with the flying of the Union Jack in public while giving
the police powers to remove any other flag or emblem on
either public or private property if they considered it might
lead to a breach of the peace.

The tendency to look back at the two decades between the
end of the Second World War and the beginnings of the Civil
Rights agitation as a period of peace and communal harmony
is at variance with the facts. The police managed to keep the
simmering discontent of nationalists under control by a combination of repressive legislation and blanket surveillance,
assisted to no little extent by the tactical and strategic inef-
fectiveness of both the IRA and constitutional nationalism.
Nationalist politicians, mainly recruited from the comfortable
Catholic middle classes, swung between irredentist demands
for a united Ireland and demands for reform of the northern
state (Buckland, 1979). Their demands for a united Ireland
met a lukewarm response from the government in the South

and their claims of discrimination were dismissed out of hand by the Stormont government, and ignored by London. The IRA similarly lacked any long-term strategy and proved incapable of mounting a serious military challenge to the state. Its elitism and conspiratorial nature divorced it from the nationalist population, rendering it incapable of tapping into other forms of protest and resistance.

Nationalist disarray allowed the Unionist state to ignore the complaints of the minority, secure in the belief that the police would be able to deal with any street disturbances. A reading of contemporary reports from the main nationalist newspaper, the *Irish News,* illustrates the level of simmering resentment among nationalists and the contempt towards their grievances shown by the state during this period. For example, taking a period at random (March 1952), the month began with a complaint at a meeting of Belfast City Council – who ran the city's public transport system – about 'discrimination in transport undertaking appointments'. It was alleged that of 105 transport inspectors 10 were from the minority community and 95 'supporters of the Unionist Party at Glengall St'. The Council was accused of 'vicious discrimination against the nationalist minority of the city' (*Irish News,* 4 March 1952). At the same meeting, the High Sheriff of Belfast proposed that flagpoles be erected in all council housing estates in Belfast. This brought a riposte from a nationalist councillor, Alderman McKeavey, 'If Mr Harpur [the High Sheriff] had a flagpole erected in the Ballymurphy estate, the Union Jack would not fly on it.'

On 5 March, the front-page headlines in the *Irish News* concerned a doctor in Altnagelvin Hospital in Derry: 'Detective escorts doctor from Derry hospital' alleging that the doctor had been 'kicked out, for refusing to swear allegiance to the Queen'. On 13 March, the paper reported extensively on the refusal of planning permission by local authorities for Catholic schools and churches. A few days later, there were the familiar reports of the police breaking up St Patrick's Day parades, this time in Derry 'for the second successive year' where 'wild scenes' resulted in 22 people being treated in hospital for their injuries. The justification for the police baton charges was the usual one: flying the tricolour. An ex-RUC officer, who served in Derry during this period, wrote in a recent letter to the *Irish Times*:

Nationalist marches on St Patrick's Day and at Easter were totally banned from the city centre and allowed only within the confines of the Catholic Bogside. Orangemen, Blackmen and Apprentice Boys could march where they liked ... As a sergeant I once stopped an Orange band which had left its legally authorised route ... and was deliberately approaching a number of Catholic houses. For three weeks a senior officer tried to make me apologise to the master of the lodge which I refused to do. Eventually in my office one afternoon he lost his temper and roared out: 'Sgt. Scott, you can stop a Catholic band any time you like but don't you ever stop a Protestant band again' (*Irish Times*, 29 September 1999).

Things did not get better as the decade wore on and unionists did not modify their determination to exclude the minority. At a 12 July parade in 1958, the Minister of Education attacked the Catholic Church as an 'implacable enemy' and went on to say that 'our tolerance has gone too far' (*Irish News*, 13 July 1958). Whether he was speaking here for the government, Orangemen, or both is not clear. In August of the same year, the *Irish News* was complaining of Catholic exclusion from voluntary positions on NHS boards: 'The percentage of Catholics nominated to serve unpaid on boards, authorities and committees under the National Health Service is relatively insignificant.'

A dense apparatus of coercion and control confronted this lack of strategic coherence among nationalists. The apparatus of control was made up of legal, administrative, electoral and territorial constraints backed up by a cabal of academics ever willing to defend the unionist position. Such a band of eminent academics came together in a book published in 1955 under the editorship of Thomas Wilson, an Ulster-born professor of economics who held the prestigious Adam Smith Chair of Political Economy at Glasgow University and who advised the Unionist government on economic issues. In his own contribution to the book, Wilson dismisses nationalist grievances:

From any objective point of view it cannot be said that the grievances of Catholics are always very real. They have less to complain about than the U.S. Negroes, and their lot is a very pleasant one as compared with that of nationalists in, say, the Ukraine ... They were made to feel inferior, and to make matters worse they often *were* inferior, if *only* in those personal qualities that made for success in competitive economic life. (Wilson, 1955, p. 208, emphasis in original)

The introduction to the book, penned by the Vice-Chancellor of Queen's University, is a hymn of praise to the Unionist government:

> ... it [the Unionist government] has been obliged to develop policies which transcend the special interests of any one class ... It can claim too, and not unjustly, that freedom of speech and opinion, the exercise of legitimate political activities ... offer their own proof that Northern Ireland can offer more than material prosperity to its citizens. (Wilson, 1955, p. xxiii)

In another chapter, the Professor of Jurisprudence at Queen's University, F.H. Newark, defended the Special Powers Act by arguing that, 'Unstable conditions and revolutionary tendencies do not permit us the luxury of unlimited freedom of the individual; just as he who wishes for peace must prepare for war, so he who wants freedom must be prepared to use restraint' (p. 50). Newark dismissed the National Council of Civil Liberties Report (on the Special Powers Act, published in 1936), in a paragraph worthy of Joe McCarthy:

> Quite apart from its contents this was a remarkable production. In blue paper cover with all the format of a Government Blue Book it was calculated to deceive the unwary into believing that in some way it emanated from Whitehall. In fact it was sponsored by a body well leavened with individuals whom we now recognise as Communists and fellow travellers. (Wilson, 1955, p. 49)

There were few books written in the 1950s that were even remotely critical of the state of affairs in Northern Ireland, and this cast of academic and establishment heavyweights, with the imprimatur of Oxford University Press, gave respectability to the unionist view of the world and justified and condoned its practices. However, in 1962 cracks began to appear in the façade of academic complacency with the appearance of Barritt and Carter's *The Northern Ireland Problem*. The book was sponsored by the Northern Committee of the Irish Association which took the position that any problems in Northern Ireland were based upon mutual misunderstandings which, with good will on all sides, could be cleared up to the satisfaction of all. It is indicative that the book, while extremely moderate and conciliatory in tone, caused considerable unease by actually writing off Northern Ireland as a divided community.

Barritt and Carter's cautious assessment that something was wrong with the Stormont regime: 'Some complaints, for instance of discrimination, seem to us well founded', is immediately qualified with the remark that 'those who complain of discrimination would in other circumstances be very ready to practice it themselves' (p. 154). None the less, from the 1962 General Election onwards, the question of discrimination and civil rights was beginning to creep on to the political agenda (Purdie, 1990, p. 73).

The ideological and cultural hegemony which unionism did its best to foster was an important component in efforts to maintain the status quo in Northern Ireland, but the linchpin that held the Stormont regime together was the operational efficiency of the RUC, a force not only dedicated to the control of the minority but also given the resources to carry out this task. This system of control was to break down at both levels with the emergence of the Civil Rights Movement in the 1960s. McGarry and O'Leary (1995) summarise the factors leading to its breakdown:

> The system of control broke down firstly because the Irish state appeared to cease to have the same interest in unification, leaving northern nationalists with no option but to pursue their interests internally, and secondly, because the Westminster government began to intervene in ways which raised Catholic expectations that their grievances could be remedied. The post-war welfare state increased Catholics' resources, their material welfare, their hope of social mobility, and their desire for equal citizenship. The brilliant strategic choice of a civil-rights movement … undermined the Stormont regime in British and international public opinion (p. 261).

The pressures which led to the introduction of Keynesian economic management and social democratic welfare reform in post-war western Europe were absent in Northern Ireland. The social and economic forces which led to the implementation of reforms in post-war Europe were rationalised through an ideology which stressed equality, democracy and a general harmony of interests. Reform was encapsulated in a new version of universalism: equality of opportunity, access to education and social mobility and the promise of a rising standard of living and a redistribution of wealth and privilege. The state, assuming a corporatist mantle, took upon itself the task of recasting the labour process in a Fordist mould and acting as midwife to the birth of a consumer society.

In Northern Ireland, there was little appetite for such far-reaching changes. Industry was mainly small scale and family owned and the larger industries – shipbuilding, linen manufacture and engineering – did not lend themselves readily to reorganisation on Fordist lines. Sharp divisions existed between the Catholic and Protestant working class in ideological, organisational, spatial and sectoral terms, which made united action around a reformist agenda difficult if not impossible. There was little enthusiasm on the part of the Unionist Party for the welfare state and the Catholic Church was downright hostile.[5] The fact that Northern Ireland was part of the United Kingdom, however, ensured that Stormont could not reject the legislation implementing the welfare state in Westminster without provoking a constitutional and political crisis.[6]

However, the unexpected, and to some extent imposed, modernisation of sections of the Stormont state was to have unanticipated and far-reaching consequences. With the crucial exception of the security apparatus, which was highly centralised, the state bureaucracy under unionism was decentralised and localised. The Unionist government was content to practice a non-interventionist and *laissez-faire* attitude towards most areas of administration, allowing local government control over areas such as housing, roads, planning, and, to a lesser extent, education. Given the nature of sectarian relations in Northern Ireland, this non-intervention had the effect of reproducing the status quo. Institutional links between the Unionist Party and the Orange Order, and the overlapping membership of the Protestant commercial and industrial class in both, ensured that established patterns of industrial location (which favoured the Protestant population) were retained. It was a system based upon stagnation and particularism: to maintain its power the Unionist Party was forced to retain the status quo, but not could be seen to be intervening directly in a partisan fashion. Sometimes the state *did* intervene directly, as in the decision to situate a new university in the Protestant town of Coleraine rather than in Derry, which already had a third-level institution associated with Trinity College in Dublin. As Purdie points out, the university issue cut across traditional sectarian political issues and pointed towards the possibility of agitation on a new political terrain (Purdie 1990, p. 165).

The introduction of Keynesian management of the economy as a component part of the post-war settlement undermined this reality and presented the Unionist system with challenges it could not meet. Having reluctantly accepted the principles of state intervention and the universalistic ideology of welfare reform, Stormont had given the minority a crucial political and ideological opening. Alongside this, the gradual implementation of welfare legislation was having its effect on the social structure. Since the general standard of living, social class position and economic status of the minority was considerably lower that that of the majority, the introduction of welfare measures affected the former in a disproportionate fashion. The pressure to emigrate lessened, educational qualifications rose, as did the overall standard of living and health. In contrast with the Republic, a comprehensive welfare system was being put in place and strong economic growth gave at least the promise of jobs. Meanwhile, the economy of the South was stagnant with growth rates of zero in some years during the 1950s (Lee, 1989, p. 271). These material and structural changes were matched by the gradual spread and acceptance of the culture of social democratic ideals. A new political agenda of rights, equality, democracy and reform was making inroads into the dominant ideology of nationalism. The discourse of the minority was gradually shifting away from the coercive, instrumental and asymmetrical nature of nationalist politics towards one based upon moral categories, such as the need to replace ritual humiliation with recognition in the form of the realisation of rights. In an interesting comment on a speech made in 1965 by John Hume (later to become leader of the moderate nationalist party, the SDLP, and one of the architects of the recent peace process), Purdie writes: 'At a mass rally in the [Derry] Guildhall ... Hume roused the crowd with a speech which made no reference to partition or nationalist grievances, but emphasised the common heritage and common interests of all the citizens of Derry' (1990, p. 165).

By the mid-1960s the situation in Northern Ireland had been transformed on a number of levels. New groups and individuals had emerged which were capable of taking advantage of political opportunities, the social structure had undergone radical change, and new cultural ideals had taken root. This transformation had taken place against a background of ongoing grievance and simmering discontent.

In 1962, the last in a long line of unsuccessful IRA campaigns aimed at destroying the Northern Ireland state came to an end. The manifest and miserable failure of the campaign brought about a rethink among individuals and groups in the trade union movement, socialist groups and elements of the republican movement. John Hume's speech in Derry in 1965, mentioned above, was typical of the new thinking: a move away from traditional republicanism and nationalism which believed that the state must be overthrown as a prerequisite of equality and democracy towards a reformist agenda based upon changing the state from within. The Civil Rights Movement (CRM) evolved from a number of interacting forces. Both constitutional and militant nationalism were seen to have failed to challenge the practices of the Unionist-dominated state, and awareness was growing that new forms of protest were possible and effective as the example of the civil rights agitation in the United States seemed to demonstrate (Dooley, 1998).

4 The Impact of Civil Rights on Policing: Collapse and Failed Reform

The Civil Rights Campaign

Stanley Palmer, writing of the rise of Irish nationalism and separatism in the late nineteenth century, comments that the nature and practice of the RIC was an important factor in the emergence of Catholic nationalism:

> Indeed, it may be argued that the diminishing independence of Protestant Ireland would contribute to the development of an exclusivist Catholic and cultural and political revolution at the end of the century. The importation of a centralised English controlled police, with a heavily Anglo-Irish officer corps dependent upon Dublin Castle, would in the long run help prepare the soil for the growth of Catholic republicanism and separatism (Palmer, 1988, p. 245).

Similarly, it can be convincingly argued that the RUC, in its handling of the Civil Rights Movement (CRM) in Northern Ireland, prepared the way for the re-emergence of militant nationalism. NICRA (Northern Ireland Civil Rights Association) was not the first group to agitate for civil rights, but its foundation in November 1966, and the broad support it enjoyed from a number of organisations, marked the beginnings of the creation of a mass movement. (For an extended discussion of NICRA, see Purdie (1990) and Ó Dochartaigh (1997).)

The aims of the new organisation were initially restricted to a focus upon legal and constitutional rights in line with the organisation's middle-class origins:

- to defend the basic freedoms of all citizens
- to protect the rights of the individual
- to highlight all possible abuses of power
- to demand guarantees for freedom of speech, assembly and association

- to inform the public of their lawful rights. (NICRA, 1978, p. 8)

For the first 18 months of its existence, NICRA avoided engagement with concrete grievances in areas such as housing, electoral practices and employment, confining itself to what amounted to a letter-writing campaign to ministers. This proved to be as lacking in success as previous attempts to pressure the British government to actively pursue a reform agenda had been (Purdie, 1990, pp. 82–120). Effectively, the political system monopolised by the Unionist Party was blocked[1] and both incapable and unwilling to engage with the pressing need for reform. As in Italy in the 1960s, the monopoly of power by one party (since 1922 in Northern Ireland, 1945 in Italy) impeded the possibility of democratic electoral change, as well as consolidating the identification of state with the ruling party of government. The Unionist Party had never felt accountable for the cultural marginalisation and political exclusion of the minority, blaming nationalists for not participating in what they considered a model democracy. Given that, in unionist eyes, nationalists had excluded themselves, the responsibility of party and government was to its loyal supporters.

In Northern Ireland there was a clear absence of a 'political opportunity structure' through which the demands of civil rights organisations could be channelled.[2] The existing 'political opportunity structures' were closed and incapable of mediating and resolving conflicts. The Unionist-dominated Stormont parliament treated the Nationalist opposition with contempt – the only Nationalist-sponsored piece of legislation to be accepted was an Act regarding the protection of wild birds – and other expressions of discontent were swiftly repressed by the RUC. The unwillingness of the Unionist government and their supporters to countenance sharing power with nationalists and their determination to retain a monopoly of power at every level of the system, down to the allocation of local authority labouring jobs, blocked any opportunities for political change. The attitude of successive British governments compounded the situation. Parliamentary convention dictated that the affairs of Northern Ireland could not be debated at Westminster, and London had consistently refused to use its position as the superior constitutional and political actor to intervene.

The constitutional and peaceful phase of agitation by NICRA lasted 18 months, amid increasing frustration at the

lack of progress. All the factors necessary for successful mobilisation were in place: a cognitive framework for collective
action – composed of traditional elements of nationalist grievance as well as new factors, particularly the growing impact of
the US black Civil Rights movement, the identification of
an adversary, the definition of a purpose and the overall objectives of the struggle (Melucci, 1996, p. 292), and by the summer
of 1968 the leadership of NICRA was, somewhat reluctantly,
ready to support taking protest to the streets.

In institutional terms, the state in Northern Ireland rested
upon two contrasting pillars. The bulk of decision making, as
it affected the everyday life of citizens, was made at local level.
Local government had control over housing, large areas of
employment, planning and infra-structural development. Local
unionist elites were entrenched in local town and county councils, and the Orange Order and other formal and informal
organisations linked to unionism, such as the Freemasons,
were capable of exerting their considerable influence to pre-
serve their privileges. This made the task of reform, even if central
government was willing to meet the demands of the civil rights
protesters, practically impossible. The very cohesion of the
unionist class alliance depended upon the semi-autonomous
nature of the local politics of exclusion.

In contrast, the security apparatus was centralised and
under the control of the Minister of Home Affairs. The organisation, culture and political direction of the RUC and USC
made them, both individually and organisationally, deeply suspicious of any political actions of the minority, and inclined
to view even the most reformist demands as a direct threat to
the state and their position within it, both as Protestants and
police officers. Indeed, as Ruane and Todd (1996, p. 127)
acknowledge, 'many in the RUC, and virtually all the B Specials
were defenders of the Protestant community first, defenders
of the Protestant state second, and normal policemen third.'
The refusal of the state to address, or even acknowledge, the
grievances of the minority made it inevitable that when street
protest began in the summer of 1968 the first line of confrontation would be with the RUC. It is interesting that in NICRA's
list of demands (see above) the nature and practice of policing
do not figure at all, nor did the question of state repression,
although this was always central to the survival of the state.
But as soon as the confrontation between street demonstrations and the police began, the question of repression rose

swiftly up the agenda of grievances. Della Porta (1995, p. 189), highlights the relationship between forms of repression and patterns of collective action when she argues that in Germany and Italy, 'political violence developed directly from interactions between social movements and the police.' This was precisely the case in Northern Ireland (Ellison and Martin, forthcoming).

The CRM did not face a regime that was secure and stable in terms of support and legitimacy despite its monolithic facade. The dependence of the state on repression for its everyday existence was an index of the precarious nature of its rule, even though this was not immediately obvious to the minority, or indeed to the Unionist establishment. The Unionist Party was exposed as little more than an empty shell when faced with concerted and determined opposition, opposition which also exposed long-repressed internal divisions within unionism. Without the political will or the structural means to grant concessions to the Civil Rights Movement, the Unionist government responded in the way it knew best: with increasing repression. It was this repression, implemented by the RUC, which fostered a sense of solidarity among the nationalist community and pushed the CRM further down the road of collective action and protest. As soon as the CRM moved into the phase of street protest, the reaction of the government became increasingly repressive and brutal. At practically every march and demonstration the state unleashed the full force of its repressive apparatus. During one of the first civil rights marches in Derry in October 1969, attended by about 400 people, 'the RUC punched, batoned and pursued civil rights demonstrators in a brutal display of concerted violence' (Ó Dochartaigh 1997, p. 5). This initial repression brought about a radicalisation of protest encouraging further militancy and the emergence of other, more combative groupings. One such group was People's Democracy (PD) an *ad hoc* group founded by Queen's University students and others immediately after the events of 5 October 1968 in Derry, when a CRM march had been involved in serious and violent confrontations with the RUC and loyalist counter-demonstrators.

In defiance of the NICRA leadership, People's Democracy embarked upon a march from Belfast to Derry on 1 January 1969. The march was consciously modelled on the famous Selma–Montgomery, Alabama march of 1966, which in the eyes of one of the organisers, 'had exposed the racist thuggery of America's Deep South and forced the US government into major reforms' (Farrell, 1980, p. 249; Dooley, 1998, pp. 54–7). The participants in this march were ambushed at Burntollet Bridge, close to their destination, by groups of attackers wearing white armbands. This ambush, which resulted in an uncertain number of injuries (the RUC put the number injured at 13 but it was most probably higher) was to provide a crucial dynamic for subsequent patterns of mobilisation. It soon became clear that the RUC response (backed up by units of the RUC Reserve) was in every conceivable sense a 'loyalist' response, since they had quite obviously aligned themselves on the side of the attackers (McCann, 1993; Purdie, 1990). However, the Prime Minister of Northern Ireland, and other members of the government were quick to lay the blame at the door of the marchers, and absolved the RUC of any responsibility.

By this stage in the CRM's development, two significant processes were in train. First, state repression was creating a myth, which had the instant effect of delegitimising the state by creating 'injustice frames' (Gamson, 1992)[3] and arousing a feeling of absolute injustice (Della Porta, 1995). Second, whatever vestige of neutrality the RUC may have had was dispelled by reports of collaboration with the loyalist attackers. After the RUC beat an elderly man in Derry, who subsequently died from his injuries, the question of policing and, by proxy the legitimacy of the state, had displaced the original reformist agenda of the Civil Rights Movement. By the beginning of 1969, the CRM had all the hallmarks of an insurrectionist movement. The preconditions for a rapid slide into confrontation and violence were in place: a blocked political system incapable of reacting energetically and creatively to the reformist demands of the CRM; the existence of symbolic events which acted as catalysts for mobilisation;[4] an extension of support for the CRM into the wider nationalist community, and an increasing focus upon the question of policing and justice, leading to direct confrontations with the RUC.

The Stormont government, crippled by internal divisions, was incapable of pushing through a coherent reform package that might have defused the situation.[5] The use of 'hard' policing had led to a radicalisation of the CRM, allowing militants to displace moderates, and outright confrontation to displace the strategy of peaceful protest. The RUC, for its part, was so used to policing a divided society in a partisan fashion that it had no conception of itself as an institution of a civil society.

Indeed, even after the collapse of the RUC and the introduction of the British Army in August 1969, the RUC still clung to the traditional interpretation of its role and refused to accept any culpability for the situation that led to a collapse of order and eventual British intervention. In 1970, the Chief Constable of the force was to reinforce this typically unreflexive stance in his introduction to the Annual Report of the same year:

> From its inception in 1922 the RUC played a dual role in the policing of Northern Ireland. Not only was the force required to provide a service of law enforcement ... it had the added responsibility of Protecting the Province from subversion from within as well as from outside Northern Ireland ... In later years, and especially during the first eight months of 1969 the police were heavily engaged in a peace-keeping role dealing with serious problems of public order on the streets of our cities and towns. (*Chief Constable's Annual Report*, 1970, pp. vii–viii)

The initial response of the Unionist government was to concede nothing – arguing that the CRM was an IRA attempt to destroy the state – and to unleash the RUC and the state militia, the USC, to forcibly resist the demands of the civil rights campaigners. The willingness of the RUC and the USC to carry out this task is aptly illustrated by the words of a former RUC officer who had previously served as a member of the USC:

> The USC regarded every Catholic as an enemy. It was as far as I know one hundred percent Protestant. I am not impartial and I have never believed in impartiality but it had got to the stage where our backs were up against the wall and something had to be done. After all our country and our government was being attacked. The Ulster government belonged to the Ulster people and the people who cared about Ulster. The Civil Rights movement was nothing more than the IRA. The Unionist government knew that but the British wouldn't listen. (cited in Ellison, 1997 p. 157)

Senior officers also shared this perception of the CRM as posing a direct challenge to the legitimacy of the Unionist government. In a memorandum that only came to light in January 1999 with the release of cabinet files under the thirty-year rule, the Inspector General of the RUC reported to the Unionist government on one of the first CRM marches between Dungannon and Coalisland, on 21 August 1968:

> It might be more correct to describe the march as a republican parade rather than a civil rights march. It was composed largely of republicans and sympathisers under the control of a local IRA man ... from the conduct and behaviour of some of the speakers it is evident that the civil rights organisation is allowing its platform to be used by extremists and troublemakers for the purpose of preaching violence and stirring up hatred amongst the people. (cited in the *Irish Times*, 1 and 2 January 1999)

This analysis of the CRM and the imputation of the motives of the participants, seems to have been widespread throughout the force if the comments of an ex-RUC sergeant are anything to go by:

> I was a policeman for many a long year and served my country well and to the best of my ability ... I have nothing against the Catholic community, never had. But I used to see it myself; you would get the Catholic who had a very bad attitude to the government and to everything else. Everything the government would do for them they were never happy – they wanted more. That civil rights business was the up-shot of it all. It turned even decent Catholics against the government and the police. It totally destroyed the RUC's relationship with the Catholic community; it was never the same after that. (cited in Ellison, 1997, p. 155)

The role of the RUC, albeit unintentional, in the mobilisation of the wider nationalist population around the demands of the CRM was to become a crucial determinant of the events which followed. The RUC were used to two types of protest from the nationalist community: street demonstrations with a clear nationalist flavour, and sporadic IRA military campaigns. In the eyes of the police, the boundary between the two was fluid, as their constant reporting of 'known republicans' at street protests shows. This mindset was applied to the civil rights demonstrations, which were dealt with in the tried and tested manner, as a threat to the security of the state.

The RUC Inspector General's report to the government, quoted above, is indicative of this thinking, and formed the basis of RUC tactics. There is some evidence, from recently released Cabinet papers,[6] that at least some members of the Stormont regime were not so sure that this was the case and were beginning to feel that they were perhaps facing into a new situation which would not be amenable to the usual solution of dispersing protests, if necessary with violence, and ignoring the complaints of nationalist politicians and others. The events in Derry on 5 October 1968 were crucial, not because the RUC had acted with its usual brutality, but because the events were televised and flashed around the globe. The report of the Cameron Commission (Cameron Report, 1969), set up in January 1969 to investigate the disturbances on and after 5 October 1968 said: '... the police broke ranks and used their batons indiscriminately on people in Duke Street ... the District Inspector in charge used his blackthorn with needless violence'. Cameron could hardly have avoided reference to this incident, since, caught by the cameras of the international media, it remains one of the iconic images of the present conflict.[7] However, the general tenor of the report is to subscribe to the 'bad apple' theory of the RUC – that is, although individual RUC officers may have overstepped the mark, in general the police showed restraint: 'In the majority of cases we find the police acted with commendable discipline and restraint under very great strain and provocation from various quarters' (Cameron Report, Para. 177, p. 73).

Although Cameron singles out acts of 'misconduct which involved assault and battery, malicious damage to property ... and the use of provocative and sectarian slogans', he immediately proceeds to comment that such actions '... obscure the restraint, under conditions of some strain, then deployed by the large majority of the police concerned' (Para. 177, p. 73). Cameron was careful to uncouple his criticisms of the discriminatory practices of the Stormont state – which he held responsible for creating a climate of discontent – from his overall endorsement of the RUC. A similar logic runs through the next, inevitable, report into civil disturbances, the Scarman Report (1972), which investigated the disturbances of 1969. Once again, the RUC as a body was exonerated: 'Undoubtedly mistakes were made and certain individual officers acted wrongly on occasions. But the general case of a partisan force co-operating with Protestant mobs to attack Catholic people is devoid of substance and we reject it utterly' (quoted in Ryder, 1989, p. 114).

Such official reports did little to convince the minority population that the RUC was not the armed wing of the Unionist government, and they were more inclined to share the view of English journalist Clive Limpkin in his description of RUC behaviour in the Bogside, 'It wasn't the RUC's stoning or rare petrol bombing that shocked; it was their hate that really stunned, matching that of Catholics. The obscenities, the threats, the religious tauntings – and all coming from a peace-keeping force' (Limpkin, 1972, p. 19). In addition, the protesters were speaking a language – that of the US civil rights movement (Dooley, 1998) – which had a global resonance, something which Cameron had anxiously noted in his report (Cameron Report, p. 55). For the first time, the Westminster Government in London was unable to ignore the plight of a substantial number of its own citizens and began to exert pressure on the Prime Minister, Terence O'Neill. However, as the Cabinet papers show, the events in Derry created a wave of international publicity that caused Harold Wilson, the British Prime Minister, some considerable concern. As O'Neill was to write in a memo to his colleagues:

> We all know, too that a strong section of left wing opinion has been pressing Wilson very hard to take some positive step. Up to now he has fobbed off this pressure, from our point of view very well. With Northern Ireland calm and a general feeling that slow but steady progress was under way, he could contain the situation … I would be failing in my duty if I did not make it clear that, in my view, London-derry has altered this situation to our great disadvantage. Whether the press or television coverage is fair is immaterial. We have now become the focus of world opinion. (*Irish Times*, 1 January 1999)

By the time the Stormont regime got around to proposing a package of reforms it was not a case of 'too little too late but rather too late too late' (Ó Dochartaigh, 1997, p. 22). For the RUC had, by August 1969, ceased to exist as a functioning police force or even as a paramilitary force. Demoralised, discredited and exhausted, it was removed from the streets and replaced by the British Army. Like its predecessor, the RIC, the RUC had disintegrated in the face of concerted resistance and the new tactics of street protest to which it was unable to respond effectively. By training, it had always been poised to deal with IRA insurgency, and by inclination to implement the low-level harassment of individual nationalists. By 1968 the RUC was neither ideologically nor tactically prepared for the subtle machinations of the CRM, with its emphasis on peaceful and non-violent protest, and demands for basic civil rights.

The decision to put troops on the streets was a fateful one, as was the decision to leave them under the control of the

Unionist government. The large-scale introduction of British troops into Ireland has historically indicated the presence of a crisis situation since such a decision contradicted the long-standing policy of using locally recruited police to hold the line (Townshend, 1983; Palmer 1988). Robert Peel, speaking in the House of Commons in 1814 in support of his Peace Preservation Bill, had already sounded a warning frequently ignored by governments in London and Ireland over the next 180 years: 'It would, in his [Peel's] opinion, be infinitely better to invest the civil powers with sufficient authority to repress these disturbances, than to call in the aid of the military. The frequent use of soldiers in that manner made the people look upon them as their adversaries, rather than their protectors'.[8]

The honeymoon period enjoyed by the British Army was indeed brief. Two events, in particular, had disastrous consequences for the Army's relationship with the nationalist community: the ill-conceived policy of internment (implemented in August 1971) which was directed almost entirely against nationalists and based on out-of-date RUC intelligence, and 'Operation Motorman' in 1972, which was an attempt by the Army (and given wholehearted encouragement from Unionist politicians) to 'smash' their way into staunchly Republican areas of Belfast and Derry (Buckland, 1979). These operations had the effect of flooding the still-embryonic IRA with young recruits, many of whom were to die or serve long prison sentences.

The CRM period demonstrated that the nationalist community would no longer acquiesce in the practices that had underpinned the operation of governance in Northern Ireland for over fifty years, and that informed the traditional demeanour of the RUC. In an attempt to diffuse the situation, the British government ordered a number of official investigations to consider the causes of the disturbances and behaviour of the police.

Reform in a Vacuum: The Hunt Report

The confrontation between the RUC and civil rights protesters and the inability of the Northern Ireland state to contain the escalating crisis were, as mentioned above, to become the subject of two Royal Commissions, subsequently published as the Cameron Report (1969) and the Scarman Report

(1972). Although these were technically instigated by the Northern Ireland Minister for Home Affairs, they were commissioned only under intense pressure from a British government which, like its predecessors, had held itself aloof from Irish affairs. Apart from becoming concerned at the level of media attention the crisis was attracting, and the consequent impact on international opinion, there was a fear in London that the conflict was in danger of getting out of control. Indeed, the traditional indifference of the British government towards the situation in Northern Ireland meant that there was little on which a rational and reasoned response to the escalating crisis could be based.

When both commissions reported, the main casualty was the Ulster Special Constabulary. The Cameron Commission, which reported in October 1969, concluded that the RUC had suffered from 'a breakdown in discipline' and had been guilty of 'acts of misconduct' involving 'assault and battery', 'illegal violence', 'malicious damage to property' and the use of 'provocative and sectarian slogans' but exonerated the police of serious institutionalised misconduct. The Scarman Tribunal (1972) was extremely critical of the sectarian nature and conduct of the USC, noting that they were 'a partisan and paramilitary force recruited exclusively from Protestants' (cited in Brewer et al., 1988, p. 51). As such, these criticisms proved a devastating blow to the standing of the USC, and provided official acknowledgement of their role in exacerbating the unrest, while confining criticism of the RUC to the actions of individual officers. At a structural level, the findings of both Cameron and Scarman highlighted the nature of dominant–subordinate relations in Northern Ireland. Of course, all police forces – along with other elements of the security apparatus – are there in the last analysis to defend the state, but the level of relative autonomy enjoyed by such institutions is crucial (Waddington, 1999). A state confident of its legitimacy and political stability can allow itself the luxury of detachment from the problem of social control, confident that the relationship between citizen and the agencies of social control will be based upon shared assumptions and a belief in the due process of law. These assumptions could not be made in Northern Ireland, where a sizeable section of the nationalist community displayed little normative loyalty to the state.

The official findings determined that reform of the police was to be of paramount importance before any realistic assessment of the situation could be made. Consequently, when the British government was forced to intervene directly to assuage the crisis in August 1969 by committing its troops to the aid of the civil power, another Commission under Lord Hunt was appointed by the Northern Ireland Ministry of Home Affairs (again under instructions from the British administration) to: 'Examine the recruitment, organisation, structure and composition of the Royal Ulster Constabulary and the Ulster Special Constabulary and their respective functions and to recommend as necessary what changes are required to provide for the efficient enforcement of law and order in Northern Ireland' (Hunt Report, 1969, p. 7).

Hunt reported on 3 October 1969, less than six weeks from the date when the inquiry began (26 August 1969), illustrating the sense of urgency that was attached to reforming the RUC, a point noted by Hunt in the introduction to his report.

Although the Commission conducted its enquiry within a relatively short period of time, the recommendations were wide-ranging and, as Hunt advised, were to be implemented as quickly as possible: 'It is our conviction that nothing less than the full implementation of the proposals ... within the shortest time possible can suffice to lay a sound foundation for the good order and security of the Province' (p. 3).

Essentially, Hunt was recommending that the RUC be reformed in terms of a liberal-democratic model of policing, which draws a distinction between routine or 'normal' police functions and the paramilitary aspect of maintaining order. For the RUC, Hunt proposed that it be disarmed and relieved of its paramilitary duties, and 'assume the character and sole function of a civil police force' (p. 41). The traditional order-maintenance and counter-insurgency role of the RUC was to be henceforth carried out by the British Army, which was now pushed to the front line in the maintenance of internal security. Operating under a colonial war model of counter-insurgency (cf. Kitson, 1971), virtual martial law and internment without trial was introduced to deal with the unrest. Apart from proving ineffective in dealing with widespread civil disturbance and an emerging IRA, the use of the Army severely damaged Britain's image abroad, prompting a new strategy to 'manage' the conflict, which was gradually put into place between 1974 and 1976.

Among the more far-reaching conclusions was the recommendation that the USC be 'disbanded' (though this was later

changed to 'replaced' by the Unionist government) and a reserve force of RUC constables and a part-time militia under
the control of the Army GOC established in the USC's place.
Hunt also recommended that a Police Authority be established to act as a buffer between the RUC and the Unionist
regime. The force was also to be open to inspection by Her
Majesty's Inspectorate of Constabulary and an independent
system of prosecution was to be established. Additionally, Hunt
argued that community relations needed to be improved –
particularly in Derry, where he advocated the appointment of
a liaison committee comprised of members of the RUC and
the local community. Among Hunt's more 'iconoclastic' recommendations were those concerning the rank structure, which
was to be modelled on the British system, and a change in the
colour of the uniform from 'Irish green' to 'British blue' (Walker,
1990). This latter recommendation was never implemented,
although a different shade of green was introduced a few years
later.

While the British government accepted Hunt's proposals
as part of an overall reform package for the RUC, the reaction
of unionists was rather more ambivalent, if not downright
hostile (Ó Dochartaigh, 1997; Ruane and Todd, 1996). None
the less, in the face of a Westminster administration which
was rapidly losing patience with what it regarded as an intran-
sigent regime determined to thwart its reform efforts, the
Stormont government had little choice but to accept reluctantly Hunt's proposals. However, this news was greeted by
fierce rioting in Protestant areas of Belfast, resulting in the
killing of an RUC Constable, the first police fatality of the
current conflict. Likewise, the ambivalence towards the Hunt
Report seems to have been reflected within the ranks of the
RUC itself. For example, one RUC Constable who was serving during this period laments the disbandment of the USC
and suggests:

> I would say that the B-force was disbanded to placate nationalists.
> There was no way in which the British government could get in on the
> Specials and the only way in which they could get a hold of security
> here in Northern Ireland was by changing the force. The Hunt Report
> was the first instance of a softly-softly policy. Take the easy way with
> the IRA and be nice to them and everything will be alright – that's
> nonsense. You see this is an on-going thing. If you want to go away
> back before the Reformation and even before, the Protestant people

were burned at the stake for proclaiming the Bible as Luther seen it. The one thing I'll always regret, and I'll tell you we would have a different situation now – was that the Specials weren't let loose on those Civil Rights ones. I'll tell you the whole thing would have been stopped dead ... it would have been stopped dead. There would be none of the problems you have today. (cited in Ellison, 1997, p. 160)

Another constable appears equally unequivocal about the rationale for the Hunt reforms:

Hunt was an idealist. He tried to superimpose English police practices on the RUC. There were a lot of things, which he didn't understand about the RUC and he was wrong to generalise. The Civil Rights campaign was localised in that it focused hostility in Belfast and Derry and outside of those areas there wasn't really much Catholic hostility to the RUC. Also, he didn't understand our rank structure, and the role we traditionally had in fighting the IRA. He didn't understand these things so he got rid of them and tried to model us on the English police. (cited in Ellison, 1997, p. 161)

An ex-USC member who later joined the RUC Reserve argued that:

... The Hunt Report I never read it. But it is the same as today. Annesley is a clever man but I am afraid they [Catholics] have got the upper hand on him too ... You know yourself from the history problem there will always be a division between the people here in Northern Ireland as far as religion is concerned. Because the Protestants – the majority of the Protestant people – don't want popery or a papish Republic. It's all right being open-minded when everything's equal ... and that was the problem with Hunt. Everything's not equal you see ... You know the history of Roman Catholics. (cited in Ellison, 1997, p. 161)

Other respondents from the RUC have suggested that, while they perceived little active opposition to the Hunt reforms, they nevertheless argue that they lowered morale and created widespread disillusionment. However, other officers suggest that they were generally agreeable to Hunt's proposals and acknowledge that the RUC had demonstrated itself incapable of dealing with a widespread and sustained pattern of civil unrest. Organisationally, their manpower was overstretched, they were furnished with out-of-date and inappropriate equipment, and logistically they relied on outmoded methods of public order policing. For example, another RUC officer who was serving at the time recalls:

With Hunt guidelines were laid down – things that before were never
written down since in those days all our directives were politically
motivated from Stormont. When the troubles started in 1969 the
really senior officers just didn't have a clue – they just didn't know
how to cope. The RUC were in serious crisis by 1969. We were in
serious crisis primarily because we were under strength and there
was so much rioting and civil unrest taking place in the whole of the
north of Ireland. We didn't have the manpower to cope with that ...
Our manpower was so stretched that we could just never have
coped. Therefore, you had to thank the English for actually showing that you had to have sufficient numbers on the ground – you
had to have a physical presence and that there is only one way you
can police and that is by being seen to be unbiased. (cited in Ellison,
1997, p. 162)

Although, the Hunt reforms did not lead to mass resignations
amongst RUC officers, the above transcripts illustrate that
their implementation was a far from facile process. For some
constables (and members of the USC), the Hunt Report
amounted to an unwarranted criticism of what they perceived
their duty and responsibility to be, namely the protection of
the Northern Ireland state. As one USC platoon sergeant, who
later joined the Ulster Defence Regiment, recalls:

The Hunt report was a face-saver for the British government. The
British had no right disbanding the Specials. I am proud to have served
in the USC – they were a noble force, and do you know we were
castigated the world over – for what I'll never know. I served 22½
years and in all of those 22½ years I never saw anything done to be
ashamed of – other than providing security for my own country. I
remember feeling very angry at that time. We didn't do anything wrong,
never as far as I was concerned. I remember there was a lot of talk in
the platoon about ... well going over to a disreputable side of life [the
UVF] but nothing ever came of it. We talked as well about handing in
our guns in protest but decided to see what the new force [the UDR]
would look like. A lot of the men joined that including myself. (cited in
Ellison, 1997, p. 162)

Evidently some RUC and USC Constables greeted the Hunt
reforms with a sense of betrayal, since from their point of view
they had been merely exercising their duty. However, this attitude is hardly surprising given the historical and political legacy
that was bequeathed to the force when the Northern Ireland
state was created in 1922. Throughout the 1950s and 1960s,
the Northern Ireland state was increasingly anachronistic in

the context of modernising influences taking place elsewhere in Europe. A political system, which remained ossified for over half a century and which depended for its very existence on the coercive tactics of the RUC and the USC, was in little position to cope with the winds of change beginning to blow across Northern Ireland in 1968. It is open to debate whether the Northern Ireland government could have delivered the demands of the CRM, given the absence of either the political will or the structural means to do so (Rolston, 1983). None the less, the historical legacy bequeathed to the RUC by the Unionist government has major implications even today for the way in which the force is perceived by the nationalist community in Northern Ireland. So close was the relationship between the RUC and the Unionist administration that their fortunes in a sense became intertwined. The Stormont government depended upon the loyalty of the predominantly Protestant RUC and USC for its very existence, while they in turn (particularly in the RUC) were rewarded by the Unionist government with what one respondent has termed 'good stable employment', which stressed the importance of family loyalty and tradition:

> You certainly had a situation way back then, though it has disappeared to some extent now, where the sons would follow their father into the RUC, the Specials or maybe join the army. It stands to sense that if your father, uncle or brother was in the police, then you would be looked on more favourably ... Employers look for people they can trust and who they know can do the job. (cited in Ellison, 1997, p. 163)

The close association between the RUC and their political masters meant that criticism levelled at the Unionist regime became *de facto* criticism of the RUC also. As such, the Hunt proposals can be regarded as an early attempt by the British state to professionalise the RUC and to free it from the charge of political partiality. Among senior officers, the Hunt reforms provided a 'breathing space' for the force by allowing it to pull back from the front line in the maintenance of internal security, and also to benefit from an injection of manpower and resources (Tomlinson, 1980b, p. 186). However, the extent to which the RUC could distance itself ideologically from its traditional role in securing Unionist hegemony was to be of crucial importance, as future events were to illustrate.

The Hunt proposals, while only reluctantly accepted by the Unionist government, were none the less implemented under the Northern Ireland Police Act (1970). However, the practice of civilianisation of the RUC was undermined by the continuing deterioration in the security situation, resulting in the rearming of the RUC in 1971, after a series of shooting incidents. The practice of internment, together with the killing of 13 unarmed civilians on Bloody Sunday, totally alienated the community from the army in nationalist areas. In addition, allegations of brutality and torture by the British Army and the RUC Special Branch in the interrogation of suspects became the subject of yet another official enquiry under Sir Edmund Compton in 1971 (Compton Report, 1971).

With the introduction of Direct Rule from Westminster in 1972 as the 'least of all evils' form of government in 1972 (Tomlinson, 1980b, p. 186), the British state assumed full responsibility for security in Northern Ireland. Nevertheless, the overall strategy remained an essentially military one, with the RUC assuming a secondary role to the Army in dealing with political violence.

Hunt: Failed Reform?

The Hunt reforms, as we have seen, were accepted somewhat ambivalently by the RUC, with senior officers being generally more agreeable to the proposals. Arguably, however, they did not go far enough, and represented a tinkering with the existing structure rather than a transformation of the force (Tomlinson, 1980b, p. 186). For example, while the USC was technically 'disbanded', it was replaced by the UDR which was heavily recruited from members of the Special Constabulary, and soon achieved the same notoriety within the Catholic/nationalist community. Additionally, it was to become (like the USC) an almost exclusively Protestant force.[9]

Also, there was little attempt to subject the newly created Police Authority to democratic control. Nor, it must be said, did the Police Authority for Northern Ireland (PANI) take its accountability function seriously, preferring to remain silent in the midst of the controversies that have dogged the RUC over the years. Similarly, little effort was made to address the issue of police complaints and discipline as recommended by Hunt, outside an annual review by the Inspectorate of Constabulary.

However, this is perhaps to misjudge what Hunt was about. The RUC respondent (see above) who suggested that Hunt was an 'idealist' who tried to 'superimpose English police practices on the RUC', has pointed to a fundamental weakness in the Hunt proposals, namely that they represented an attempt to 'Anglicise' the RUC in line with something that was alien to its very character. Much of what was contained in the Hunt Report had previously been outlined for England and Wales under the 1964 Police Act. As such, it posited a very English policing solution to a very Irish policing problem.

5 Criminalisation and Normalisation: The Counter-Insurgency Solution

Introduction

The initial response of the British state to civil disorder in Northern Ireland was hesitant and incoherent. It was only after the collapse of the RUC as a disciplined force during the widespread street disturbances of 1969 that British troops were sent to Northern Ireland in a policing role. The British Cabinet was reluctant to intervene directly, and half a century of disinterest and neglect had left the London administration with a dearth of concrete and realistic information on which to base reasoned response to the crisis on its own doorstep. Sending troops allowed a breathing space and the opportunity to institute a package of reforms to existing and contentious state practices. A number of reports were commissioned into local government, the police, electoral reform and the causes of the disturbances which were designed as a prelude to reform in these areas. In retrospect, it is clear that this process was fatally flawed. The process of inquiry followed by the drafting and passing of legislation was tortuous and protracted in any event but was made more difficult by elements within the Unionist power structure who refused to accept the existence, much less the legitimacy, of Catholic grievances. On 14 August 1969, Northern Ireland Prime Minister Chichester-Clark, speaking in Stormont, said: 'This is not the agitation of a minority seeking by lawful means the assertion of political rights. It is the conspiracy of forces seeking to overthrow a government democratically elected by a large majority' (Farrell, 1980, p. 261).

More importantly perhaps, the reforms were seen at best as tinkering with what was a fatally discredited system. The establishment of a Community Relations Commission, and later a Ministry for Community Relations is a case in point. The legislation was based upon the British Race Relations Act and demonstrated little understanding of the historical complexities of the situation in Northern Ireland. For example, some paragraphs in the legislation appear to have been drafted simply by substituting the word 'religion' for 'race'. In addition, the compartmentalisation of the problem in a separate Ministry and Commission effectively ignored the fact that the question of community relations, discrimination and sectarianism was central to the very process of governance in Northern Ireland. Both organisations were ineffectual, and both were soon to sink without trace (Rolston, 1980). The reform of the police was equally flawed. No attempt was made to tackle the organisational and cultural problems of the RUC and the replacement for the USC, the Ulster Defence Regiment (UDR), was soon embroiled in controversy over the recruitment of ex-members of the 'B' Specials. Attempts to recruit Catholics foundered and fell from an initial recruitment figure of 18 per cent to 3 per cent.

The general approach of the British government was based upon a reluctance to embark upon fundamental reform in the hope that problems could be either administered out of existence or would fade away as their momentum dissipated over time. Given the attitude of the majority of the Unionist establishment, this approach was a recipe for disaster. The consequent failure of the reform process in the eyes of the minority ensured that the political vacuum was filled by an ever-rising level of confrontation between nationalists and the British Army.

Suppressing Dissent: the Colonial War Model

In the decades after the Second World War, Britain was engaged in a retreat from empire, forced by anti-colonial and nationalist movements to cede independence to its former colonies in a manner reminiscent of its withdrawal from the Southern part of Ireland in 1922. The British Army, almost constantly at war during this period, built up an unrivalled expertise in low-intensity operations and the coordination of military and administrative measures designed to curb armed resistance. Experience of urban guerrilla warfare was gained in Aden and Cyprus while conflict in Kenya, Malaya and elsewhere, supplied ample exposure to rural-based campaigns. The colonial war model of suppressing dissent was distilled from these experiences and essentially involves a militarisation of the administrative and legal systems and their integration into an interlocking strategy of strangling support for insurgents prior to their military defeat. Special legislation replaces the normal process of law and even administrative decisions – such as those relating to town planning, for instance – are subject to military approval and, if necessary, modification. Censorship and media manipulation are used to hinder the mobilisation of public opinion, both domestic and international. One expert on counter-insurgency, a serving officer in Northern Ireland at the time, puts the matter succinctly:

> The law should be used as just another weapon in the government's arsenal, and in this case it becomes little more than a propaganda cover for the disposal of unwanted members of the public. For this to happen efficiently the activities of the legal services have to be tied to the war effort in as discreet a way as possible. (Kitson, 1971, p. 66)

Central to this strategy is the 'winning over' of the local population by inducement, persuasion and, if necessary, coercion to isolate and eliminate opposition. The decision to remove the RUC from the front line in Northern Ireland was based upon operational and political considerations, but it removed a necessary buffer between the military and the civilian population. As the semi-official historian of the British Army in Northern Ireland comments about this period, 'The underlying fact remained; no army, however well it conducts itself, is suitable for police work' (Dewar, 1985, p. 38).

In the event, the situation in Northern Ireland and in Belfast in particular, moved rapidly into one of direct confrontation between the military and the local population. Faced with a rising tide of violence from Protestant paramilitaries, escalating street protests in nationalist enclaves and an emergent IRA, the British Army adopted a policy of direct confrontation in an attempt to regain the initiative. Despite the commitment of large numbers of troops – by July 1970 there were 11,000 British soldiers in Northern Ireland – the overall everyday control of security was left in the hands of the Unionist government and local regional military commanders. The security committee was made up of the then Prime Minister of Northern Ireland, Brian Faulkner, the GOC Land Forces, the Chief Constable of the RUC and a number of civil servants. This was a fatal combination. The British Army, hardened in the crucible of colonial war, was quick to identify the nationalist community and the IRA as the real enemy, a perception that was reinforced and nurtured by unionist hard-liners. After all, it was Brian Faulkner who, as Minister of Home Affairs, had directed the campaign against the IRA in the 1950s. Some of the most senior British officers in the North at the time were experts in colonial counter-insurgency; one senior officer, Brigadier Kitson, had written a number of works on counter-insurgency, including a standard text, *Low Intensity Operations* (1971), which was to become a definitive handbook for the CIA and NATO (Faligot, 1983). Kitson served in Northern Ireland between 1969 and 1972, and soon came into conflict with his superior officers, arguing that the strategy being pursued was counter-productive as it alienated the civilian population and drove them into the arms of the IRA, thus breaking one of the central dogmas of counter-insurgency doctrine (Faligot, 1983, p. 23). In particular, he opposed the introduction of internment without trial in 1971, seeing it as heavy-handed, indiscriminate and based upon inadequate and out-of-date intelligence information. However, the presence of Unionist politicians on the security committee probably made the introduction of internment inevitable since their mindset would hardly be amenable to the argument that the nationalist population should be won over.

Kitson was not against internment in principle, since he had advocated its use in a number of colonial situations, such as Malaya, Oman, Cyprus and Palestine. In one sense, this was an argument about tactics since Kitson's book laid down ideological and political parameters governing the conduct of counter-insurgency operations which were to become received dogma for over two decades. According to this approach, subversion is the product of attitudes and the manipulation of attitudes by small, highly motivated groups. It is not accepted that dissent can have an objective basis or even have widespread support. The problem is essentially a security one; to prevent the enemy gaining a hold over the civilian population, which is seen as easily manipulated and intimidated by small and determined groups. The solution is to put into place an integrated system of intelligence gathering, evaluation and a coordinated military and police strategy to eliminate subversive elements. Without this coordinated approach, internment was bound to fail, and indeed be counter-productive.

As Kitson (and many other observers) predicted, the introduction of internment in August 1971 did not have the desired results. The initial internment operation netted 342 men – all allegedly nationalists – and within six months, 2,350 people had been arrested and interned. However, contrary to expectations, the level of republican violence did not decrease but rose to unprecedented levels. The total number of violent deaths rose from 25 in 1970 to 467 in 1972, and explosions from 153 to 1022. During the same period (1970–72) the number of British soldiers killed rose from zero to 103 while the number of indigenous forces who died as a result of political violence was 17. It was not until 1975 that British Army deaths fell below the combined total of UDR and RUC fatalities (see Barzilay, 1981, p. 232).

Along with increased violence, many middle-class Catholics withdrew from public office, and there was widespread civil disobedience in the shape of a rent and rates strike. The shooting dead of 13 civilians by British paratroopers at a civil rights demonstration in Derry in January 1972 led to widespread reaction and protest. Two months later, the Stormont parliament was prorogued, and direct rule from London introduced. A significant shift in security policy was to follow.

There are a number of reasons why the colonial war model, as applied in Northern Ireland, had failed. First, Ireland was not some far distant colony where repression could be practised out of the view of the world media. It was not possible to isolate the North, the media could not be effectively gagged or controlled and, as the Six Counties were constitutionally part of the UK, draconian measures such as martial law could not be introduced. (For a discussion of state attempts to regulate the media, see Coulter, 1999.) Second, Irish nationalism was adept at mobilising international opinion through the Irish diaspora in the US and elsewhere, using the rhetoric of civil rights. Third, a considerable section of British opinion was sympathetic to the nationalist cause, as were both government and people of the Irish Republic. These pressures severely constrained the military options open to the British state and forced a considerable modification in strategy which went some way towards accepting the text-book analysis of Brigadier Kitson.

In *Low Intensity Operations,* Kitson argues that any campaign of insurgency will progress through three phases: a preparatory phase, a non-violent phase, and an open-insurgency phase. For Kitson, the opportune time to introduce military tactics (for example, internment without trial) is during the non-violent phase (with intelligence data collected and collated during the preparatory phase) so as to quickly neutralise and discredit the 'insurrectionist' movement before it can attain widespread popular support. However, the relatively late intervention of the British Army to the situation in Northern Ireland meant that the 'insurgency' campaign had already entered its third and final stage. This, argued Kitson, would make it impossible to defeat the 'insurrectionists' by military means alone and could actually have a counter-effect in generating support for the movement. A successful counter-insurgency strategy would therefore, have to rely more on what Kitson termed a 'unified approach' and would by necessity include 'Psychological Operations' ('Psyops') as well as a combination of direct military operations and political initiatives. The Joint Warfare Establishment, a department of the British Ministry of Defence (MOD) has defined the aim of Psyops thus:

> The primary aim of psychological warfare is to support the efforts of all other measures, military and political, against an enemy, to weaken his will to continue hostilities and to reduce his capacity to wage war. Psychological warfare relates to an emergency or a state of hostilities, and it is with the further subdivisions of strategic psywar, tactical psywar and psychological consolidation that its employment can best be examined. (cited in the *Irish Times*, 27 October 1976)

For Kitson, the aim of any successful counter-insurgency strategy was to isolate the insurgency movement from its base of support. In order to achieve this effectively, 'hard-line' tactics must co-exist with 'softer' community initiatives. In 1969 he had already outlined the essential requirements for a successful campaign in the appendix to the *Army Land Operations Manual: Counter-Revolutionary Operations, Vol. III*. These can be listed as follows:

1 The passing of emergency regulations to facilitate the conduct of a national campaign [against the insurgents].
2 Various political, social and economic measures designed to gain popular support and counter or surpass anything offered by the insurgents.

3 The setting up of an effective organisation for joint civil and military control at all levels.
4 The forming of an effective, integrated and nation-wide intelligence organisation, without which military operations can never be successful.
5 The strengthening of indigenous police and armed forces, so that their loyalty is beyond question and their work effective.
6 Measures of control designed to isolate the insurgents from popular pressure. (cited in Faligot, 1983, p. 18)

The 'unified approach' advocated by Kitson encompassed close liaison and coordination between all aspects of civil, military and judicial authority so as to deal precisely and effectively with insurgency on a number of levels, and also to identify potential weaknesses in the overall strategy: 'The fundamental concept is the working of the triumvirate, civil, military and police, as a joint and integrated organisation from the highest to the lowest level of policy making, planning and administration' (Kitson 1971, p. 66).

Ex-Colonel Robin Evelagh, who commanded the 3rd Battalion Royal Green Jackets in Northern Ireland between 1972 and 1973, subsequently reiterated the rationale for this 'unified approach'. Evelagh in his own exposition of counter-insurgency tactics, *Peacekeeping in a Democratic Society*, argues that:

> Insurrection and terrorism are based on a multiplicity of interacting and connected causes; their origins are seldom simple, and they must be combated in the same dimension, i.e. across the whole spectrum of the activities of society. It is dangerously simplistic to see terrorism and insurrection as an economic problem, or a political problem or a security problem; they are almost certainly all of these. Just as the problem is one of the whole system of society, so the Government must meet it on the basis of a co-ordinated response by the whole system of government. (Evelagh, 1978, p. 108)

The Interregnum: 1972–75

The introduction of direct rule in March 1972 ushered in a period of reassessment of security policy, and the structure of the security apparatus. It was tacitly accepted that the attempt to destroy the IRA with the blunt weapon of internment had failed, and that the use of the military in a policing role had led to the politically damaging events in Derry in January 1972, which once more focused international attention on the problem. The sight was not a pretty one. Allegations of torture and ill treatment at the hands of the British Army and RUC Special Branch – later to be substantiated by the European Court of Human Rights – were being made against a backdrop of internment camps surrounded by barbed wire and images of troops in combat gear escorted by heavy armoured cars rumbling through the streets of Belfast. Such images did little to enhance the image of Britain abroad or its capacity to deal with an increasingly violent conflict.

The policy adopted by the British government was a twin-track one. Attempts were made to forge a political solution involving talks with the IRA leadership (who were flown to London in an RAF aircraft) while at the same time a power-sharing executive was set up involving both the SDLP and the Unionist Party. Parallel to these political moves, the security apparatus was being radically overhauled. When the first round of talks with the IRA foundered in 1972, the state still went ahead with modifications to the process of internment with the introduction of a judicial commissioner with powers to release internees. This constituted the first step in the process of distancing the executive from the administration of security policy.

Of more central and far-reaching importance was the report of the Diplock Commission that was published in 1972. This report was central to the policy of criminalisation, that is, the attempt to delegitimise politically motivated crime by dealing with it through the 'normal' legal process. The full title of the Report unambiguously states the objective: *Report of the Commission to Consider Legal Procedures to Deal With Terrorist Activities in Northern Ireland* (Diplock Report, 1972). The Commission did not visit Northern Ireland as a body and the chairman, Lord Diplock, only visited twice. Evidence was oral and taken in the main from British Army personnel and civil servants directly concerned with security matters. Effectively, the report reduced the complex ethnic, social and political problems of the North to one of combating terrorism and, indeed, it was only with the report's publication that the term 'terrorism' became a staple feature of official discourse on the conflict (Coogan, 1995, pp. 472–85).

Most of the Commission's recommendations were incorporated into the Northern Ireland (Emergency Provisions) Act

1973 (EPA), which gave widespread powers of arrest and detention to the RUC and the British Army. However, the most
important aspect of the EPA (for the policy of criminalisation)
was that it redefined the range of activities commonly associated with terrorism/political violence as 'scheduled offences'
which carried a mandatory prison sentence, for example, the
possession of arms or explosives. In addition, special 'non-jury'
courts were established which were presided over by a single
judge. Confession evidence and witness statements (it was
not a requirement that the witness actually appear in court)
were accorded an extremely high level of admissibility within
the court's proceedings. For the purpose of obtaining such
evidence, special interrogation centres were to be established
at Castlereagh in Belfast and Gough Barracks in Armagh. Both
centres were operational by 1977. The establishment of these
centres led to a phenomenal increase in the number of complaints made against the RUC in respect of ill-treatment during
interrogation. In 1975, Amnesty International initiated an investigation into the allegations which sparked an official British
government inquiry to examine RUC interrogation procedures
(Bennett Report, 1979).

Since the emphasis of the new security strategy was now on
criminalising both the IRA and their activities, it was axiomatic
that there would have to be a fundamental reorganisation of
the role that the security forces (that is, the RUC, UDR and
British Army) were to play in this process. The military strategy implemented after 1969 to deal with the violence had
explicitly recognised the political nature of the conflict, both
in the tactics used (internment and intelligence screening),
and in the treatment of prisoners (special category status). It
was becoming increasingly obvious that any attempt to depict
the IRA as 'criminals' would be severely undermined by allowing the British Army to continue in the front line and that the
high-profile use of the military allowed the IRA to portray
themselves as anti-colonial freedom fighters. The policy of
criminalisation illustrates the ambiguities inherent in the British government's strategy. The venerated principles of British
justice became, in the context of Northern Ireland, just another
strategy to deal with political violence. Any technique of repression could, if it were seen to have a legal foundation, be
portrayed as legitimate and conducted within the law
(Tomlinson, 1980b). Broadly speaking the changes to the
security structure can be summarised under four headings:

1 A reorganisation and rearming of the RUC to allow the introduction of police primacy
2 The setting up of interrogation centres to contain suspects on the basis of a new centralised intelligence gathering system
3 The introduction of 'special' legislation to deal with political violence through the 'normal' legal process
4 The 'professionalisation' of RUC practice and discourse.

The overall strategic intention of the changes in policing was to present a picture of the normalisation of a society which was, apart from the activities of a small unrepresentative minority, carrying on with its activities under the benign eye of a professional and neutral police force. The reality of a protracted and bloody internal war was, where possible, evaded and there was constant stress upon the proposition that the IRA had no widespread support but only continued to exist through coercion and intimidation.

Since police forces do not operate in a political and social vacuum, organisational and other reforms are a response to a specific situation or situations and are not simply part of some abstract process of professionalisation or liberalisation. The discourse of professionalisation adopted by the RUC had its roots in the wider strategy implemented by the British state to manage political violence in Northern Ireland.

The new security strategy, designed to strengthen the legitimacy of the administration and deny the political nature of IRA violence, was developed from 1974 and incorporated two overlapping components: criminalisation and Ulsterisation. Criminalisation was designed to isolate the republican movement from a wider support base, and depended upon a number of factors. First, in 1974 the Secretary of State announced that 'full responsibility for law and order' was going to be transferred from the Army to the RUC. Second, internment without trial was to be stopped from February 1975, and the courts were to be used as the sole means of dealing with those suspected of violence. Finally, special category status – which gave prisoners the *de facto* status of prisoners of war, allowing freedom of association, the right to wear their own clothes and considerable autonomy within their own compounds – was to be withdrawn for any prisoner sentenced after 1 March 1976. Criminalisation depended upon the denial of any vestige of legitimacy to the IRA campaign, and its members were to be regarded as 'ordinary' criminals. The impetus for criminalisation was provided by the Gardiner Report of January 1975 which commented that:

> The introduction of Special Category Status was a serious mistake ...
> It should be made absolutely clear that Special Category prisoners
> can expect no amnesty and will have to serve their sentences ... We
> recommend that the earliest practicable opportunity should be taken
> to end the Special Category (cited in Coogan, 1995, p. 482).

The ideological rationale for criminalisation is neatly summarised by Sir Kenneth Newman, who became Chief Constable of the RUC in 1976:

> It [criminalisation] is based on the idea of separating the terrorists
> from the support they obtain in their communities. The object is to
> prise open and progressively widen a gap between the terrorist and
> the ordinary people so that they will be increasingly perceived as crimi-
> nals and not as wayward political heroes (Sir Kenneth Newman, *A
> Force Under Fire*, Ulster Television, 1 April 1992).

Since criminalisation meant that political violence was to be dealt with through the normal legal process – assigning it the status of a basic law-and-order problem – it was axiomatic that there would have to be a fundamental reorganisation of the RUC to reflect this new emphasis. The RUC and UDR were to be the face of normality dealing with the situation as a law-and-order problem. The problem was as much about image as anything else since the need to placate international opinion dictated that the British Army could not be seen to be acting as a colonial army in an occupied territory.

The chief vehicle by which this was to be achieved was through the policy of 'police primacy', also referred to as 'Ulsterisation'. As was suggested above, the policy of police primacy was first mooted in 1974. However, even by 1976, Ulsterisation was not proceeding as quickly as was hoped, with large areas of Belfast, Derry and South Armagh effectively designated 'No-Go' areas and inaccessible to the RUC (Evelagh, 1978). In order to reassess the situation and to put the Ulsterisation process back on track, a ministerial working party under the leadership of John Bourn (a senior civil servant seconded from the Home Office) was established by the Secretary of State, Merlyn Rees in January 1976. The Bourn Committee's proposals were outlined in an unpublished document entitled 'The Way Ahead', which effectively laid the foundation for the future structure, role and organisation of the modern RUC (Ryder, 1989, p. 140). (The document, lodged in the House of Commons library, was never published.) The Bourn Committee reiterated the importance of police primacy as a principle element in the security strategy favoured by the British administration as the then Secretary of State for Northern Ireland, Merlyn Rees, made clear in the House of Commons:

> I would like to have published its results. But by their very nature it would not be in the public interest to disclose the details ... the only way forward is the way in which law and order has always been established in this country – by the police working to the law and securing its effective administration ... At the heart of the Committee's conclusions is therefore the idea of *securing police acceptance and effectiveness.* By securing police effectiveness is meant the integration and acceptance of the police in the community to enable them to administer law and order effectively. It does not mean a return to the past. This is a particularly difficult and challenging task because of the legacy of Irish history. There is a traditional sensitivity and antipathy to the police ... We have to accept that the police are not acceptable in all areas of Northern Ireland today. The police will consequently have to overcome the legacy of the past as well as the experience of the last seven years.
>
> To increase the effectiveness of the police the Committee's main conclusions are as follows:
>
> 1 An increase in the size of the force.
> 2 The continuing introduction of special investigation teams.
> 3 Improved arrangements for the collecting and collating of criminal intelligence.
> 4 Flexible use of resources to concentrate upon serious crime and preventative policing.
> 5 A special effort will be made to make the RUC more representative.
>
> This will depend to some extent upon political factors and opinion leaders in the minority community speaking up more frequently for the RUC [emphasis added].

Predictably, the recommendation to make the RUC more representative was hedged around with qualifications, and the onus placed on external factors (such as intimidation) to explain the low level of the force's acceptability among nationalists. The new Chief Constable of the RUC, Sir Kenneth Newman, swiftly endorsed the recommendations of the Bourn Committee. It was considered essential – if the strategy of criminalising political violence was to be effective at all – that the RUC be seen to deal with the situation (Newman, 1978b). In order to assist the RUC in this role as the lead agency in a revamped counter-insurgency operation, the recommendations contained in *The Way Ahead* were swiftly implemented. There was to be an increase in the size of the regular RUC (from 5,000 to its present level of 13,000); the RUCR was to be expanded to free regular officers for patrolling duties; the force budget was to be increased from £49 million to £69 million; regional crime squads were established to deal more effectively with IRA active service units; the Criminal Investigation Department (CID) was restructured to make more efficient use of forensic science techniques, and intelligence data was to become computerised and organised centrally. According to Geraghty (1998, pp. 158–9), there are two main computer systems, one linked to the vehicle licensing office, called 'Vengeful' and another 'Crucible', which contains personal files. Geraghty claims that initial efforts to integrate both systems failed, but that attempts to develop a knowledge-based integrated system have continued during the IRA cease-fire.

In addition, more efficient and modern equipment was commissioned for the force, such as the NATO 7.62 mm rifles, M1 carbines, Federal riot guns, and a new fleet of armoured Land Rovers and armoured civilian patrol cars (Ryder, 1989, p. 141). Finally, the Police Authority earmarked £25 million for the refurbishment of police stations and the construction of new ones. Newman also commissioned a number of studies within the force to estimate future training and manpower requirements and to devise a public order manual (Ryder, 1989, p. 142). In this respect, the Bourn Committee represented the initial impetus for the professionalisation of the RUC on a purely technical and administrative level. The policy of police primacy came into operation officially on 1 January 1977, when Sir Kenneth Newman and the Army GOC signed a joint directive to relegate the Army to a 'military aid to the civil power' role and to position the RUC in the front line in the maintenance of internal security. Additionally, in 1979, Sir Maurice Oldfield, a career 'securocrat' who had been chief of MI5, was appointed as security coordinator in Northern Ireland, by the Prime Minister, Margaret Thatcher. Teams of 'expert assessors' were seconded to Oldfield from the RUC and Army. This development followed closely from that advocated by

Kitson, who as we have seen above had argued for the establishment of an 'effective organisation for joint civil and military control at all levels' to coordinate security policy and tactics.

The success of the new security strategy depended on more than technical professionalism, however. Of crucial ideological importance was that the RUC's historical role as a paramilitary force be downplayed in favour of one that stressed an 'ordinary' or 'normal' policing dimension (Newman, 1980b). Indeed, Robert Evelagh who, as we have seen, informed the British government's counter-insurgency strategy, argued that the success of the criminalisation strategy would be undermined if the RUC were seen to be performing an overtly paramilitary role, since this might inadvertently highlight the political dimension to the conflict (Evelagh, 1978). On a similar basis, he has also argued for the 'necessary fiction' of having the RUC maintain a presence, even in those areas where they are unable to do so without British Army support (Evelagh, 1978, p. 81). Once again, this fitted neatly with the counter-insurgency strategy advocated by Kitson in *Low Intensity Operations*, where he stressed the importance of 'psychological co-ordination' in any attempt by the state to deal with insurrection. In particular, the nationalist community must be 'won over' and made to perceive the security forces as their protectors. This is highlighted in a confidential document entitled 'Future Terrorist Trends' (dated 15 December 1978), distributed by MI5 and the Intelligence Branch of the Ministry of Defence to the Secretary of State and British Army commanders based in Northern Ireland, which fell into the hands of the IRA under mysterious circumstances. In a section entitled 'Terrorist Counter Measures', the necessity of cultivating popular support for the security forces among nationalists is emphasised as a priority of the security strategy. (A copy of this document, written by a senior counter-insurgency officer, General Glover, is reprinted in Appendix 4, Faligot 1983, pp. 221–42. See also Coogan, 1995, p. 468.)

Kenneth Newman supplied the ideological component of the new criminalisation strategy when he became Chief Constable of the RUC. Newman argued vehemently for the centrality of 'British' policing methods in defeating the IRA (Newman, 1978a, 1978b, 1980b). His thesis was influenced by his time spent as a Detective Constable in the Palestinian police force, where he came to acknowledge that the exercise of physical force was by itself not enough in waging a successful counter-insurgency campaign (Ryder, 1989, p. 136). Newman insisted that the RUC articulate a discourse of professional policing, a discourse that was to be manifested on a number levels. One element of this professional discourse stressed the importance of the RUC adopting 'British' policing methods drawn from what is referred to as the Westminster model of policing. Newman's rationale was that the 'criminal problem of terrorism' could only be successfully countered by the application of 'normal' policing strategies and tactics. This is a point highlighted by Cain, who emphasises the ideological importance attached to 'British' policing methods in obtaining legitimacy for the colonial administration:

> The ideal of the British 'bobby' (now shown decisively to have been forever a myth) was part of the rhetoric and strategy of British colonial administration worldwide, from Queensland to Kenya, and from Cape Town to Bengal. Policing by consent is fundamentally cheaper than military control or paramilitary policing both in money and legitimacy costs. (Cain, 1991, p. 320)

Particular importance was attached to the extent to which the RUC acted impartially, within the law and with the widespread support and consent of the community. The emphasis for Newman was one of 'total strategy' – mirroring as it did Kitson's 'unified approach' – whereby 'terrorism' would be eradicated only through 'an unspectacular process – the persistent, impartial and professional application of the law', coupled with increased liaison and cooperation between the RUC and the local community (Newman, cited in Ryder, 1989, p. 158). To 'isolate the terrorists' from the local community, Newman set about cultivating public support for the RUC through an expansion of the Community Relations Branch (increasing the complement of officers from ten to sixty) and through his advocacy of a 'multi-agency' initiative between the RUC and governmental organisations and community groups (Hillyard, 1983, pp. 46–7). However, community relations officers were to be an integral part of the counter-insurgency strategy and:

> ... continually emphasise that they are policemen first and community relations officers second, and that the Community Relations Branch is just another specialised unit which a modern police force requires if it is to serve the community properly by reducing or preventing the production of irresponsible citizens (a senior RUC officer, cited in *Ulster Commentary,* May 1975).

Newman's commitment to 'professionalise' the RUC, in line with the principles that are said to guide British policing, was driven by what he termed the 'debacle' surrounding the policing of the Ulster Workers' Council strike of 1974 where the RUC (and the British Army) fraternised openly with striking loyalists.

The RUC and the Ulster Workers' Strike

Direct Rule from Westminster was implemented as a crisis measure, a means of allowing a space to create political structures to allow the establishment of a local system of government, which would include the participation of the minority. The establishment of a power-sharing executive by the British government in January 1974 was seen as a first step towards this objective. The executive was made up of representatives of the Unionist Party, the moderate Alliance Party and the SDLP and had the support of the Dublin administration. However, there was formidable opposition to this measure amongst Unionist hard-liners in the United Ulster Unionist Coalition (UUUC), which was committed to bringing down the power-sharing executive and demanded a return to the old Stormont system. The UUUC threatened a major programme of industrial action unless the British administration capitulated to its demands. This campaign was to be orchestrated by the Ulster Workers Council (UWC) and the Ulster Army Council (UAC) – both comprised of loyalist paramilitaries – who had already begun to recruit sympathetic trade union leaders and 'key' employees in the power stations. The UUUC demands were ignored, and the euphemistically-termed 'constitutional stoppage' started on Tuesday, 11 May 1974. The strike resulted in the widespread intimidation of workers in factories throughout Northern Ireland, forcing them to close for the duration of the strike. Additionally, petrol was banned to all but essential users and the UWC used their influence with power station workers to stage widespread power-cuts. Consequently, thousands of families were left without light or heat. The British government still refused to meet the UWC's demands and the Northern Ireland Secretary Merlyn Rees declared a State of Emergency on 19 May, authorising the use of troops to maintain essential services. In late May, a number of Unionists who were participants in the power-sharing

executive met Rees and pleaded with him to talk to the UWC
in the hope of calling an end to the strike. When he refused
they resigned, which effectively brought an end to the power-
sharing experiment. The UWC had achieved their goal and
the strike was called off the next day. (For an overview of the
UWC strike, see Fisk 1975.)

The UWC strike had severe repercussions for the image of
the RUC and the British Army. They were seen to be collud-
ing with loyalists in the overthrow of a power-sharing process
that offered Catholics a say in the governance of Northern
Ireland for the first time in fifty years. Contemporary newspaper reports cite incidences of RUC officers chatting to members
of loyalist paramilitaries at barricades and refusing to act on
calls for assistance from workers who were intimidated for
attempting to cross picket lines (*Irish News*, 18 May 1974).
Likewise, Farrell suggests that a secret loyalist group in the
Ulster Defence Regiment (UDR) and RUC, calling itself 'For
Ulster', was planning to mutiny if the British government
attempted to use force to break up the strike (Farrell, 1980).
In the eyes of the Catholic community, there was little evidence that the RUC was paying anything other than lip service
to the reforms set out by the Hunt Commission. This point
was illustrated by evidence from some RUC officers themselves,
one of whom suggested that there was a policy decision taken
by the RUC hierarchy to adopt a policy of non-intervention
during the strike:

> During the UWC strike the police deserved all the criticism they got.
> They stood back and let it happen. They could if they had put their
> minds to it quelled the strike. However, more generally manpower
> was also lacking in '74. You didn't have a strong police force – it took
> a few more years before the RUC's strength was built up. (cited in
> Ellison, 1997, p. 166)

It would appear that in 1974, four years after the Hunt Committee reported its findings, the RUC were still inclined to
adopt a differential approach to the policing of nationalist
and loyalist dissension. Indeed, many RUC officers were able
to engage ideologically with the aims of the strikers. One
officer viewed the strike as a 'legitimate protest' about 'loyalists
standing up for their rights'. The same officer justified the strike
by referring to the civil rights protests: 'You had the nationalist parades and marches a few years earlier and they seemed

to get what they wanted. So why shouldn't the loyalists have been allowed to protest?' (cited in Ellison, 1997, p. 167).

Policing after the UWC Strike

In the aftermath of the UWC strike, the British government was resigned to the idea that an internal political solution to the troubles was unlikely, given the reaction of hard-line union-ism to the power-sharing executive, and that Direct Rule would remain exactly that for the foreseeable future (McGarry and O'Leary, 1995). The principal element in any revised secu-rity strategy would have to concern itself with the defeat of the IRA so as to break the unionist and loyalist impasse on the possibility of any future power-sharing arrangement. In order to deflect international criticism, this new strategy would have to be compatible with either the due process of law or else be enacted under state of emergency legislation. However, this latter option was unattractive to the British government, since it highlighted their failure to reach a politi-cal solution and in some respects would have been similar to the unsuccessful and counter-productive military strategy pursued at the time.

According, to one contemporary, Newman 'was incensed by what he saw and was determined never to allow a situation like that to arise under his leadership' (a senior RUC officer, and personal friend of Newman, cited in Ellison, 1997, p. 183). Newman's first priority as Chief Constable was to instil into the force an ethos of political impartiality by emphasising its assurance to serve all sections of the community 'without fear or favour'. He argued that the RUC could not operate effec-tively without the active consent and support of the community, particularly, the nationalist community. This would not occur, he maintained, if the nationalist community perceived the RUC to be a partisan force which defended loyalist interests (Newman, 1979). A further rationale was that the very success of the criminalisation strategy depended on the neutralisation of nationalist support for republican paramilitaries. It should be noted that for Newman, republican paramilitaries represented the biggest obstacle to the attainment of peace and stability in Northern Ireland. Indeed, he argued vociferously that loy-alist paramilitary activity was essentially reactive (See Ryder, 1989). The extent to which the RUC could depict itself as an

impartial force operating above politics, in the interest of the
'whole community' was therefore, imperative. As such, the
RUC under Newman adopted a 'professional commitment'
to act as the 'the thin green line' between order – what the
RUC and all right-thinking people want – and the 'terrorists' –
who were wreaking havoc and chaos on the community.

The second element in Newman's professional strategy for
the force was symbolised by two related developments: first,
the expansion of the RUC Special Branch to deal with intelligence gathering and surveillance, and second, the formation
of the Bessbrook Support Unit (BSU) in 1977. This BSU represented professionalism at the level of technical efficiency
and its manifestation was an elite squad of highly equipped
and SAS-trained RUC officers who were deployed along the
South Armagh border to intercept IRA active service units in
the region. The BSU was replaced in 1979 with a Special
Patrol Group, which was itself replaced in 1981 with Headquarters and Divisional Mobile Support Units (HMSU/DMSU).
Indeed, a short time later, a number of similarly equipped and
trained Special Support Units were gradually extended throughout Northern Ireland for the same purpose (that is, engaging
IRA active service units) and a specialised Special Branch
unit (E4A) was established for deep surveillance purposes in
1980.[1]

These special units represented the cutting edge of Newman's
professional strategy for the RUC. Ostensibly, the training,
techniques and tactics of these units – 'firepower, speed and
aggression'[2] – might seem at odds with Newman's emphasis
on 'normal' policing discussed earlier. However, he regarded
their implementation as another component in his 'total strategy' and perceived them to be fully concomitant with the
orthodoxy of Ulsterisation (Newman, 1978a, 1978b). The SAS
had been operating in Northern Ireland officially since January 1976, and unofficially from 1970 (Faligot, 1983), so for
Newman the deployment of RUC units for a similar purpose
merely occupied the lacuna until the RUC came to assume full
responsibility for law and order. As Ryder suggests:

> Pouring resources into the undercover war was another major devel-
> opment sponsored by Newman. These operations were initially
> centred on the border but the Special Support Unit, modelled on the
> SAS, soon began to operate throughout the province when the Spe-
> cial Branch undercover surveillance teams and informers came up

with tip-offs for them to act upon. The strategy was founded on Newman's belief that if the RUC was successfully to replace the army then the 'gap' in its capabilities for this type of work must be closed. That involved not only developing a capability to deal with public order situations but also acquiring the means to handle sieges, counter surveillance operations and other similar kinds of incident. (1989, pp. 215–16)

The end result of the changes in security strategy was that the RUC returned to its original role as a counter-insurgency force with vastly enhanced capabilities and technology, as well as the full and open backing of the British government, and the tacit support of the government in Dublin. At the operational level, the traditionally reactive role of the police was reversed. One major effect of the restructuring was to put an information-gathering apparatus in the hands of the police which allowed the targeting of deviant populations, and the collection and collation of vast amounts of information, however trivial. To give one example, records were kept of the furnishings and wallpaper in the houses of suspects (see Geraghty, 1998). Policing became highly proactive, with large numbers of people being treated as deviant on the basis of religion, residence and association. Whole populations were subject to an intense level of covert and overt surveillance.

6 Legitimacy, Counter-Insurgency and Policing: The Legacy of the 1970s

Criminalisation, Interrogation and the Bennett Report

In December 1977, the Irish police seized an IRA document during a house search in Dun Laoghaire near Dublin; the document outlined the organisation's concern with the success of the RUC and British Army in arresting and convicting volunteers and in disrupting operations. The document, which outlined measures to counter security forces' successes, was frank in admitting serious weaknesses in the structure and organisation of the IRA:

> The three-day and seven-day detention orders are breaking volunteers, and it is the Republican Army's fault for not indoctrinating volunteers with the psychological strength to resist interrogation. Coupled with this factor, which is contributing to our defeat, we are burdened with an inefficient structure of commands, brigades, battalions and companies. This old system with which Brits and Branch are familiar has to be changed. (Taylor, 1980, pp. 345–7)

The counter-insurgency measures put in place between 1974 and 1976 had, by the following year, begun to have a severe effect on the operational capabilities of the Provisionals. During 1996, over 2,000 suspects, the majority charged with IRA-related incidents, were convicted through the non-jury Diplock courts. Most of those arrested confessed within two days (it was said that if a suspect could resist the RUC interrogators for two days, the next five days of the detention period could be managed without breaking), and were swiftly convicted on the basis of their confession. Such confessions were often used to implicate others, who were then interrogated leading to an almost assembly-line process of arrest, interrogation, confession and conviction. Arrests were generally made on the basis of intelligence gathered through undercover operations or the use of informers. Both the British Army and the RUC were involved in these types of operation with the Army concentrating on covert operations and the RUC Special Branch focusing on the use of informers. According to one source, by 1980, there were some 300 specially-trained British Army surveillance operators, supplemented by another hundred from the RUC (Urban, 1992, p. 47). The military structure of the IRA was traditionally modelled on the British Army pattern of brigade, battalion and companies and members were invariably recruited from specific geographic areas which made it extremely vulnerable to the intelligence-gathering operations of the security forces. The main advantage of the traditional military structure – that it gave the IRA a high profile in nationalist areas ensuring credibility through visibility – was now transformed into a fatal weakness. The RUC and British Army used their successes to undermine the morale of suspects. Clearly and visibly placed in security forces' installations, ready to greet a suspect dragged out of his bed in the middle of the night, were charts of the local IRA organisation with photographs of the members, or suspected members, of the unit. The photos of those already imprisoned were crossed out in heavy black ink.

The security establishment seemed convinced that the war was almost won. The Secretary of State, Roy Mason, who had little time for political initiatives, was backed up by a team of military and RUC commanders (Chief Constable Newman and Assistant Chief Constable Hermon) who favoured an aggressive security response to the problems of Northern Ireland. Mason was fond of soundbites, and comments such as 'we are squeezing the terrorists like a tube of toothpaste', or that 1977 was the year that the 'noose tightens on the terrorist', are indicative of the extent to which the authorities thought that the 'war' had been won. Newman, too, was convinced by August 1977, that they had the 'terrorists on the run'. However, by December of that year, Mason was being a little more cautious, talking only of 'considerable progress' having been made.

The IRA document mentioned above had pinpointed the weaknesses of the IRA, and also proposed solutions. The unwieldy military structure was to be replaced by a cell structure, 'we must gear ourselves toward long-term armed struggle based upon putting unknown men and new recruits into a new structure. The new structure shall be a cell system' (Taylor, 1980, p. 346). In addition, and equally important for the IRA,

was the introduction of training in anti-interrogation techniques. The reorganisation of the IRA had both political and
military implications, with the latter defining the former. It
was essentially a defensive move based upon the awareness
that the British Army could not be defeated militarily and
that Britain could not be forced to withdraw from Ireland by
the combined efforts of the IRA and a popular mass movement. In effect, the reorganisation was a *de facto* recognition of
the success of the new security tactics in bringing the IRA to
the verge of defeat. The new political reality, flagged up in the
reorganisation document, was publicly articulated during a
speech in June 1977 at the Bodenstown commemoration, an
annual occasion (ostensibly to honour the memory of Wolfe
Tone), which has been traditionally used by the republican
movement to signal changes in policy and tactics. A new strategy of the 'long war' was put forward: instead of following the
textbook model of guerrilla warfare, the IRA was to reverse
the process to achieve the same ends. The size of the military
membership was to decrease, command was to be decentralised, and preparations were to be made for a long, slow war of
attrition. It has been estimated that the number of active IRA
operatives decreased from about a thousand in 1975 to less
than 250 a decade later (Bishop and Mallie, 1987, p. 264). In
addition, Sinn Féin was to become the propaganda and political arm of the IRA. The reorganisation was successful in
stemming the successes of the security forces. The introduction of the cell system led to a decrease in arrests and
convictions, and although operations were curtailed, those
that were carried out were more carefully planned and more
economically damaging. In addition, the IRA had effectively
rearmed with modern weapons and improved their bomb-
making capabilities by 1978. However, despite the increased
efficiency of IRA operations, it is doubtful if the bombing campaign in the North had any significant economic impact other
than to prepare the city centre for the wave of property development which took place from the 1980s onwards. The decision
to launch a bombing campaign in England may well have followed from this realisation.

However, it was not the military dimension of the conflict
that was to dominate the scene after 1978, but rather political questions concerning the direction and execution of
security policy and, in particular, the role of the RUC in the
latter. The successes of the security forces prior to 1978 were

based upon a number of interlocking factors: the inefficiency of the IRA as a organisation, the success of the Diplock system, the use of undercover units, the suppression of dissent in nationalist areas, and the ideological erosion of the nationalist domination of the propaganda war through the rhetoric of terrorism and the policy of normalisation. The role of the RUC had become central to this effort. Special Branch interrogation units ensured the flow of confessions to the Diplock courts, the liberal use of plastic bullets and riot squads in nationalist areas suppressed overt expressions of dissent, and special police units were taking their place alongside the SAS and other British Army undercover squads.

It is quite clear, both from the public statements of senior RUC officers, and the findings of any number of commentators, that the RUC enthusiastically embraced its counter-insurgency role, and indeed fought numerous turf battles with the British Army to achieve primacy in counter-insurgency operations. Yet the optimistic scenario of a quick victory over the IRA began to unravel almost as rapidly as the republican hope that 'one more push' would drive the British out of Ireland. From the end of 1977 onwards, the tactics involved in the policy of criminalisation came under increasing scrutiny and criticism from groups other than the IRA and Sinn Féin.

Allegations about the mistreatment of suspects under interrogation by the RUC Special Branch gathered momentum during 1977. The allegations, which were originally confined to Sinn Féin and other republican groups and well known to local lawyers dealing with Diplock cases, began to gain support from the SDLP, some Catholic priests and a few Westminster MPs. The RUC and the Northern Ireland Office emphatically denied that any ill-treatment had taken place. The Chief Constable suggested that the injuries were self-inflicted with, for example, the plastic knives and forks supplied to prisoners. It was not until the screening of a television programme about the allegations of ill-treatment in October, followed by statements by members of the medical and legal professions, followed by the Churches and a damning investigation by Amnesty International in 1978 that the state began to show signs of embarrassment. The Amnesty Report was blunt: 'Maltreatment of suspected terrorists by the RUC has taken place with sufficient frequency to warrant the establishment of a public inquiry into interrogations' (cited in Taylor, 1980, p. 286).

In June 1978 a limited inquiry under Judge Bennett was set up with restricted terms of reference which excluded any investigation of allegations of brutality. The terms of reference were to investigate 'police procedures and practice' relating to interrogation rather than to look at the question of ill-treatment. In March 1979, nine months after the Bennett Report had been commissioned, two police doctors felt constrained to speak out publicly and confirm that suspects had been ill-treated while in custody. Within days of the appearance of one doctor on LWT's *Weekend World,* the Bennett Report was published and, although hampered by its terms of reference, the report made clear that evidence of ill-treatment was overwhelming.

The Chief Constable and the Secretary of State refused to admit that ill-treatment had occurred, the latter being somewhat economical with the truth when responding to questions in the House of Commons: 'The Bennett report has not said that ill-treatment has taken place.' Since MPs had been given no time to study the report before the debate, they were not in a position to ask the Secretary of State how he reconciled his statement with Paragraph 163 of the report: 'There can, however, whatever the precise explanation, be no doubt that the injuries in this last class were not self-inflicted and were sustained during the period of detention at a police office' (Taylor, 1980, p. 324).

The system of interrogation was a crucial link in the chain between the initial identification of suspects and the extraction of a confession, and conviction in a Diplock court. The first link was managed by Special Branch and military intelligence on the basis of information from covert surveillance and informers and the second was totally in the hands of the RUC. According to Peter Taylor, one of the doctors who had spoken out, Dr Elliott, in his letter of resignation to the Chief Constable, said: '... he had been driven to two conclusions: results were expected and were to be obtained even if a certain degree of ill-treatment were necessary, and that a degree of ill-treatment was condoned at a very high level' (Taylor, 1980, p. 334).

Dr Elliott seems also to have been convinced that ill-treatment had continued between the publication of the Amnesty Report and the publication of the Bennett Report and this was admitted, with qualification, by the Police Authority (Taylor, 1980, p. 335). Peter Taylor's own research shows clearly that complaints of ill-treatment decreased during the visit by Amnesty International representatives, but swiftly rose again, to decrease on publication of the report. A further rise ensued, to be followed by a drop on the publication of the Bennett Report. Perhaps those in charge of operational policy imagined that the process of rolling up the IRA would be sufficiently rapid and successful to counter and silence any criticisms that might be made of interrogation procedures. The Bennett Report was essentially an attempt to defuse the questions surrounding detention and interrogation without having to confront the more basic questions inherent in the strategy of depoliticising and delegitimising the aspirations of large numbers of nationalists, whether supporters of the IRA or more moderate constitutional nationalists. Despite the overwhelming evidence of ill-treatment, no police officer was charged with an offence related to the events in the interrogation centres and the Chief Constable probably saw no reason to revise his statement, made when allegations of brutality first began to surface:

> In recent months I have found it necessary to issue instructions to the force warning them that they must take precautions to prevent self inflicted injuries by prisoners. There have been incidents of prisoners wounding themselves with eating utensils, a nail, a tin of lemonade or by butting their heads against a wall or smashing a window. (*Irish Times*, 24 June 1977)

The ill-treatment of suspects during interrogation was only one aspect of RUC tactics designed to defeat the IRA. The emergency legislation used to arrest suspects had effectively become the primary means of policing republican areas. The refusal of Sinn Féin and the IRA to participate in the political process and their policy of not standing for election played into the hands of the state propaganda machine. Central to the policy of normalisation was the contention that the IRA had little support, and only survived by intimidating the Catholic population into silence. This approach gave the RUC, in particular, a basis on which to build its own claims to legitimacy: in the absence of any clear evidence to the contrary, they could maintain that they had considerable support among the Catholic population, but were unable to engage in 'normal' policing because of the activities of the terrorists (Mulcahy, 2000).

This left the IRA essentially in a no-win situation. Although they had managed to restrict the damage done to their organisation during 1976–78, their military campaign had been contained and they had no organisation capable of capitalising on the widespread unease created by the British government's single-minded obsession with a security solution. The levels of popular protest existing during the civil rights campaign were a thing of the past and any attempts at popular protest were swiftly repressed by the RUC. The northern leadership of the IRA was acutely aware of the problem of translating the war with the security forces into political capital. The IRA 'Staff Report', which fell into the hands of the Irish police, outlined a more active role for Sinn Féin:

> Sinn Féin should come under Army organisers at all levels ... Sinn Féin should be radicalised (under Army direction) and should agitate about social and economic issues which attack the welfare of the people. Sinn Féin should be directed to infiltrate other organisations to win support for, and sympathy for, the movement. Sinn Féin should be re-educated and have a big role to play in publicity and propaganda departments, complaints and problems (making no room for RUC opportunism). (Taylor, 1980, p. 347)

Although short on detail, there is a clear acknowledgement here that the 'securocrats' were winning the propaganda battle, and that a political dimension to the struggle would have to be developed particularly with regard to attempts by the RUC to present an image of 'normal' policing. Those living in middle-class areas, and towns and villages not affected by the conflict, were presented with a police force that was polite, reasonably efficient and careful to present an image of an organisation that was making every effort to restore normality, even in the midst of a murderous IRA campaign.

The picture in many nationalist areas was radically different and the reality of policing far from 'normal'. The exigencies of the political situation and the use of emergency legislation replaced any pretence at normal policing and anyone living in a republican area was a likely target for police attention. In a twelve-month period during 1977–78, 2,800 people were arrested under the three-day detention powers, of which 35 per cent were subsequently charged, usually on the basis of confessions extracted during interrogation. Of those arrested under all the various pieces of emergency legislation – four-hour, three-day or seven-day detention – 90 per cent were released without charge. Anyone, whether a resident or not, found frequenting bars, clubs, or even visiting friends in republican areas was automatically suspect and likely to attract the attention of the security forces. (Boyle and Hadden, 1980; Walsh, 1983; Scorer and Hewitt, 1981). Effectively, emergency powers were used to impose blanket policing in republican areas. The usual police practices for gathering intelligence, information and evidence were replaced by the use of emergency powers of arrest, detention and interrogation to gather information. Incidents of normal crime were dealt with in this fashion: 40 per cent of those charged before Diplock courts were charged with 'ordinary', that is, non-terrorist related, crimes. The evidence against most of those charged (75 per cent) was based upon confessions made during interrogation, many of which would not have been admissible under common law (Greer and White, 1986).

The attitude of the RUC was to treat all Catholics as potential IRA supporters, until they could prove otherwise. Such markers as address, occupation, dress, age, gender and general demeanour were used by officers on the ground to make decisions which could lead to the immediate arrest and detention of anyone, particularly young males, who might have aroused the slightest suspicions in the mind of the police officer. Such police practices were rendered invisible by a generally compliant media and the constant barrage of state propaganda (Curtis, 1984).

Policing the Hunger Strikes

However, events were to overtake the hesitant steps of the republican movement towards developing a more political stance, and were simultaneously to undermine a central tenet of the normalisation strategy: namely, that the IRA enjoyed no significant support. The hunger strikes by republican prisoners in 1979–80 had the unintentional effect of changing the political landscape (Guelke and Smyth, 1992; Smyth, 1988).

The decision of republican prisoners to embark upon a hunger strike had its roots in the abolition of special category status for prisoners in 1975. Those convicted of an offence committed after March 1976 were to be treated as 'ordinary

criminals' with no special privileges and committed to a cel-
lular regime. This was an essential element in the policy of
criminalisation, since it denied convicted members of illegal
organisations any claim to political legitimacy through special concessions – such as rights of association, right to wear
their own clothes, etc. – because of the political nature of
their offences. Although this decision struck at the heart of
republican ideology, and the perception of being engaged in a
legitimate armed struggle, reaction to the prisoners' decision
to refuse to accept the new regime was slow. The first prisoner
to reject the new regime, by refusing to wear prison issue clothing, did so in September 1976. Three hundred others, imprisoned
in cells less than three metres square and clad only in blan-
kets soon joined him.

The republican movement was hesitant in offering significant support to the prison protest. The IRA leadership saw
the protest as a distraction from the armed struggle, and feared
that any attempt to mobilise mass protest would fail, thus
further demoralising their supporters. Their response to the
protest was to kill prison officers: 18 died at the hands of the
IRA between 1976 and 1980. In the meantime, conditions in
the prison worsened significantly. Attempts by the Archbishop
of Armagh, Cardinal Ó Fiaich, to mediate with the British authorities came to nothing. After a visit to the prison in August
1978, Ó Fiaich described the conditions he had seen in the
following terms:

> One would hardly allow an animal to remain in such conditions, let
> alone a human being. The nearest approach to it I have seen was the
> spectacle of hundreds of people living in the sewer pipes in the slums
> of Calcutta. The stench of filth in some of the cells with the remains of
> rotten food and human excreta scattered around the walls was almost
> unbearable. (*Irish Times*, 2 August 1978)

In the following year, relatives of protesting prisoners formed
themselves into the Relatives Action Committee (RAC), which
led to the calling of a conference against repression in Coalisland
attended by a large number of people from fringe political
groups. An attempt by the Provisionals to take over the meeting was frustrated, which led to their refusal to take part in
any broad-based campaign of protest. As one commentator
put it: 'The prevailing militarism and authoritarianism of
Republicans does not predispose them to collaborating on a

basis of equality with those who are not under their discipline, much less those who do not share their views' (*Magill*, April 1981).

It became clear that the Provisionals had seriously underestimated the support for an anti-repression agenda when one of the leaders of the RAC, Bernadette McAliskey, stood for election to the European Parliament on an anti-repression platform, and got over 30,000 votes, despite the determined opposition of the Provisionals. The decision of the prisoners to embark upon a hunger strike in response to the refusal to meet their demands in October 1980 came from within the prison, and was opposed by an unlikely alliance of the Provisionals, the Catholic Church, political parties north and south and many family members of the prisoners. Once the strike got under way, it tapped a huge reservoir of support across the island. Demonstrations in support of the prisoners were the largest ever seen since the civil rights demonstrations of a decade earlier. There were numerous marches and demonstrations throughout the country, most of which went unreported in the press. The larger marches, in Belfast and Derry attracted many thousands of protesters, moving one seasoned commentator on the Irish scene to write:

> Many of the demonstrators are painfully poor ... a lot of women with strained tired faces, dressed in thin clothes against the biting wind and rain. Many of them walk with young children or stand silently watching on the pavements, putting coins and notes into collection boxes that pass by. For the past decade they have borne the brunt of the suffering, the violence, and in recent months the economic cuts in some of the most deprived areas of the United Kingdom. (Mary Holland, *New Statesman*, 5 December 1980)

The first hunger strike ended in confusion in December, with little or no progress having been made by the prisoners in pursuit of their demands. The position of the British government on the question of political status was unyielding, and a second hunger strike began on 1 March 1981. The sudden end to the first strike might possibly have opened the way to changes in the prison regime, without loss of face, but instead there is evidence that a harsher regime was introduced. A section of the political and security establishment viewed the facing-down of the hunger strikers as a new opportunity to defeat the IRA once and for all (Mary Holland, *New Statesman*,

5 December 1980), reasoning that a defeat would demoralise both IRA supporters and volunteers, thus opening the way to a final military solution. The Sinn Féin and IRA leadership on the outside shared this view. In a communication to Gerry Adams, the IRA leader in the prison wrote: 'I know you are strategically opposed to a hunger strike, but you are not morally opposed to it.' To which Adams replied: 'Bobby, we are tactically, strategically, physically and morally opposed to a hunger strike' (*Magill*, August 1981).

At the height of the hunger strike, some three weeks after the death of Bobby Sands (who had been elected MP for Fermanagh South Tyrone in April) the British Prime Minister, Margaret Thatcher, visited Belfast and stated her attitude towards republicanism in general and the hunger strike in particular. In her view, the hunger strike represented the 'last card' in the IRA campaign. In spite of mounting evidence to the contrary, she persisted in the belief that there was little support for republicanism among the nationalist population. As she was to argue:

> Faced with the failure of their discredited cause, the men of violence have chosen in recent months to play what may be their last card. They have turned their violence against themselves through the prison hunger strike to death ... In so doing the PIRA have put the Catholic community on the rack. Our heart goes out to those who are finding themselves in an increasingly intolerable position especially perhaps to the parents. Our encouragement goes to the many including the clergy of the Catholic Church who are urging the rejection of the arguments of the extremists. (*Irish Times*, 28 May 1981)

The situation on the ground was rather different. Support for the prisoners was surprising in its depth and intensity. However, it was still possible to see this support as being of an emotional and transitory nature. Even the massive turnout for Sands' funeral – over 70,000 according to the *Irish Times* – could not dent the optimism of the British state. The Secretary of State, Humphrey Atkins, in a statement made to coincide with the funeral, commented that Sands may not have made the decision to die himself, but rather 'under the instructions of those who felt it useful to their cause that he should die' (*Irish Times*, 8 May 1981).

The hunger strike eventually came to an end at the beginning of October 1981, as a consequence of pressure from the relatives of those remaining on the strike. The British government had won a pyrrhic victory. Although the term 'political status' was avoided, the concessions given in the aftermath of the hunger strike came very close to the original five demands of the prisoners. Far more important, however, was the effect of the protest on the political landscape, so long dominated by a single-minded war between the state and the IRA. As the then northern editor of the *Irish Times*, Ed Moloney, wrote in the wake of the strike:

> From the hunger strikes have flowed not only the deaths inside and outside the prisons, but a regenerated IRA and a growing INLA. There has been friction in Anglo-Irish relations, instability on both sides of the border, increased polarisation, a weakened SDLP, and internationally a changed perception of the problem. The Government's criminalisation policy has emerged from the experience barely intact. Indeed the growth in support for the Provisionals, electorally or otherwise, which resulted from the 10 deaths has given them a political profile and importance which would have been unimaginable before. (*Irish Times*, 5 October 1981)

The hunger strikes, and the massive unrest in nationalist areas, tested the doctrine of police primacy. The RUC, for the first time since 1969, was now in the front line in confronting unrest across the North, but particularly in Belfast and Derry. The British Army acted as back-up to the police, who set about their public order function with a will.

Some 30,000 plastic bullets were fired during the protests, leading to the death of eight people, three of them children under the age of 15 (Jennings, 1988a, p. 135). RUC tactics were brutally effective. Nationalist areas were effectively sealed off – often for days at a time – and police in armoured Land Rovers undertook high-speed patrols through nationalist areas, firing plastic bullets through gun ports at any semblance of trouble. These tactics were successful in containing the rioting and restricting damage, death and injuries to the Catholic ghettos.

This tactical success was far outweighed by the long-term damage done to the policy of criminalisation. The IRA had forged new links with the Catholic community and the mass mobilisation undermined the contention that the organisation had little or no support. The success of hunger-strike candidates in elections convinced Sinn Féin that it could achieve a legitimate mandate on both sides of the border. The role of the RUC during the hunger strikes convinced many

Catholics that the force could never change or be trusted: 'It was an irony of the episode that it began with the Government attempting to impose on the prisoners the status of prisoners and ended with the IRA restoring their credentials among sections of the Catholic community as freedom fighters' (Bishop and Mallie, 1987, p. 299).

The Consolidation of Police Primacy

The decision to remove the British Army from ultimate control of the counter-insurgency operation in favour of the RUC was ratified by a joint directive signed by the new GOC, General Creasey, and Newman in January 1977. Newman's task, after his appointment in 1976 was effectively to militarise the RUC. There were a number of reasons behind the policy of police primacy, one of which was concern over the effects on British public opinion of the sight of young soldiers – more often than not, teenagers – being transported home in coffins for military funerals. The fear that the British presence in Northern Ireland would become a domestic political issue was reinforced by concern over the image presented of heavily-armed British troops patrolling the streets and country lanes of the North. This image was one that served to reinforce the republican movement's interpretation of the conflict as a colonial one, fought out on Britain's own doorstep. The British government was keen to present the war as one between two internal factions, with Britain playing the role of honest broker, ultimately responsible for preventing the situation in Northern Ireland from descending into bloody civil war. The RUC were presented as a force representing the eternal verities of justice and the rule of law, fighting a battle against terrorism on behalf of the 'vast majority of the people of Northern Ireland'. The then Secretary of State, Roy Mason put this point of view in his usually trenchant style:

> No one who views the situation in Northern Ireland from close at hand, the influence seven years of bloodshed have had on the minds of the young people there, the paramilitary on both sides who would like us to get out so that they can get on with the slaughter, the ingrained nature of the violence and the racketeering associated with it, and, last but not least, the Irish temperament, would give much chance for peace if British soldiers were pulled out. (Workers Research Unit, 1982)

The transition to police primacy was not achieved without considerable friction with the Army hierarchy. From its initial deployment in 1969, the Army had a very low opinion of the abilities and skills of the RUC and suspicion of the political allegiances of some police officers went right to the top of the military establishment. The Chief of the British General Staff in the mid-1970s, Lord Carver, voiced his suspicions in his memoirs:

> The Army's frustration ... led to a gradual and increasing pressure that it should rely less on Special Branch and do more to obtain its own intelligence, a tendency which I was initially reluctant to accept, all experiences in colonial fields having been against this and in favour of total integration of police and military intelligence. However, the inefficiency of the RUC Special Branch, its reluctance to burn its fingers again, and the suspicion, more than once proved, that some of its members had close links with Protestant extremists, led me finally to the conclusion that there was no alternative. (quoted in Urban, 1992, p. 22)

The situation was complicated by Roy Mason's close relationships with the British Army hierarchy. He had been Secretary of State for Defence and during his tenure had taken a strong interest in the campaign against Marxist guerrillas in Oman (*Daily Telegraph*, 31 December 1975). Coincidentally, the post of General Officer Commanding, Northern Ireland (GCONI) had gone to General Creasey in 1977, who was one of the British Army's leading counter-insurgency experts and practitioners (Bloch and Fitzgerald, 1983, pp. 141–2). Creasey was a strong advocate of undercover operations against the IRA as a means both of restricting Army casualties and demoralising the movement. Although the RUC had misgivings about the use of British Army undercover units – particularly the SAS – the argument that the key to success was the collection and collation of intelligence was hard to counter since, although the Special Branch ran informers, the RUC did not yet have the capacity to mount sophisticated surveillance operations. The nearest thing the RUC had to a specialised anti-terrorist unit was the Special Patrol Group, which was expanded from 100 to 300 officers by Newman. The SPG was given upgraded weaponry and training in riot control and then dispersed in units across the North. The British Army was not happy with the increasingly active role being give to the SPG, as their semi-official historian makes clear:

It [the SPG] operated province wide, was totally autonomous and the
Army felt that it was too paramilitary in nature. The Army believed
those resources, particularly manpower, should not be committed to
a paramilitary organisation when troops were in the province to carry
out a similar function, and felt the group should be disbanded.
(Barzilay, 1981 p. 12)

British Army undercover units operating in Northern Ireland
have gone under a bewildering number of names to cause
deliberate confusion and disguise the destination of soldiers
transferred to such units. However, the three-tier system of
undercover units put in place in 1977 remained the operational
model for the next decade or so. A specialised surveillance force,
known as 14 Intelligence Company, was set up for the purpose of covert observation from fixed positions or unmarked
cars. In addition, close observation platoons were recruited
from resident Army battalions in the North to collect basic
intelligence information through stop and search powers, house
searches, checkpoints, etc. The SAS had the function of setting
up operations, particularly ambushes, designed to disrupt the
activity of IRA active-service units.

The use of the SAS during 1976–78 was less than successful. In the two years after 1976, the SAS was responsible for
the death of three innocent civilians and seven members of
the IRA, all of whom died in disputed circumstances (Asmal,
1985; Urban, 1992). The operations involving the death of
the civilians were a public relations disaster and may have led
to the downturn in SAS operations over the next five years
and the emergence of similar specialised RUC units. The
experience of SAS-style undercover operations during this period was to bolster the case of the RUC for its own undercover
squads, but was also to expose weaknesses in this particular
anti-terrorist tactic, weaknesses which were to come back to
haunt the RUC in the early 1980s.

The killing by the SAS of three IRA men and an innocent
passer-by in Belfast in June 1978 was followed by a particularly inept attempt at media management. The killings had
taken place during an ambush on an IRA unit about to bomb
a Post Office installation and the initial version of events from
the Army press office was that the passer-by, William Hanna,
had been killed in crossfire: a few hours later the admission
was made that no weapons were found at the scene. Some
days later, press reports appeared claiming that a fourth

IRA member – who had escaped – had opened fire. At the inquest in 1980 no evidence of the use of weapons, apart from by the SAS, was produced. Army press officers also claimed that the target of the bombers had been under surveillance prior to the attack. This was a mistake that the security forces were to avoid making in the future, as they refined both the tactics of ambush and their news management skills. To admit to foreknowledge of such paramilitary activity is to raise the question of whether the use of force was necessary or whether the suspects could have been apprehended. A month after the Post Office depot incident, the SAS shot dead a Co. Antrim teenager in Dunloy, Co. Antrim. The teenager, John Boyle, had discovered hidden weapons in a disused graveyard and had told his father, who in turn had contacted the RUC. Four SAS men staked out the graveyard and subsequently shot the teenager dead as he returned, out of curiosity, to the cache of weapons he had found.

Coming so soon after the Post Office incident, the shooting of John Boyle was to prove another public relations disaster. Initially, the story was that the soldiers had intercepted three terrorists in the vicinity of the arms dump. When this version collapsed, it was claimed that John Boyle had pointed a loaded Armalite rifle at the soldiers, who then shot him in self-defence. At the subsequent trial of the soldiers, it transpired that the rifle was unloaded and that no warning had been given. As was to become the norm in cases of soldiers charged with murder, they were acquitted.[1] In September of the same year, a man out duck-shooting in east Tyrone was shot by the SAS. He had returned from duck-shooting to find the tyres of his car slashed. When he asked a nearby British Army patrol for an explanation, they shot him dead. No prosecutions followed, although it was later admitted that he had been shot in error.

The shooting of an IRA auxiliary, Patrick Duffy, in Derry in November of the same year was to further demonstrate the need – as far as the security forces were concerned – to produce an immediate and credible story. Duffy, a 50-year-old man, was shot in an unoccupied house in Derry that contained an arms cache hidden in a wardrobe. Duffy himself was unarmed. The initial Army story was that Duffy was shot after picking up a gun from the arms dump and turning around to confront soldiers who had hidden themselves in the house. At the inquest it emerged that the SAS unit involved had entered the house before the arms had been hidden. No reason was given why those who had brought the weapons to the house were not apprehended, nor why the house had been staked out in the first place. The autopsy report showed that Duffy had been shot 52 times and the entry wounds were consistent with him being shot while he faced the wardrobe where the guns were stored.

The embarrassment caused by the antics of SAS undercover squads gave the RUC the opportunity to reorganise its own units and become lead agency in this area, thus cementing the reality of police primacy. Criticisms of the Special Patrol Group, which was generally seen as something of a cowboy outfit, led to the establishment of 'Bronze Section' within the SPG, combining observation and disruption operations. The unit seems to have been modelled on the MRF (Mobile Reaction Force) introduced by Brigadier Kitson, and enjoyed a similar lack of success. Subsequently, the RUC followed the lead of the British Army and set up separate intelligence-gathering and operational units. These were put under the control of E Department (as the revamped Special Branch was now officially known), which was itself subdivided into five sections. The operations unit is E4, which comprises two sub-units, E4A, which carries out surveillance, and E4B, the operational unit involved in ambushes, etc.

A further element in the transformation of the RUC into a counter-insurgency force was the establishment of Divisional Mobile Support Units (DMSUs). These units receive riot control and special firearms training. In addition, HMSUs (Headquarters Mobile Support Units) were established as a back-up to rural units, with training in ambush techniques and other undercover skills. HMSU members generally operate in plain clothes, under the control of Special Branch. The disbanded Bronze Section was replaced by a secretive and little-known unit called the SSU (Special Support Unit), which was subsequently trained by the SAS and organised on similar lines.

These covert-action teams were to replace the SAS from late 1979 onwards: it was to be five years before the SAS killed again. Between January 1979 and December 1983, eight people were killed by undercover units, six by the RUC and two by an undercover surveillance officer in Derry when confronted by an armed IRA team. It was the questions raised by the shooting of six people by the RUC within a space of three weeks which were once again to raise the spectre of a 'shoot to kill' policy and to have long-term consequences for the RUC which have still not played themselves out.

In 1979, those elements within the British military establishment opposed to police primacy made one last effort to return the military to a lead role against the IRA. In the wake of the killing of 18 soldiers at Narrow Water in Co. Down in an IRA ambush on 27 August (on the same day that Lord Mountbatten was killed by another IRA bomb), Prime Minister, Margaret Thatcher flew to Northern Ireland for a series of meetings with the RUC and the military. General Creasey and his staff made a concerted effort to reassert control over the security operation by calling for a 'security supremo' – presumably a person of military background – to be appointed. Such a move would have effectively removed the RUC from operational control of security, at least for a period. The arguments of Newman and his staff, who met separately with the Prime Minister on the same day, proved to be more persuasive (Urban, 1992, p. 85). Newman played upon the political implications of an increased military role, arguing that the whole point of the exercise was to decrease the numbers of soldiers on the streets, not increase them. He argued further that the situation on the border – where the ambush had taken place – was not typical and that he could contain the situation if given more policemen. Thatcher agreed with Newman, and gave the go-ahead for a thousand new RUC recruits. As a sop to the Army – as well as an attempt to clean up the rivalry over intelligence information which existed between the police and military – she appointed Maurice Oldfield, a one-time director of MI6 brought out of retirement from All Souls College, as security coordinator. This was not a new position, but previous incumbents had the limited and inefficient brief of 'tasking' – defining the operational role of the different agencies – and arbitrating disputes between rival outfits. Oldfield was given the brief of taking overall control of all intelligence gathering and collation and he swiftly established a directorate known as 'The Department'. The head of this department was to chair a committee drawn from the various security agencies: SAS, military intelligence, MI5, MI6, the RUC Special Branch, and the Bronze section of the SPG. The Committee was to organise and coordinate tasking for the RUC Special Branch and the Army (*Sunday Tribune*, 5 April 1981).

Oldfield lasted six months in Northern Ireland before he was quietly removed. Despite Oldfield's departure, officially

because of 'mental fatigue', the tighter liaison between the
undercover units of the RUC and British Army was to continue and during the 1980s there seems to have been a merging
of units at the operational level.

Telling Tales: the Supergrass Years

The modification of the legal system to combat threats to the
state from militant republicanism has been a feature of policy
in both parts of Ireland since partition, carrying on a practice
long established under British rule. Since 1922, practically
every known legal modification has been practised: military
courts, exile, non-jury courts and internment have all been
given an imprimatur in emergency legislation. Such modifications to the legal system cause a special type of problem for
the state. The very terminology used – 'special' or 'emergency'
legislation – is based upon the assumption that the problem
is a passing or transitory one, not endemic to social or political structures, and that such extraordinary measures are aimed
at eliminating small pockets of dissent. Unfortunately, temporary measures of this nature have a tendency to become
permanent in themselves, both affecting the general body of
law and corrupting the institutions charged with their implementation. A case in point is the Prevention of Terrorism Act,
enacted in 1974 in the immediate wake of the IRA bombings
in Birmingham, in which 21 people died and a further 164
were injured. A strong case has been made that this particular
piece of legislation has been used by the state to gather information on large numbers of people, who, if the figures on
convictions under the Act are anything to go by, have had no
involvement in terrorist-type activities (Scorer and Hewitt,
1981). For those in charge of the operational end of security
policy – as the RUC has been since 1978 – there is a strong
temptation to extend the powers given to them through informal practices designed to increase their success rate. For the
policy makers in the Northern Ireland Office, the problem has
been to strike a balance between the need for legitimacy and
at least a semblance of normality with the need to eliminate
militant dissent as swiftly and as surgically as possible. It was
on the rocks of this contradiction that internment foundered
as a weapon against the IRA, since it could not be made legitimate in the eyes of either domestic or international opinion.

The use of Diplock courts ran into the same problem as allegations of ill-treatment in police custody began to mount and gain credence. By confining the investigation to police practices and procedures, the Bennett Report attempted to restrict the problem and, indeed, the judiciary emerged from that particular scandal untainted. The Diplock system was carefully constructed to give the appearance of legitimacy and normality to extraordinary judicial processes. The fact that confessions were extracted with the use of torture and intimidation, or at best the use of dubious interrogation procedures, did not directly taint the judicial process itself. Indeed, it could be argued with some justification that the Diplock courts were an improvement on the previous practice of internment without trial and a far cry from the option of military tribunals used not only by openly repressive regimes such as Turkey, but also by the Irish Republic for a considerable period of time and in the face of a very limited IRA threat. (On the use of emergency legislation in Ireland, see Farrell, 1986.) However, the effects of the controversy over interrogation and the impact of the Amnesty and Bennett reports deprived the RUC of a potent weapon in their battle with the IRA. Combined with the increased efficiency of the IRA as a result of reorganisation, anti-interrogation training and a more focused military campaign, the need for more caution during interrogations led to a significant decline in convictions. It was also not clear that the increased use of undercover operations was having any effect other than to offer a propaganda weapon to republicans.

The next phase in the security operation was set in motion with the arrest of an IRA member, Christopher Black, in late 1981, who, when promised immunity from prosecution, made statements which led to the arrest of 38 people. The following year saw the emergence of some 25 other informers, or 'supergrasses' as they were commonly known, leading to the arrest of more than six hundred suspects. It is not clear whether the use of informers in this way was part of a conscious strategy on the part of the RUC or whether the apparent success of Black's information in leading to the arrest of such large numbers led to the decision to embark upon a strategy of actively recruiting informers in this manner.

In any event, as a consequence of the Bennett Report, the number of suspects complaining of ill-treatment dropped dramatically, as did the numbers charged on the basis of confessions made during interrogation. Although Bennett did not confirm the reality of ill-treatment in Castlereagh interrogation centre and elsewhere, the suggestions he made to curtail the opportunities for abuse seem to have had a significant effect. The report recommended increased access to a solicitor, medical checks at least once every 24 hours, measures to inform prisoners of their rights, and the installation of closed-circuit television cameras in interrogation rooms.

Given the reality of a declining success rate in convicting suspects on the basis of confessions, it is not surprising that the RUC viewed the use of supergrasses as a viable alternative. The RUC denied that there was a deliberate policy of recruiting informers for the purpose of launching mass trials on the basis of their information, preferring to talk of 'converted terrorists' coming forward of their own free will. In his 1982 Report, the Chief Constable, Jack Hermon, who had taken over from Newman in January 1980, wrote: '[The] emergence of the supergrass phenomenon was due to a combination of public recognition of the true nature and futility of terrorism and of the growing disillusionment within the ranks of paramilitary organisations' (*Chief Constable's Annual Report*, 1982).

However, the available evidence points towards a high-level decision to embrace the use of informers in this particular fashion. Dermot Walsh, in his analysis of the use of emergency legislation found that 35 per cent of his survey of 60 individuals detained between September 1980 and June 1981 and subsequently released without charge were put under pressure by their RUC interrogators to become informers (Walsh, 1983, p. 68). It has also been pointed out that the levels of expenditure and staffing resources necessary would have had to be sanctioned at the highest level (Greer, 1988, p. 85).

The attitude of the judiciary was crucial to the strategy of using supergrasses. In effect, the judiciary and the courts were integrated into the counter-insurgency campaign in a more direct manner than before. The judiciary was left relatively untainted by the controversy over ill-treatment under interrogation, as judges were able to distance themselves from the question of how confessions were obtained and confine their role to the sentencing. The use of supergrasses drew the judiciary, the majority of whom came from unionist backgrounds, uncomfortably close to acting as direct agents of state policy in the war against terrorism.[2] Two aspects of the use of supergrasses were crucial in this process: first, the acceptance of evidence from supergrasses which, by its very nature is questionable whether because of a promise of immunity from prosecution, a short sentence, financial inducement, or a combination of these factors. There is evidence that the police supplied at least some supergrasses with a script to memorise (Gifford, 1984). The judge, sitting alone, decided on the credibility of the evidence presented and convicted individuals on the basis of those parts of the evidence he accepted. The irrationality of many of the subsequent judgments is well documented. Such irrational and inconsistent judgments were inevitable as long as the judiciary failed to question the moral and evidential implications of the process of granting immunity and the police practice surrounding it.

Second, convictions on the word of a supergrass necessarily involve the acceptance of uncorroborated evidence and although this practice had been abandoned in British courts, the Diplock judges did not regard corroboration as necessary. The judges decided what parts of the evidence were 'tainted' or had a 'ring of truth' and convicted accordingly. It can hardly have been accidental that those convicted were generally regarded by the RUC to be dangerous and guilty. The RUC exerted great pressure to extend and justify the use of supergrasses claiming that the system might well deal a 'death blow to the terrorists' in the words of the then Deputy Chief Constable when asked if the use of supergrasses was the first major turn against the IRA:

> Probably. It is probably the most significant. We have a long-term strategy, and we have a short-term strategy. In the short term we are looking for something that will deal a death blow to the terrorists, and certainty this is probably the most significant that has appeared on the scene from the outset ... After all, maybe tomorrow we will get a converted terrorist who will put the finger on the top people who are now very worried. (*Irish Press*, 8 August 1983)

This confidence echoed that of the Chief Constable in his Annual Report for 1982: 'Terrorist organisations regard the supergrass technique as a fundamental threat to their continued existence ... The outcome [of the supergrass process] is crucial to the well being of Northern Ireland' (*Chief Constable's Annual Report*, 1982).

Even as the Deputy Chief Constable was affirming the success of the 'supergrass technique', the process was beginning to unravel. More than half the number of those agreeing to become supergrasses retracted their evidence before the cases could be heard, or during the trial itself. The performance of the others in court often verged on the farcical, and left a lot to be desired as far as the quality of evidence was concerned. Public disquiet was also growing. During 1982–83 relatives of the accused formed protest organisations on both sides of the community; bishops, politicians, community groups and even the Criminal Bar Association of Northern Ireland joined the protest. A pamphlet written by a leading English lawyer, Lord Gifford, did much to undermine the process by pointing to legal problems with the court procedure itself (Gifford, 1984). The judiciary also began to have a change of heart after an initial willingness to convict on the evidence of a single informer as in the first three cases to come to court. Subsequently, convictions became rarer as the courts looked upon the evidence of informers with an increasingly jaundiced eye. It is impossible to pinpoint with any certainty the exact factors which led the judiciary to abandon its initial uncritical stance, but judges may well have thought that they were being sucked into the implementation of a discredited counter-insurgency strategy. They may also have recognised that the process had alienated large numbers of loyalists as well as nationalists and while alienating the latter was not problematic, to foster a Protestant disenchantment with state policy was potentially very dangerous (Greer, 1988). The freeing of most of those convicted on appeal effectively ended the use of supergrasses. In the final analysis, the use of supergrasses did little to influence the course of the conflict in the North. Of the six hundred or so individuals arrested on the word of an informer, some two hundred came to trial. Fifty-three of these lost their appeals and of these, fifty had made confessions, or alleged confessions, of guilt.

The central, and purely pragmatic, argument put forward by the RUC in support of the use of supergrasses, that it had resulted in a reduction in the level of politically-motivated violence, is questionable. The general level of violence had been decreasing steadily since 1976, but this had more to do with changing tactics on the part of both the security forces and paramilitary groups.

The other side of the equation is perhaps more intangible but of considerable long-term importance. The legal system was called into further disrepute and the integrity of the judiciary questioned and the sight of members of the legal profession earning vast fees by engaging in supergrass trials was not a pleasant one. The alienation of the Catholic community from the system was given a further twist as opinion polls taken at the time show (see *Fortnight*, no. 209, 1984; *Belfast Telegraph*, 6 February 1985). The security forces, in particular the RUC, had once again embarked upon a high-risk strategy to defeat the IRA with no appreciable success apart from damaging their own battered reputation.

7   Shooting to Kill?

Background

By the beginning of 1980, the RUC had specially-trained surveillance and operational units in place, and the new Chief
Constable, Jack Hermon saw these units as a means of curtailing the operations of British Army special units and pushing
the RUC to the forefront in this area. At the same time as
Newman departed General Creasey was replaced by General
Lawson. Lawson was, unusually for the incumbent of the post
of GOC Land Forces, a cavalry officer, and his appointment
was intended to cement police primacy and resolve the crisis
in RUC–Army relations which had existed under his predecessor.

From the beginning of 1980 until November 1982, 19 people were to die at the hands of the security forces. None were
members of a paramilitary organisation, and nine were killed
by plastic bullets. In none of the incidents were shots fired at
the security forces and in only one incident was the victim
armed (see Jennings, 1988c and Asmal 1985). The extensive
use of plastic baton rounds, generally against the nationalist
population, has been a contentious issue for decades (see CAJ,
1990 and Jennings, 1988a). In all, plastic bullets have killed
17 people, not including three killed by rubber bullets, which
were phased out in 1973. According to the Patten Report,
41,657 plastic bullets have been discharged by the RUC since
1981 and a further 14,572 by the British Army, leading to eleven
deaths and 651 injuries (Patten Report, 1999, p. 54). Eight
children have been killed by plastic bullets, and all but one of
the victims was a Catholic. One member of the security forces
has been charged in connection with a death caused by a plastic
bullet and he, a member of the RUC, was acquitted. The stock
response of the RUC and Army to a fatal incident involving
plastic bullets is to state that the weapons were used in a 'riot
situation' and that the security forces had been under attack for
several hours resulting in injuries to soldiers and policemen.

Eyewitnesses frequently contradict such statements, but it is, in general, difficult to disprove the official version. A more intractable problem is that of identifying the soldier or police officer responsible. Plastic bullets cannot be forensically examined to determine the weapon from which they have been fired: in the single case of a prosecution being taken, it was photographic evidence, which formed the basis of the state case. This was the killing of Sean Downs on 12 August 1984 during a demonstration on the Falls Road. (See *The Best Documented Killing*, Belfast, Springhill Community House, 1988). None the less, the police officer involved was acquitted.

The comparatively high number of deaths from plastic bullets in 1980 can, on the surface, be attributed to the massive street disturbances over the hunger strike issue in during which some 30,000 plastic rounds were fired. (If this figure is added to those in the Patten report over 86,000 plastic bullets have been discharged since 1980.) However, a closer analysis of the nine deaths during 1980 from baton rounds shows that most were not killed in a riot situation. Four of the nine were children under the age of 15 (the youngest eleven years old), and only one was clearly engaged in rioting – if a group of teenagers tossing stones at armoured police Land Rovers can be described as such – and he was shot at a range of 15–16 feet well below the regulation 60-feet range for firing (Asmal, 1985, pp. 60–65). During the same year, the IRA campaign continued unabated. Ten members of the UDR, seven regular soldiers (including one member of the Territorial Army) and seven RUC officers were killed by the IRA, with one IRA member killed in a gun battle with the RUC (Barzilay, 1981, p. 232).

The decline in the number of IRA casualties had a number of reasons. Better-trained volunteers and more selective and carefully-mounted operations contributed to the drop in casualties, but the suspension of undercover SAS operations involving ambushes was an equally significant factor. The 'official' reason given for the suspension of this type of operation was that the IRA benefited from the cult of martyrdom which resulted from the death of its members at the hands of the SAS (Urban, 1992, p. 83). The bad publicity caused by the level of 'collateral damage' suffered by innocent civilians during these operations in the late 1970s was perhaps a more decisive factor in the decision to call a temporary halt to SAS ambushes. In addition, the RUC was keen to use the deficiencies in SAS tactics to push for their own, broadly similar, surveillance and operational units in line with their interpretation of police primacy. What is interesting about this period is that despite the suspension of the undercover ambush tactic, IRA violence had fallen to a level not seen since the early 1970s. The numbers of explosions, deaths and shootings had fallen off dramatically; shooting incidents for instance were down from 728 in 1979 to 169 in the following year (Barzilay, 1981, p. 232). Of course, this was the period of the hunger-strike agitation and it may well be that IRA units were stretched in dealing with the levels of street violence. It is none the less debatable whether the ambush tactic, which was to become the central occupation of undercover units and their Special Branch masters during the 1980s had any effect in reducing the overall level of violence. Mark Urban is in little doubt about the negative effect of the tactics followed, under the direction of police primacy, for over a decade after 1982: 'When I began this study, I was open to the idea that ambushing the IRA might help to lower the level of terrorist violence. All of my research, however, convinces me that it does not and that, on the contrary, such operations carry significant human and moral costs' (Urban, 1992, p. 241).

Undercover Operations and the RUC

In 1982, a series of dramatic events in the Lurgan/Armagh area involving the RUC was to show that the latter had learned little from the experiences of the SAS in the late 1970s. Within the space of less than three weeks, six people were shot dead by RUC undercover squads who seemed determined to fill the vacuum left by the SAS. These killings were unusual for a number of reasons. They were the first deliberate killings by undercover units since the SAS shot James Taylor in September 1978. The three incidents, occurring in quick succession, were to engulf the RUC in the most serious crisis it had faced since the early 1970s. A central component in the ensuing controversy was the stark contradiction between the initial RUC version of events and the facts as they later emerged.

The first incident was the shooting dead of Sean Burns, Eugene Toman and Gervaise McKerr on 11 November in Lurgan, Co. Armagh. The initial RUC version of events claimed that a police officer, carrying out a routine traffic check, had attempted to stop a car by signalling with a torch. The car, it was claimed, stopped momentarily, then accelerated and struck a policeman. A police car, parked by chance nearby, saw the incident and pursued the car. The officers believed that they had come under fire from the car and they themselves then opened fire. When the car being pursued came to a halt, all three occupants were dead from gunshot wounds. Superficially, the RUC story contained all the elements of a classic cover-up designed to exculpate the RUC men involved:

- The police had come across the suspects by accident, not as part of an undercover operation.
- The alleged attempt to run down a policeman gave justifiable reason to suspect terrorist involvement.
- The pursuing car was also in the area fortuitously.
- The pursuing police believed that they were under fire.

The RUC's version of events began to unravel almost immediately. No weapons were found on the victims and witnesses stated that shots had been fired both from a police checkpoint and an unmarked car. The contradiction between the police version of events, and that of the forensic evidence – 109 shots had been fired and the body of Eugene Toman was found dead outside the car – indicated that he had been shot after the car had come to a halt, and led subsequently to the prosecution of three police officers. At the trial in September 1983, serious conflicts between the original RUC version of events and prosecution evidence emerged. The RUC version, as presented in court, insisted that Toman and Burns had planned an attack on the security forces and that a unit of the HMSU was brought in to capture them. No evidence was produced regarding the police officer who allegedly had been injured while trying to stop the car. Despite prosecution evidence to the effect that shots had been fired by the RUC after the car had come to a halt, the three officers were acquitted.

During the trial, the Deputy Chief Constable, Michael McAtamney, responded to Judge Gibson on the tactics of E4A officers:

> McAtamney: Once you have decided to fire, you shoot to take out the enemy.

Judge Gibson: Do you mean, permanently out of action?
McAtamney: Yes.

(*Irish News*, 5 June 1984)

The judge, in finding the three officers innocent, went out of his way to offer a boost to police morale and criticised the Attorney General and the DPP for bringing the case in the first place:

> I wish to make it clear that having heard the Crown case I regard each of the accused as absolutely blameless in this matter. That finding should be put in their record along with my own commendation for their courage and determination in bringing the three deceased men to justice, in this case the final court of justice.[1]

The judge then offered an implicit criticism of the DPP for bringing the case:

> Those who brought the prosecution on such evidence undoubtedly did not take into account that these men's personal security was at risk … The case is going to have a more widespread effect among other members of the security forces generally. When a policeman or soldier is ordered to arrest a dangerous criminal and on the basis of that order to bring him back dead or alive, how is he to consider his conduct now? (*Irish Times*, 6 June 1984)

The Assistant Chief Constable of Manchester, John Stalker, who was subsequently called in to investigate the circumstances of the killings encountered a similar attitude from the Chief Constable, John Hermon, who made it plain to him that police officers engaged in undercover operations would be fully protected and shielded from external investigation at the highest level (Stalker, 1988, p. 76). Stalker also concluded that the police investigation into the shootings had been slipshod and incomplete. Crucial forensic evidence had been overlooked, witnesses had not been traced and cartridge cases had been removed from the scene in order to mislead the forensic scientists.

In November and December of the same year, the RUC was to become further embroiled in controversy over the killing by undercover units of three people in two separate incidents. Two teenagers were shot – one, Michael Tighe, fatally – in what the RUC subsequently described as a result of 'a routine patrol investigating suspicious activity around a hayshed'. The HMSU unit had opened fire when one officer allegedly heard the sound of a rifle cocking. There was no prosecution for the killing of Michael Tighe. However, his companion, Martin McCauley, who was badly wounded in the incident, was charged with possession of firearms – three 60-year-old rifles found in the hayshed without ammunition. During the trial, it transpired that the hayshed had been staked out by the HMSU and doubts were cast on the police version of the events leading to the shootings. In particular, the forensic evidence indicated that the HMSU officers probably had not opened fire on 'identified targets'.

The hayshed incident was followed in December by the shooting dead of Seamus Grew and Roddy Carroll in Armagh City. Grew was driving the car up a hill leading to his home when an unmarked police car intercepted him. Constable John Robinson got out of his car and fired 15 shots, killing Carroll. He then reloaded his weapon, walked around the car and dispatched Grew with four shots. The initial RUC version of events claimed that the suspects had driven through a roadblock, injuring a policeman. The police then radioed for another car that gave chase and, believing that the occupants were about to fire, a police officer shot and killed both men. It later transpired, at the trial of Robinson for the murder of Seamus Grew, that the incident was a carefully planned – if eventually botched – HMSU operation to ambush Dominic McGlinchy, who was then leader of the republican splinter group, the Irish National Liberation Army. Robinson testified in court that he had been instructed by his superiors to tell a series of lies about the incident to make it appear that the encounter with Grew and Carroll was by chance, that a policeman was injured at the roadblock, and that he had pursued Grew in an ordinary marked police car. It transpired in court that immediately after the shooting, a debriefing was held by senior Special Branch officers who then issued a false version of events (Asmal, 1985, p. 38).

The attempt by the RUC to take the lead role in undercover operations in 1992 was a disaster from any point of view. Six people were dead and police credibility was at an all-time low. The efforts of the political establishment to deflect criticism by ordering an inquiry under John Stalker backfired dramatically when he took his brief seriously and came into direct conflict with Chief Constable Hermon and other elements within the security establishment. In the meantime,

British Army undercover units began to reassert themselves.
Between December 1983 and January 1990, 28 people were
killed by British Army undercover units, not including the three
members of the IRA shot by the SAS in Gibraltar in March
1988. The shooting dead of eight IRA members (two active
service units) in Loughgall in May 1983 was a significant blow
to the IRA and the largest number of IRA operatives killed in
a single engagement. Unlike the killings in the Lurgan/Armagh
area, the ambush at Loughgall was meticulously planned and
executed. The IRA unit was intent on blowing up the RUC
station in the town, but clearly the security forces had knowledge of their plans. The area was staked out, and the IRA unit
was allowed to detonate the bomb before being cut down in a
hail of gunfire along with a passer-by who happened to be in
the line of fire.

The initial press release was terse and carefully worded. It
stated that the IRA unit had opened fire on the police station
and was then engaged by the security forces before the bomb
was detonated. The press release also claimed that two soldiers and one policeman had been injured. The RUC press
office refused to elaborate further as to whether the security
forces had prior knowledge of the attack or whether any of the
IRA weapons had been fired. It emerged later that the three
injured members of the covert unit (which seems to have been
made up of a mixture of British Army and RUC personnel)
had suffered minor injuries from debris caused by the explo-
sion and not, as had been implied, from gunfire. Clearly lessons
in managing the press in the wake of such ambushes had been
learned after the debacle of the Lurgan/Armagh shootings. No
hostages were given to fortune by the press statement and the
question of reasonable force – that might form the basis of a
later prosecution – was carefully obscured.

Three further incidents where people were shot in disputed
circumstances demonstrate the increasing sophistication of
the RUC press office in dealing with problems left in the wake
of security force killings. To avoid the charge of deliberate or
premeditated shooting, it is initially stated that the police or
Army units involved came across the incident 'by accident' or
just 'happened to be in the area' (as in the initial response to
the killing of Brian Robinson 1989 and three men outside a
betting shop in West Belfast in 1990), or that the victims threatened or injured a soldier or police officer thus offering a
justification for the use of lethal force (*Irish Times*, 15 January

1990; *Independent on Sunday*, 12 August 1990). The initial statement from the security forces is generally terse and further elaboration is not forthcoming. However, the official statement is followed by a series of unattributable 'steers' to selected journalists. This practice was very effective in the wake of the Gibraltar killing of three IRA members, though the shootings in Gibraltar, carried out as they were, overseas, aroused suspicion that the operation must have been sanctioned at the highest level in London (see Kitchin, 1989; Jack, 1989). The shooting dead of Pearse Jordan in November 1992 by a police unit on the Falls Road was a classic example of the use of this 'steering' tactic.[2]

The 'steer' implied that Jordan was acting as lookout on a bombing run when his car was in collision with an RUC vehicle. There were also hints of a raid on a nearby bomb factory, a burning refuse bin and talk of a mercury tilt switch (used in the making of booby-trap bombs) having been found. These unattributable rumours – and they were no more than that – were turned into fact by sections of the press and served to fix the notion of a bombing run having been foiled in the minds of the public. No evidence ever emerged to substantiate any of these claims.

The manipulation of the media and public opinion by the RUC press office in the wake of incidents involving fatalities caused by the security forces has become a key component of undercover operations and essential to their success. The difficulties facing journalists are immense. The immediate vicinity of the location of a killing by the security forces is immediately sealed off and the units involved swiftly removed from the scene for debriefing.

The soldiers and police on the ground in the aftermath of an incident have no knowledge of what went on. The official statement is of little value and can rarely be checked. Eyewitnesses, particularly in nationalist areas, are unwilling to come forward; although they may talk to journalists, they are generally unwilling to make official statements for fear of harassment by the RUC. Journalists are forced to fall back on informal briefings and, naturally, reporters considered sympathetic to the security forces will receive such briefings. With a few honourable exceptions, journalists are not prepared to undergo the hard slog necessary to get at the truth in such circumstances.

The Role of RUC Special Branch

By the time of the Lurgan/Armagh killings, the Special Branch (SB) was officially in complete control of the intelligence operation in Northern Ireland. There is also evidence that the British Army set up a parallel undercover unit called the FRU in 1980 which was involved in running agents inside the IRA and loyalist paramilitary groups (see Urban, 1992, p. 109; Geraghty, 1998, p. 155). Although the SB's own specialty was the running of informers, access to British Army intelligence – primarily the result of surveillance – gave SB a lead role. Within the RUC itself, SB acted with impunity, as it had the authority to override other sections of the RUC such as the drugs squad and even the CID. According to one senior officer in charge of West Belfast, he was rarely aware of the activities of SB in his area and even junior SB officers could issue him with orders. The Patten Report on policing makes a similar point: 'Several respondents have described it [SB] as a "force within a force" and RUC officers, serving and retired, have made similar comments to us, a common observation being that sub-divisional commanders often knew very little about the activities of the Branch in their areas' (Patten Report, 1999, p. 72).

The power of Special Branch, and its ability to engineer massive cover-ups of the true nature of its operations became apparent during the Stalker inquiry. The relationship between the CID and the Branch was a crucial factor in the engineering of covert operations during the 1980s. The main task of the CID is to investigate the circumstances surrounding a crime and to present to the DPP (Department of Public Prosecutions) evidence upon which a decision to prosecute or not can be made. In law, the circumstances of the CID investigation should be the same whether the investigation involves an 'ordinary' crime, a killing by a paramilitary organisation or a death caused by the security forces. In reality, the circumstances surrounding the various types of crime are different. When the police or Army are involved, as opposed to a paramilitary operation, the CID should have no difficulty in identifying the relevant personnel. The investigation then hinges on the question of whether those involved acted within the law, particularly the law relating to the use of 'reasonable force'. In the case of paramilitary crimes, the identification of suspects is crucial and the question of the lawfulness of the killing is less important. In addition, members of the security forces have the safeguard of immediate and specialist legal advice and are not normally subjected to seven-day detention orders and intensive interrogation.

There is also a distinction to be made between killings carried out by regular units and those that result from covert operations, such as in Lurgan/Armagh in 1982. When undercover units are involved in ambushes, the likelihood of fatalities is high and accepted in advance by Special Branch officers running the operation. The role of SB is crucial and central as it has initial responsibility for obtaining and collating information, for targeting particular individuals or groups (such as IRA active service units) and then for the planning of the actions of covert units. When such units are involved in an incident leading to fatalities, Special Branch officers are first on the scene and in charge of debriefing the soldiers or police involved, preparing a story for the media and, finally, deciding at what point the CID should get involved. Since the Stalker investigation, it is clear that the Special Branch has total control of such situations, allowing it to tailor the information given to the CID and if necessary withhold information. Undercover units are routinely removed from the scene of a killing, making immediate forensic examination of weapons, clothing, and transport, etc., impossible. The SB carries out the initial debriefing enabling the concoction of a story and a selective part of the evidence to be presented to the CID. The conflict of evidence presented at the inquest of Francis Bradley (killed in the vicinity of an arms dump by an undercover unit near Toomebridge in 1986) is illuminating in this context.

The shooting occurred at 9.50 p.m. and the soldiers involved had a similar story concerning the weather conditions. Soldiers A, D and E (as they were identified at the inquest) stated that there was a 'good moon', soldier B talked of 'good visibility' and soldier C testified that there was 'a moon and good visibility'. In contrast, a witness from the local weather centre told the inquest under oath that the moon did not appear in the sky that night until 11.23 (Urban 1992, pp. 214–16).

A further problem for the CID investigation is that crucial forensic evidence, such as spent cartridges, can vanish from the scene, as in the case of a number of fatal shootings by undercover units. In the case of the Lurgan killings in 1982, forensic examinations were carried out in the wrong area and cartridge cases went missing. Stalker stated: 'My conclusion in relation to the missing cartridge cases was that as many as twenty were deliberately removed from the scene. I could only conclude that this was in order to mislead the forensic scientists and to hide the true nature and extent of the shooting' (Stalker, 1988, p. 42).

In the wake of the shooting of three IRA members outside Strabane in 1985, a forensic scientist discovered that 42 cartridge cases were unaccounted for. He was refused permission by the RUC to re-examine the scene for 'operational reasons'. The allegation that the three IRA men had been finished off while lying wounded could not be properly investigated as the police had destroyed the victims' clothing before it could be forensically examined. In the course of an undercover ambush in the grounds of Gransha Hospital in Derry in 1986, two IRA operatives were shot dead. At the inquest, the jury found that the soldiers should have tried to arrest the men. No doubt the evidence of a CID Detective Chief Inspector to the Coroner influenced this finding: 'I cannot say what information was available to the forces prior to the incident.' Decoded, this indicates that CID are denied access, by Special Branch, to operational information concerning covert units and therefore cannot assess whether alternative courses of action – such as an arrest in this case – might have been possible.

The most detailed analysis of the role of the RUC Special Branch in undercover operations emerged during the Stalker inquiry into the killings in Armagh by RUC units in 1982. The controversy surrounding the killings resulted in the setting-up of an official investigation under the direction of John Stalker, the Deputy Chief Constable of Greater Manchester. His interim report appeared in 1985. Stalker uncovered a multitude of procedural failures relating to the CID inquiry and concluded that the SB debriefing of the police officers involved was used to concoct a fabricated version of events. This fabrication of the events surrounding the shootings was presented at a subsequent murder trial, but when Stalker looked at the police files on all six killings, he concluded:

> We had expected a particularly high level of inquiry in view of the nature of the deaths, but this was shamefully absent. The files were little more than a collection of statements apparently prepared for a coroner's inquiry. They bore no resemblance to my idea of a murder prosecution file. Even on the most cursory of readings I could see why the prosecution had failed. (Stalker, 1988, p. 40)

Stalker went on to criticise the unexplained failure to seek out and present all the forensic evidence, the failure to contact or seriously attempt to contact eyewitnesses, and the complacency involved in not seeking the views of the victims' families. The attitude of the RUC towards the families is shown in the case of one of those shot dead, Gervaise McKerr. Immediately after the shooting, the police raided his home and questioned his wife as to his whereabouts. At no time did they inform her that he had been shot dead (Asmal, 1985, p. 40). Stalker was also disturbed that the Special Branch detective with Constable Robinson – who was later charged and acquitted of murder – never gave evidence to the CID.

The central problem pinpointed by Stalker was the role of the Special Branch in the planning and execution of the ambushes and the subsequent cover-up. The history of the Special Branch during the last decades has been one of mixed fortunes. Having miserably failed in its primary task, to counter political subversion in giving some indication of the importance of the events leading to the deployment of British troops in 1969, in the years thereafter the Branch went on to make a further series of strategic errors. The importance of the burgeoning Provisional wing of the IRA was fatally underestimated and the intelligence used to select candidates for internment in 1971 was woefully inaccurate and out of date. The interrogation practices used by the Special Branch during this period eventually led to the British government being taken before the European Court of Human Rights.

The manifest failures and inadequacies of the SB during this period led to its replacement in the mid-1970s by the CID in the key areas of interrogation and the collation of intelligence. But the fate of the CID was to mirror that of the Branch: the backwash of the Bennett Report on ill-treatment during police custody pushed Special Branch to the forefront of the counter-insurgency campaign once again. Under Chief Constable Newman, the new head of SB, Assistant Chief Constable Slevin, reorganised the SB to assume the primary role in both intelligence gathering and the planning and execution of operations. The central role of SB in anti-terrorist operations became clear during the Stalker inquiry. For instance, immediately after the shooting of Burns, McKerr and Toman, the undercover officers involved were driven from the scene, with their weapons, to be debriefed by Special Branch officers. The CID investigation team was given incorrect information as to the sequence of events surrounding the shootings, and weapons and clothes needed for forensic examination were not made available for a number of days. Stalker was astonished at the power of Special Branch within the RUC. He concluded that SB officers had both obstructed his own investigation and were instrumental in covering up the events surrounding the shootings. He describes the role of the Special Branch:

> The Special Branch targeted the suspected terrorists, they briefed the officers, and after the shootings they removed men, cars and guns for a private de-briefing before the CID officers were allowed access to these crucial matters. They provided the cover stories and they decided at what point the CID was to be allowed to commence the official investigation of what occurred. The Special Branch interpreted the information and decided what was, or was not, evidence; they attached labels – whether a man was 'wanted' for an offence, for instance or whether he was an 'on the run terrorist'. I have never experienced, nor had any of my team, such an influence over the entire police force by one small section. (Stalker, 1988, pp. 56–7)

Although Slevin had effectively rebuilt the Special Branch, he fell foul of Chief Constable Hermon soon after the latter's appointment. Slevin was a career plain-clothes officer, yet Hermon moved him to Complaints and Discipline Branch, replacing him with Trevor Forbes who was then languishing in the Traffic Department. Forbes was close to Hermon and both had been involved with the RUC pipe and drum band for some years (Urban, 1992, p. 156).

The attempts of the RUC to take the lead role at the sharp end of counter-insurgency, surveillance and covert operations were thwarted after the killings in Co. Armagh. Questions were raised as to the ability of the RUC to replace the SAS in the undercover war against the IRA and a decision was made to rein in the extensive and dangerous autonomy which the RUC Special Branch had acquired under Hermon. This led to the appointment of John Whiteside, who had previously been in charge of CID, as Senior Assistant Chief Constable in charge of both SB and CID. Although the Chief Constable still retained final operational control over the use of covert units, the involvement of the RUC in such operations was effectively discontinued. Some units may have remained in back-up roles, for example securing the perimeter of an operational area, but British Army units, in particular the SAS, were to be responsible for undercover killings until the RUC shot Pearse Jordan dead on the Falls Road in November 1992.

The experiences in Armagh in 1982 did not lead the security hierarchy to the conclusion that such operations were counter-productive but that the RUC was not competent to carry them out. Another lesson learned was the importance of cover stories and the ability to manipulate the media in the wake of shootings in disputed circumstances. As the one-time British Army intelligence officer, Colin Wallace put it: 'The important thing is to get saturation coverage for your story as soon after the controversial event as possible. Once the papers have printed it, the damage is done. Even when the facts come out, the original image is the one that sticks' (*Irish News*, 2 November 1988).

Two central questions – whether such operations had any effect on the overall level of violence and whether such a policy made a political solution more difficult by alienating the nationalist population further from the RUC – do not seem to have been addressed.

A Shoot-to-kill Policy?

In the days leading up to the shooting and death of 14 unarmed civilians in Derry on 30 January 1972, the Commander Land Forces, General Ford wrote to his superior, General Tuzo, on the situation in Derry:

> I am coming to the conclusion that the minimum force necessary to achieve a restoration of law and order is to shoot selected ring leaders among the DYH [Derry Young Hooligans], after clear warnings had been issued ... In other words, we would be reverting to the methods of IS [internal security] found successful on many occasions overseas. (*Sunday Tribune*, 5 September 1999)

If the security authorities actually took this advice before Bloody Sunday, the outcome was less than satisfactory as far as they were concerned. Fourteen civilians died and the subsequent loss of faith in peaceful protest among the nationalist community gave the IRA a significant boost. What the memorandum also chillingly demonstrates is the willingness of at least some sections of the security establishment to countenance the killing of unarmed civilians in the pursuit of dubious political ends. Perhaps the lesson learnt from Bloody Sunday was simply a tactical one: the shooting of unarmed civilians under the gaze of the world's media is counter-productive, to say the least. During the late 1970s, after the deployment of the SAS in Northern Ireland, the number of people killed as a result of undercover operations rose steadily culminating in the killings of three unarmed civilians between June and September 1978. The shootings in Co. Armagh in 1982 ushered in a period of increased undercover activity initiated by RUC undercover squads and continued by SAS and related units. Undercover units killed 23 people between 1982 and February 1985 (Jennings, 1988a, p. 104). All but one were known or suspected republican activists and many of the killings were carried out in disputed circumstances. The RUC caused six of the deaths and the remainder were at the hands of British Army covert units. Clearly, the botched RUC operations in Armagh did not lead to any serious reassessment of the tactics of ambushing republican suspects apart from removing the RUC E4A unit from the scene.

The shootings in Armagh, in particular, led to widespread allegations that a shoot-to-kill policy was in operation in Northern Ireland, and that it was being used as a tactic when circumstances seemed opportune. The fact that suspected republican activists were being killed by special undercover units as a result of intensive surveillance seemed also to point in the direction of a consistent policy. The experience of John Stalker, the obstruction of his investigation at the highest levels within the RUC, and the use of cover stories at the trial of the E4A operatives all indicate a complicity in, if not direct support for, shoot-to-kill operations. Although Stalker found no direct evidence of high-level complicity in the activities of undercover units, he did come to certain conclusions: 'There was no written instruction, nothing pinned up on a notice board. But there was a clear understanding on the part of the men whose job it was to pull the trigger that that was what was expected of them' (*The Times*, 9 February 1988). Writing of the Armagh killings, he concluded: 'The circumstance of those shootings pointed to a police inclination, if not a policy, to shoot suspects dead without warning rather than to arrest them. Coming as those incidents did, so close together, the suspicion of deliberate assassination was not unreasonable' (Stalker, 1988, p. 253).

The use of the term 'shoot to kill' has in some ways obscured the issue and allowed the authorities to focus on this phrase as a means of avoiding the broader issues involved. Strictly speaking, there cannot be a shoot-to-kill policy under British law. For any minister to attempt to institute such a policy would be unlawful. However, the bureaucratic structure under which the security forces operate in Northern Ireland allows significant latitude to the securocrats.

Day-to-day operations are under the overall control of the Chief Constable and the Army Commander, with the former having final say under the doctrine of police primacy. Operational matters do not come under direct political control. There is, therefore, the possibility of the creation of an unofficial space to carry out operations that are in line with general strategic and political objectives. The success or otherwise of such operations is a matter for the police or Army: their political masters can always hide behind the shibboleth of operational autonomy. For instance, when James Prior (who had served as Secretary of State for Northern Ireland in the early 1980s) was asked in 1988 about his knowledge of undercover operations when he was secretary of state, he had this to say to Tom Mangold of the television programme *Panorama*:

> Mangold: Were you personally involved in the decision to use the SAS?
> Prior: No, not at any time.
> Mangold: Did you ever ask to be told?
> Prior: No, I am not aware that I ever asked specifically to be told when the SAS was going to be used. (quoted in Urban, 1992, p. 166)

Since the 'unofficial' actions of the security forces are not, legally speaking, policy at all, the initial decision to sanction such operations is informal and bounded by rules that are tacitly understood within the subculture of the Army and RUC. That such an operation space exists can be demonstrated only indirectly. One indication is the way in which the use of undercover units had been switched on and off, and transferred between different units and between the Army and RUC. The attitude of the courts to security personnel brought before them as a result of undercover killings is a further index of high-level approval of such operations (Jennings, 1988b, p. 109). Not a single soldier or policeman has been found guilty of murder during undercover operations, although 72 people have died as a result of such operations, mostly in disputed circumstances.

The inherent difficulties involved in implementing a strategy of shooting suspects rather than arresting them and bringing
them to trial became apparent once this strategy was merged
with the doctrine of police primacy. The collapse of the supergrass trials and the determination of the RUC hierarchy to
implement police primacy in all areas can be seen as the background to the killings in Armagh. The botched operations
carried out by the RUC led to the Stalker inquiry, which did
not proceed as the RUC had hoped. It may well have been
that the appointment of Stalker was a sop to public opinion
intended to defuse the situation initially and then produce a
report that would clear the RUC of having acted illegally.
Stalker was given the impression that this was his brief from
the Chief Constable:

> The Chief Constable obviously took the view that I was in Northern
> Ireland to 'review' what had happened in the three separate cases
> involving the deaths of the six men. He expected, I think, that I would
> read papers, speak to some key people about what had undoubtedly
> gone wrong, and submit a report containing a few operational recom-
> mendations for the future. (Stalker, 1988, p. 30)

The investigation did not follow the course mapped out by
Hermon. Stalker's investigation was wide-ranging and impinged
upon every aspect of undercover operations. Before he could
complete his report, Stalker was suspended from duty on the
basis of a disciplinary inquiry initiated in Manchester. Although
he was eventually exonerated, Stalker was permanently removed
from the investigation that was completed by another senior
policeman and submitted in April 1987. The results of the
investigation were never published and the British Attorney
General, in a statement to the House of Commons in January
1988, said that although there was evidence of police officers
attempting to pervert the course of justice, no prosecutions
were contemplated because of considerations of 'national
security'.

Despite the controversy surrounding undercover operations,
there was no let-up in the numbers killed; the only change
was that the RUC were replaced by the SAS, although Special Branch continued to play the lead role in intelligence
collation and targeting under the overall control of the Chief
Constable. Between 1984 and 1988, 18 people were killed by
undercover units, mainly the SAS, including the shooting of

three unarmed IRA members in Gibraltar. The latter operation exposed once again the inherent dangers of a policy of the execution of suspects. Two prerequisites for a successful cover-up were absent: the three were not caught red-handed and there were a number of witnesses willing to testify that the SAS unit opened fire without warning. The political fall-out from that particular operation, which involved criticism from the Dublin government, large-scale street violence in Belfast and the attempt to block two television programmes on the incident by the British government, was considerable.

It is difficult to understand the logic behind the undercover tactics practised during the 1980s under the overall direction of the RUC. To be effective in crushing dissent, the policy would have to be part of an overall strategy of state terror – as practised in Argentina in the mid-seventies – carried out in a situation where the rule of law had been suspended, the media gagged and critics silenced. The tactics of undercover ambushes did not led to a diminution of IRA activity except on a very temporary basis, as units reorganised after members had been killed. For instance, three years after the Loughgall ambush, the IRA returned to demolish the half of the RUC station left standing after their first attack. Although the IRA never came close to winning the war in any military sense, nor was it ever close to military defeat. Indeed, during the decades after 1970, it became increasingly proficient at the business of killing: in 1970 the Provisionals needed 191 attacks to kill one member of the security forces, by 1984 this had fallen to 18 (*Fortnight*, November 1989). Covert operations may have had a deterrent effect, but this cannot be demonstrated: indeed, the opposite may well be the case, as such killings may harden republican and nationalist opinion.

It would seem that with the restrictions put upon interrogation practices after the Bennett Report, and the collapse of the supergrass system, the shooting of suspects was seen by the RUC as the only option open to a security apparatus frustrated by the constraints put upon its activities. The corrosive effect of the tacit support of government for such activities upon democratic institutions has been incalculable.

8 Collusion and Death Squads

Since the beginning of the current conflict, there has been a constant flow of allegations of collusion between different elements of the security apparatus and loyalist paramilitaries. Collusion, in the Irish context, refers to the use of members of loyalist paramilitary organisations to carry out operations, such as assassinations or bombings, with the aim of eliminating individuals or terrorising the nationalist population as a whole. Collusion can be informally or formally structured. Formal collusion would consist of the sanctioned use of loyalist gangs with directives coming from the operational and/or political levels. This would involve conscious decision on the part of the authorities to engage in extra-legal activities, including murder, to achieve the objective of eliminating dissent. Informal collusion would include members of the security forces operating in tandem with paramilitary groups or the passing-on of intelligence information by individual security personnel to loyalist paramilitaries without official sanction. As with the shoot-to-kill tactic, while such activities would not be officially condoned, an operational space is created in order to make such operations possible. Essentially, collusion is a local term used for the widespread practice of using 'counter-gangs' or 'death squads' to eliminate or terrorise those who oppose the policies and actions of the powerful.

That there has been informal collusion between individual members of the security forces, whether they be Army, RUC or UDR personnel, is beyond doubt and members of the UDR, before its metamorphosis into the Royal Irish Regiment, were deeply involved. The Stevens inquiry, set up to look into allegations of collusion in 1989, concluded that while there was no evidence of instutionalised collusion with loyalist groups, there was evidence of security documents reaching loyalists through members of the security forces

The murder of the Lurgan solicitor and human rights campaigner Rosemary Nelson in March 1999 led to renewed accusations of formal collusion, particularly against the RUC, as was the case in the wake of the murder of the Belfast solicitor Pat Finucane in 1989 (see Pat Finucane Centre, 1999; BIRW, 1992). A significant number of human rights organisations and agencies are convinced that there is sufficient evidence of formal collusion to merit a full inquiry. Amnesty International, Helsinki Rights Watch, The Committee for the Administration of Justice and the UN Special Rapporteur, Dato Cumaraswamy, are among those organisations and individuals concerned that formal collusion has taken place (see Amnesty International, 1994; Human Rights Watch/Helsinki, 1992; LSEW, 1995; LCHR, 1996). In February 1999, the London-based non-govermental organisation British Irish Rights Watch (BIRW) sent a report to the Irish and British governments containing new evidence of collusion between the security forces in Northern Ireland and loyalist paramilitaries in the Pat Finucane case. Although the report is not publicly available, the reaction to its contents from the Irish government and the UN Special Rapporteur was swift. The Irish Minister of State for Foreign Affairs, Liz O'Donnell, in a letter to Mo Mowlam, the Secretary of State for Northern Ireland, called for a public inquiry and the UN Special Rapporteur, unconstrained by the diplomatic niceties of Anglo–Irish relations, was blunt in his response to the BIRW report. In a statement to the 55th Session of the Human Rights Commission in Geneva on 12 April 1999, he said: 'From the materials seen by the Special Rapporteur, there is at least prima facie evidence of such [state] collusion.' Previously, Cumaraswamy had been trenchant in his criticism of the RUC concluding after a fact finding trip in 1998 that 'the RUC has engaged in activities which constitute intimidation, hindrance, harassment or improper interference' and that the RUC has 'identified solicitors with their clients' causes as a result of discharging their functions' (UNCHR, 1998).[1]

Death Squads and Counter-insurgency

The use of clandestine but organised groups, sponsored by the state or other organisations to eliminate those considered to be enemies or critics, has become a feature of low-intensity wars since 1945. The nomenclature regarding such groups is varied: 'counter-gangs' or 'pseudo-gangs' are the favourite terms of the military, while the more appropriate term 'death squads' has gained currency among more critical commentators (See

Human Rights Watch, 1994; Stanley, 1996; Huggins, 1991). The best-known use of such groups was in Central and South America during the 1970s and 1980s when the US sponsored, usually through puppet regimes, death squads to eliminate leftist opposition. During the twelve-year civil war in El Salvador between the US-backed government and the leftist Farabundo Marti National Liberation Front (FMLN), 75,000 people were killed, many of them at the hands of death squads. The use of death squads first became visible during the Mau Mau campaign in Kenya in the 1950s. A British officer, the ubiquitous Major Kitson, organised 'turned' Mau Mau guerrillas into 'counter-gangs', which were than sent out to track down and eliminate their erstwhile comrades. Kitson, who was later to serve in Northern Ireland – organising undercover operations during the 1970s (see Chapter 5) – wrote of his experiences in Kenya in a book entitled *Gangs and Counter-Gangs* (1960). Kitson makes it quite clear in his book *Low Intensity Operations* (1971) that the purpose of using counter-gangs in Kenya was to kill insurgents and while he does not directly apply his experiences to other situations, the implications are clear: 'Suffice it to say that there are innumerable ways in which the principle [the use of counter gangs to eliminate opposition] can be applied under various circumstances and it is up to those involved to invent or adapt such methods of achieving their aims as may be relevant to the situation' (1971, p. 126).

Kitson was not the only senior British Army or RUC officer to have had experience of the sharp end of counter-insurgency operations. The first Chief Constable of the RUC, Sir Arthur Young, was appointed by the then Prime Minister, James Callaghan, in the wake of the Hunt Report. Young had extensive experience of colonial wars, having served in the Gold Coast, Kenya and Malaya (Ryder, 1989, p.116). A former member of the Palestine Police, he had commanded a 500-strong counter-insurgency unit in Malaya (Beckett and Pilmott, 1985, p. 12). Chief Constable Newman had also served with the Palestine Police and his Army counterpart, General Creasey made extensive use of a clandestine group, the Firqat, in Oman during the counter-insurgency campaign waged there by proxy in the early 1970s. Many regular soldiers in the British Army had extensive counter-insurgency experience when first sent to Northern Ireland in 1969: 'By the time of the initial deployment to Northern Ireland in 1969 ... it was not unknown for an infantry battalion to contain men (particularly senior NCOs) who had already fought three or four campaigns' (Beckett and Pilmott, 1985, p. 24).

Other wars carried out against liberation and nationalist movements were characterised by the use of death squads, such as the Algerian war of independence, and more recently the extensive use of both outside mercenaries and internal gangs in South Africa to eliminate opposition. Recent events in East Timor, involving genocide on a massive scale, show that the tactical use of irregular gangs by the military is by now well-established and the US-trained Indonesian Army had no hesitation in using irregular militias to eliminate dissent. The *New York Times* was moved to comment: 'The US should immediately end all programs involving the Indonesian military: training, sharing of intelligence, military aid' (7 September 1999). The essential element in the use of such groups is deniability on the part of government and the regular forces. The 'bad apple' approach is one such device to distance the authorities from such operations by putting them down to the actions of misguided individuals. However, the longer a low-intensity conflict goes on, the more likely it is that the use of death squads will increase, thus making the possibility of exposure more likely. The use of death squads against suspected ETA members living in France is a case in point.

In July 1998, the ex-Interior Minister in the socialist government of Felipe Gonzalez, Jose Barrionuevo, along with a Security Minister, Rafael Vera, was sentenced to ten years in prison. The charges related to the activities of a group called GAL (Anti-Terrorist Liberation Group) which was responsible for 28 murders during the period 1983–87. Of this number, about one-third had no connection with ETA, the Basque separatist movement. GAL was set up to demoralise ETA by wiping out its leadership and issued communiqués claiming credit for the shooting and bombing of alleged ETA members. GAL was made up of both members of the security forces, and hit men and contract killers who were recruited from the ranks of former French paratroopers and the criminal underworld of Lisbon and Marseilles. It emerged in court that GAL was financed by a secret government fund and directed by Spanish military intelligence to achieve the aim declared by the socialist leader Gonzales in a 1992 interview: 'The only road to finish ETA is to fight it using their own weapons.'

What is unusual about the case of GAL is that the operation seems to have been sanctioned, financed and led from inside the Security Ministry, thus leaving a clear bureaucratic paper trail. In contrast to the system in Britain, for instance, Spanish judges have powers of investigation that allowed members of the judiciary to pursue the matter independently. The operation itself followed a pattern familiar to anyone who has observed the security operation in Northern Ireland in recent years. A front organisation is used to disguise security force involvement in the killings, information is fed to the killers from security files, and when the operation does unravel, it is often because those lower down the operational hierarchy are unwilling to carry the can for those higher up who sanctioned the operation in the first place.

The UDR and Collusion

The Hunt Report into policing recommended the disbandment of the B Specials and the establishment of a new part-time military force. The new regiment was to be lightly armed and under the command of the British Army. However, when recruitment began in November 1969 (the regiment was to become fully operational in April 1970), nationalists were incensed to find that the recruitment campaign was being run by the Stormont government with no obvious input from either the British Army or the London government. There was suspicion that the new force would have a distinctly unionist ethos and be recruited from the ranks of former members of the B Specials. Nationalists called for the full implementation of the recommendations of the Hunt Report: a more neutral name, a reduction in the proposed size of the force, and a ban on the recruitment of B Special county commanders as UDR battalion commanders. Nationalists feared that the new outfit would simply be the B Specials by another name and this fear seemed confirmed when it transpired that all the new battalion commanders were ex-B Specials and, in Co. Derry at least, half the members of the local UDR were ex-B Specials (Ó Dochartaigh, 1997, p. 144). Initially, the UDR was about 17 per cent Catholic, but this figure fell steadily to about 3 per cent.

The existence of links between the UDR and loyalist paramilitary organisations soon became apparent. In September

1972, the British Army shot dead a UDA gunman on the Shankhill Road in Belfast who was also a serving member of the UDR. In the same month, the weapons of a newly-formed battalion in Craigavon were stolen without opposition from the unit's armoury (Farrell, 1976, p. 305). By 1976, some 316 UDR weapons had been stolen in loyalist paramilitary raids on UDR armouries with no resistance from the soldiers on duty. Large numbers of personal weapons were also taken from UDR members in their homes, again without any evidence of resistance.

The British government did not ban the Ulster Defence Association (UDA) until 1992. Membership of the UDA was no hindrance to joining the UDR and relations between the two organisations were close. The areas from which the UDR was recruited, loyalist working-class areas and small towns in rural areas, were precisely those localities where the UDA had support. There were also links to the more openly sectarian UVF (Ulster Volunteer Force), which was banned in 1966, then legalised in 1974 only to be banned again 18 months later.

In August 1975, three members of the Miami Showband (a popular group based in the Republic) were killed after being stopped by a fake UDR patrol near the border. Four members of the 'patrol' were also members of the UVF. By 1976, 28 UDR members had already been convicted of arms and explosives offences and twelve were on remand (*Hibernia*, December 1976). Although the UDR was deployed across Northern Ireland, it was its activities in rural areas that most irritated nationalists. Following the practices of its predecessors, the B Specials, the UDR engaged in low-level intelligence gathering and general harassment of nationalists while some of its members became involved in serious crime. In 1977, five members of the regiment were convicted of sectarian murders; this rose to a total of 14 convictions for murder by 1989. Since 1972, there have been 30 convictions for firearms and explosives offences and numerous convictions for other scheduled offences.

Within the particular context of Northern Ireland, the UDR can be seen as a form of pseudo-gang, with functions broadly similar to the Yeomanry of the eighteenth and nineteenth centuries. The common functions were to relieve pressure on the regular Army, act as means of controlling the worst excesses of loyalist sectarianism by placing loyalists in uniform under the command of English officers and contain unrest by tactics of intimidation and harassment. Both organisations share another feature: their criminality. Within this context, the British authorities were always careful to keep the UDR rank and file at a distance. British Army officers were soon to replace those with a past in the B Specials, and soldiers recruited locally had little access to sensitive intelligence. Until 1988, UDR soldiers had access to security intelligence files which contained names, addresses, photographs and other information on republican suspects (*Independent*, 31 August 1989). Literally hundreds of these files found their way to the UDA and UVF and, in a bizarre incident in 1989, copies of police and Army files were pasted on walls in Belfast by loyalist paramilitaries. The extra-curricular activities of members of the UDR had no significant effect on the IRA directly as, with the help of leaked documents or otherwise, loyalist gangs had little success in assassinating active IRA members. According to research carried out by the Irish Information Partnership, loyalist groups were responsible for about 700 deaths between 1969 and 1989, 25 per cent of all those killed during this period (Irish Information Partnership, 1990, p. 295). The Partnership figures show that over 90 per cent of those killed by loyalists were uninvolved civilians. Loyalists have claimed that the majority of those killed by them were targeted because they appeared on security files supplied by members of the UDR, RUC or British Army. Allegations have been made that security files are 'grossly inaccurate' and contain the names of Catholics not involved with the IRA (*Independent*, 31 August 1989). In any event, figures collated by the Irish Information Partnership indicate that of the 37 people killed by loyalist death squads in 1988 and 1989, only three were clearly identifiable as members of the IRA.

The UDR in the two decades or so of its existence operated a system of low-level state terror that was tolerated by the authorities because it fitted into the overall goals of the security apparatus. As well as being a central plank in the policy of police primacy, by replacing regular British Army troops, the UDR fulfilled a number of other functions not least the important task of instilling fear into the nationalist population. Collusion between members of the UDR and loyalist paramilitaries was inevitable given the geographic, social class and religious background of those recruited to the regiment. The state, by tolerating a certain level of collusion was demonstrating that such collusion fitted the overall goals of the counter-insurgency campaign. In sociological terms, the organisational structure of the UDR (including its place within the overall security structure) allowed access by rank-and-file soldiers to basic intelligence documents listing suspect persons. Grimshaw and Jefferson's general point concerning the structure of an organisation – what they term the 'vertical dimension of rules, policies, approved procedures, command and control' – allowed the UDR access to sensitive British Army intelligence documents (1987, p. 19). The British Army authorities also ignored a second feature of the UDR as a sub-element within the security structure, namely the occupational culture of the regiment. This refers to the 'horizontal dimension of the norms and practices of colleague groups' (Grimshaw and Jefferson, 1987, p. 19) and given the background of the majority of UDR soldiers, and the loyalist culture to which they belonged, the misuse of security information and its transmission into the hands of loyalist death squads was inevitable. That such actions were tolerated and perhaps tacitly approved by the authorities is clear from the refusal to take the issue seriously and it was not until the UFF (Ulster Freedom Fighters), the name under which UDA death squads operate, leaked an official list of IRA suspects in August 1989, that the question of collusion was pushed firmly onto the political agenda.

The British Army and the Use of Death Squads

In June 1988, the Northern Ireland Police Authority rejected, by a slim margin, calls for further investigation into the behaviour of the Chief Constable and his deputies during the Stalker and Samson investigations. Between January 1988 and December 1992, 27 people were killed by the security forces, 16 in undercover operations, including a member of E4A shot by another member of the RUC in North Belfast. The last person to be shot in an undercover operation was Pearse Jordan, killed by a RUC undercover unit on the Falls Road in November 1992. Of the 27 people killed by the security forces during this period, 13 had acknowledged paramilitary connections and many of these killings were controversial (see Cain Web Service, n.d.). By any standards, the use of undercover units was becoming less and less productive. The 'clean

kill' of Loughgall was never replicated, and the average of three
IRA operatives killed each year during this period should be
set against the controversial nature of many of the killings
and the fact that over half of the victims of undercover operation had no obvious paramilitary connections.

During the same period, the number of people killed by
loyalist murder gangs rose dramatically. From January 1977
to December 1987, loyalist gangs killed 72 people: in the following six years to September 1994, loyalists were responsible
for the killing of 229 people. The increased activity of loyalist
death squads from 1987 onwards has been attributed to a
number of factors, including the successful importation of a
large consignment of modern weapons from South Africa in
1988 and the flow of intelligence information on republican
suspects which was reaching the UDA and UVF from members of the security forces. The Dublin government, in its
response to the BIRW report in 1999 points to the 'stark
change in the volume and precision of loyalist lethal force
between 1988–1994, the failure to apprehend those involved,
the failure to convict members of the UDA/UVF for murder
...' (*Irish Times*, 5 May 1999). The South African arms shipment contained rocket launchers, 400 grenades, 200 automatic
assault rifles and 90 pistols. The security forces were aware of
the shipment, which more than doubled the armed capacity
of the UDA/UVF but chose not to intervene. (It has been
suggested that the security forces did not intervene to seize
the weapons because this might have exposed their agent,
Brian Nelson (see Cain Web Service, n.d.).)

Although the security authorities were aware that extensive leaking of security files was taking place, it was not until
the killing of Loughlin Maginn in 1989 that an official investigation was launched. After the killing of Maginn, the UDA
attempted to justify his murder by claiming that RUC files in
their possession indicated that he was a member of the IRA.
They released the files on Maginn, and then leaked to the
press a list of over 250 names, addresses and photographs
culled from security files. This led to the setting-up of an
inquiry under the direction of a senior British police officer,
John Stevens, to investigate the leaking of security documents.
The full terms of reference of the inquiry were never published and the complete text of the inquiry's results was never
officially revealed, although a summary, containing 83 recommendations, was released in May 1990. The inquiry led to

the charging of 59 people mainly with the handling of classified documents, the possession of classified documents, and collecting and recording security information. Two members of the UDR were charged and convicted of the murder of Loughlin Maginn, but the vast majority of those charged, 39 people in all, were members of the UDA. The inquiry directed its investigations towards those who had allegedly been the recipients of leaked security files rather than those members of the security forces who may have leaked the documents in the first place. The inquiry confirmed that documents had been passed into the hands of loyalist paramilitary groups from sources within the RUC, the British Army and the Prison Service but concluded that the problem was not widespread or institutionalised. Others were less convinced. Amnesty International pointed out that the investigation had restricted itself to the question of leaked security documents at the time and did not confront the evidence that collusion between loyalist death squads and the security forces had been going on for many years. The Amnesty report continued:

> It did not look at ... the overall pattern as it related to both targeted and random killings of Catholics. It did not examine the authorities' record during this time in bringing criminal proceedings against security personnel in this regard, or the official response to evidence of partiality and discriminatory treatment, for example, soldiers shouting verbal abuse at Catholics or writing sectarian graffiti on walls. (Amnesty International, 14 February 1994)

The Case of Brian Nelson and the FRU

During the course of their investigation, the Stevens team came across the name of a UDA operative, Brian Nelson, who was a senior UDA intelligence officer heavily involved in collecting intelligence on, and setting up the assassination of, Catholics suspected of association with the IRA. The Stevens team planned to arrest Nelson on a minor charge of possession of information likely to be useful to terrorists. However, when eventually arrested, Nelson in a series of detailed statements revealed his role as a double-agent working for a little-known undercover unit within the British Army called the Force Research Unit (FRU). The FRU was set up in 1980 to run agents and to penetrate paramilitary organisations (Urban,

1992, p. 109; Geraghty, 1998, p. 155) and it recruited Nelson, an ex-soldier, around 1983. Shortly before his trial in January 1992, the most serious charges against Nelson, including two charges of murder, were dropped. According to the prosecution the charges were dropped 'after a painstaking and scrupulous assessment of possible evidential difficulties with the prosecution and a rigorous examination of the interests of justice' (*Irish Times*, 23 January 1992).

Because of the dropping of the more serious charges, and the plea of guilty entered by Nelson, only one witness was called, an anonymous British Army officer, 'Colonel J'. The relationship between Nelson's role as a British agent and his activities on behalf of UDA death squads was not probed in court, nor was the question asked why Nelson's information was rarely, if ever, used to ambush loyalist gangs going about their murderous business. In the course of his evidence, 'Colonel J', who was probably the officer commanding the FRU, mentioned that Nelson had brought his FRU handlers a large cache of intelligence documents from various sections of the security forces in 1987. These documents were photocopied by Army Intelligence and copied to senior RUC officers (*Irish Times*, 4 February 1992). It later transpired when the BBC *Panorama* team gained access to Nelson's prison diary, that military intelligence had weeded out-of-date targets from the files and returned a more up-to-date and selective list of targets to Nelson (BBC *Panorama* programme, 'The Dirty War', June 1992). Suspicions of direct collusion between the FRU and the UDA were strengthened when *Sunday Telegraph* reporters John Ware and Geoff Seed published the results of their investigation into the Nelson Affair (5 April 1998): 'We have seen files that, for the first time, provide evidence that the British Army's Force Research Unit, a branch of military intelligence responsible for running agents in Northern Ireland, was complicit in a series of murders carried out by the UDA between 1987 and 1990.' According to the report in the *Sunday Telegraph*, the final draft of the report of the Stevens inquiry put forward convincing evidence that the FRU had colluded with the UDA, via Brian Nelson, to target individuals identified by the unit as members of the IRA. Although this information was available to the DPP at the time, the decision was made not to prosecute 'Colonel J' or any other member of the FRU. According to the article, 'Colonel J' was subsequently awarded the OBE.

The Role of the RUC

One constant of the counter-insurgency campaign in Northern Ireland has been the continual friction between the British Army and the RUC, particularly concerning the conduct, control and direction of undercover operations. The hands-off attitude of the political establishment with regard to operational matters has meant that while the overall goal of defeating the IRA has remained constant, the tactics used have been deployed and changed in a somewhat disjointed and arbitrary fashion. Often the tactics employed and the choice of implementing agencies have been dictated by the ebb and flow of inter-service rivalry and the level of access to politicians open to different sections of the security establishment. Politicians and senior bureaucrats prefer to keep their hands clean and, just as the idea of a centralised police force was anathema to nineteenth-century English politicians, the idea of placing responsibility for security in the hands of a single ministry fills the contemporary establishment with horror. (For a discussion of rivalries between Special Branch and MI5, see Hollingsworth and Fielding, 1999.)

Direct political intervention into security matters, when it does occur (such as after the Warrenpoint ambush and the killing of Mountbatten) has tended to focus upon sorting out inter-service rivalries and shifting the lead role to one or the other agency in the war with the IRA. Public opinion can trigger political intervention as in the wake of the killings in Lurgan/Armagh in 1982, but such interventions can also trigger another round of jostling for position between the RUC and the British Army. The conflict between police and Army surfaced in a dramatic fashion during the Nelson trial. The Army argued that it had passed on crucial information on UDA targets to the RUC who had then failed to act. It was indicated at the trial that the FRU had detailed information of at least 92 planned UDA assassinations but the RUC Special Branch claimed that only two such reports contained information specific enough to take preventative action.

It is clear that by 1988 the British Army and the FRU were in the ascendant as far as counter-insurgency operations were concerned. This may have been, as Geraghty contends (1998, p. 156), as a result of pressure from the Thatcher government to respond to the bombing campaign then being waged in Britain by the IRA, but whatever the cause, the operations of loyalist death squads were stepped up with the clear assistance and collusion of the British Army. The manipulation of loyalist death squads by the FRU followed a tried and tested pattern of counter-insurgency tactics used against liberation movements the length and breadth of the declining British Empire, tactics which, as we have seen, were a particular speciality of the British Army. The role of the RUC is less clear during this period. Although the doctrine of police primacy was still in place, the lead role, which the RUC had attempted to carve out for itself in the war against the IRA in the early 1980s, did not survive the debacle of the Stalker affair. The Special Branch had considerable success in infiltrating the IRA right up to command level and had achieved even deeper penetration of loyalist groups. Although most of the security information reaching loyalist groups originated in RUC files, there is no evidence that the RUC were running active double-agents in the mould of Nelson or that they had the expertise and ability to do so. What is however clear is that elements within the RUC were willing to encourage loyalist paramilitaries to take action against people they regarded as dangerous, as in the case of the solicitors Pat Finucane and Rosemary Nelson. What is well documented in both these cases is that members of the RUC issued death threats to both these lawyers via clients who were in custody and, in the case of Pat Finucane, there is mounting evidence that the UDA killers operated with information supplied by the RUC. The UN Special Rapporteur is unequivocal on the matter of death threats to Pat Finucane: 'Prior to his murder, Patrick Finucane also received a number of death threats from RUC officers, mainly delivered via his clients' (UNCHR, 1998, Para. 62). The report also refers to the comments of a Home Office minister, Douglas Hogg, in the House of Commons less than a month before Finucane's murder: 'I have to state as a fact, but with regret, that there are in Northern Ireland a number of solicitors who are unduly sympathetic to the cause of the IRA.' Refusing to substantiate his statement, Hogg subsequently said 'I state it on the basis of advice that I have received, guidance that I have been given by people who are dealing with these matters, and I shall not expand on it further' (Para. 61). The Irish government, in its analysis of the BIRW report, points firmly towards formal collusion in the murder:

The report makes four primary and over arching allegations:

- that the security forces were complicit in the murder of Pat Finucane
- that elements within the RUC incited his murder in a number of ways, that named officers in the RUC procured his murder and that RUC Special Branch had detailed advanced knowledge of the murder plot.
- that his murder was part of a 'systematic strategy' directed by a unit (Force Research Unit) within British military intelligence whose purpose was to murder republicans in what the report describes as 'state murder by proxy'. (*Irish Times*, 5 May 1999)

When faced with the accusation of links between the RUC and loyalist death squads, the RUC falls back on the 'bad apple' explanation which takes the position that while there may be some rogue policemen, no systematic collusion with loyalist paramilitaries has ever taken place. In a recent interview, the Chief Constable, Ronnie Flanagan, stressed that no evidence of collusion has ever been presented to support what he calls 'general allegations':

> It's all very well to lay out those general accusations and you use very sweeping phrases such as 'collusion' I want to see evidence produced of any such collusion. We don't want within our ranks anyone who would collude with criminals or paramilitaries. I think our record stands the closest scrutiny. You are probably thinking of, for example, the murders of Pat Finucane and Rosemary Nelson. Both those cases are under vigorous investigation and so it makes it difficult to comment in detail. But in the past, there hasn't been produced any evidence to support the sort of general allegation to which you refer. We've been ruthless with any officer who has fallen from the high standards we require. (Interview by Anne Cadwallader, *Ireland on Sunday*, 13 June 1999)

Of course, it is highly unlikely that the sort of evidence alluded to by the Chief Constable would ever come to light or even exist. Like the evidence pointing towards a 'shoot-to-kill policy' discussed in the last chapter, any decision to involve the security forces in planned collusion – to eliminate troublesome lawyers, for instance – would not be based upon a normal bureaucratic decision involving a paper trail through the files showing official sanction of collusion and the use of death squads as a counter-insurgency tactic. The Chief Constable is aware of this and, within the context of the bureaucratic process, collusion and the use of death squads could hardly exist as official policy. On the other hand, a significant number of human rights organisations are convinced that collusion has taken place and that it is not confined to the action of a few maverick individuals but may well reach into the higher echelons of RUC Special Branch and military intelligence. In a recent letter to the then Secretary of State, Mo Mowlam, the Dublin Minister of State for Foreign Affairs, Liz O'Donnell wrote: 'The accumulated evidence [of collusion] is sufficient to give reasonable cause to the public to believe that collusion may have taken place' (*Irish Times,* 5 May 1999).

During the past thirty years, practically every available counter-insurgency tactic has been used in Northern Ireland. As each tactic has failed, or faced public hostility, it has been replaced with another. Internment, the favourite solution of unionists, failed because of bad RUC intelligence and hostile international opinion. The killing of civilians in Derry in 1972, instead of stemming the tide of militant nationalism, fanned the flames and has now returned to haunt the security establishment – in 1998, the British Prime Minister set up an inquiry, under Lord Saville, into the events on Bloody Sunday (see Saville Inquiry, n.d.). The Diplock solution failed to deliver the deathblow to the IRA because of the exposure of the interrogation practices of the RUC and the faith placed in supergrasses proved illusory. The use of undercover ambush units of the British Army and the RUC during the 1980s may have restricted the activities of the IRA, but as well as failing to be militarily decisive, embroiled the RUC in particular in embarrassing controversy.

The operations of death squads have a particular objective aimed at the elimination of civilians, not involved in guerrilla activity, but regarded by the security forces as a threat to state policy. Such actions can be seen, from the perspective of the security authorities, as complementing SAS-type operations designed to disrupt actual guerrilla operations. The killings of Rosemary Nelson and Pat Finucane should be seen in the context of RUC threats issued to solicitors involved in defending republican clients. As the Special Rapporteur reported, a large number of solicitors were subject to such threats. He writes of a 'large number of solicitors' who were 'able to provide testimony that corroborates the reports that the Special Rapporteur has been receiving for the past four years concerning the harassment and intimidation of defence solicitors' (Para. 20). The main function of death squads is to create a climate of terror through the murder of selected targets. During the period of increased death-squad activity, between 1988 and 1994, a significant number of Sinn Féin members, political representatives and alleged sympathisers were targeted. It is hardly a coincidence that the same period saw a considerable expansion of political activity on the part of Sinn Féin and an increase in their political influence.

The operational autonomy enjoyed by the RUC and British Army in Ireland is a key element in the ability and willingness of both organisations to engage in illegal activities in the pursuit of what was the overall political and military goal: the defeat of the IRA. Coupled with the unswerving support of the judiciary, this gave the RUC and British Army *carte blanche* to run through the repertoire of counter-insurgency tactics in search of a military solution. The Patten Report on policing, in a long section on the use of covert operations by the RUC (discussed in Chapter 10), makes recommendations which, while not challenging the overall system which allowed such operations to proceed unchecked, would make it more difficult for the police to engage in such tactics as collusion and ambush, but would, of course, have no effect on the activities of the British Army.

9 Symbolism, Surveys and Police Legitimacy

The publication of the Patten Commission Report in September 1999 reopened the debate on this divisive issue of policing in Northern Ireland and catapulted the question of RUC reform to the top of the political agenda at a crucial juncture in the search for a political settlement. While nationalists and republicans have broadly welcomed the report, unionists have denounced it in no uncertain terms. A coalition of oppositional interests swiftly emerged which was determined to resist any fundamental reform of the RUC, including all the main Unionist political parties, the ex-Chief Constable, Sir John Hermon, the Orange Order, the Northern Ireland Police Federation and the editor of the conservative London *Daily Telegraph* newspaper. At a meeting in the Ulster Hall in Belfast about a thousand people voiced their opposition to the report's recommendations (*Irish Times*, 20 September 1999). The former Secretary of State for Northern Ireland, Lord Mason, also joined the campaign describing the Patten report as 'petty and mean-spirited' (*Belfast Telegraph*, 27 October 1999).

Unionist opposition centres on the question of the legitimacy and acceptability of the RUC and the contention that the Commission misunderstood the level of support for the force that exists among nationalists. According to this view, Patten's incorrect assumption that such support is wanting plays into the hands of militant republicans intent on destroying the RUC on the road to a united Ireland. The RUC is seen as the crucial bulwark against terrorism preventing 'Northern Ireland from descending into an abyss of the kind seen in Bosnia, Rwanda and Kosovo' as an editorial in the *Daily Telegraph* would have it (28 September 1999). Those opposed to the report pursue two lines of argument: that the level of support among Catholics for the RUC is high and that this is demonstrated by survey evidence, and that the symbolic trappings of policing, uniform, insignia, the flying of

the Union Jack, and so on offer no threat to nationalist identity, but are symbols shared by both nationalists and unionists.

In the immediate wake of the publication of the Patten
Report, the First Minister of the Northern Ireland Assembly,
David Trimble, trenchantly restated the unionist position. In
an article in the *Sunday Times* (12 September 1999), he reiterated the familiar arguments: if Catholics did not join the RUC
it was because of 'intimidation and social pressures emanat-
ing from republicans'. The recommendation that the symbols
of the RUC be changed 'lacks all logic' as 'The badge of the
RUC is perhaps the finest example of parity of esteem we
have in Northern Ireland, including, as it does, symbols of
both unionism and nationalism side by side.' A few days later,
another unionist commentator offered an interpretation of the
survey data on the RUC to demonstrate that there is broad
support among Catholics for the RUC including the reten-
tion of the name. The author also argued that, in general,
Catholics had little objection to the RUC and its current practices (*Belfast Telegraph*, 16 September 1999).

This chapter will consider both the problems presented by
the interpretation survey data and the question of policing as
a cultural category. First, the social and cultural dimensions
of policing in Northern Ireland will be examined, drawing
upon recent theoretical arguments which suggest that policing should not be regarded simply in terms of what men and
women in blue (or whatever colour) uniforms actually *do* but
rather what they *represent* in cultural and symbolic terms
(Brogden 1999; Loader, 1997; Ellison and Martin, forthcoming). Indeed, it is only by considering policing as an 'idea' as
opposed to a material practice that we can fully appreciate
the basis of opposition – amongst unionists and Protestants
at least – to the Patten proposals to transform the symbolic
world of the RUC. Second, the body of survey evidence that
has been conducted in recent years to evaluate communal
attitudes towards the RUC will be examined.

Policing as Cultural Category

In his discussion of English policing, Loader (1997, p. 2) argues
that the British bobby acts as a 'condensation symbol' of the
national character, representing 'dominant' forms of English
national identity. The traits of the idealised 'English' citizen:

benign, steady, decent, tolerant, and so on, are commonly associated with the police. For instance, Sir Robert Mark, Commissioner of the London Metropolitan Police during the 1970s, claimed that 'the English police system ... is undoubtedly one of the most sophisticated and successful institutions to emerge from the English way of life' (1977, p. 13). The hardship and constant threat of physical injury associated with the job, he argued, 'is a price we are willing to pay for the preservation of the English way of life ... We, the police, are in fact the most accurate reflection of British society, its tolerance, its strengths and its weaknesses' (p. 33).

Thus, within English society, the police occupy a privileged position and as Loader (1997, p. 7) acknowledges, are 'embroiled in and animated by, a set of cultural mentalities and sensibilities. Policing too, communicates meaning and plays its part in the creation of culture.' Therefore, for some, the police embody an emotional and effective appeal against unforeseen threats and act as a focus for national identity, even if only in Anderson's sense of an 'imagined community' (Anderson, 1983). However, as Loader acknowledges, the symbolic capital of the police is invariably associated with particular forms of dominance and certain groups invariably find it difficult to engage with the kind of 'identity' promoted through the police and other social institutions. In other words, while policing can promote feelings of belonging and security for some, it can also deny recognition to others, not just at the level of day-to-day policing practices, but also symbolically at the level of culture, and emotionally at the level of 'belonging' to a particular group (Honneth, 1995).

By considering the cultural dimension, we can connect the 'symbolic form to social structure' (Zald, 1996, p. 264) and demonstrate the ways in which social and economic inequalities, and relations of dominance, can be promoted, reflected and articulated through the cultural and signifying practice of policing. Similarly, we can examine the ways that such issues impact on feelings of alienation, public security and modes of exclusion and inclusion within the state. The significance of these issues can be illustrated by considering what young, black people in Britain 'see' when they meet a British police officer (whether white or black). Do they 'see' a symbol and embodiment of a multicultural, multiracial society? Similarly, what do young Catholics 'see' whenever they encounter an RUC officer (again whether Catholic or Protestant)? Do they 'see', for instance, a member of an organisation committed to the equal treatment and acceptance of the competing cultural and political aspirations in Northern Ireland?

At the symbolic and cultural level, policing in Northern Ireland has reflected the sensibilities of one ethno-religious bloc to the virtual exclusion of the other. This can be seen in terms of the RUC's historically-based institutional links with the Unionist party, its central role in the control and management of nationalist dissent and protest, and its overwhelming identification with unionism through its cultural symbols, institutional ethos and occupational culture (Ellison 1997; Weitzer, 1995; Mulcahy, 1998; McGarry and O'Leary, 1999).

In Northern Ireland, policing has played a key role in animating the collective folk memories of Protestants and unionists, Catholics and nationalists, albeit in starkly divergent and mutually exclusionary ways. For many Protestants, the RUC is still seen as 'their' police. Historically, the force played a key role in consolidating the position of the Unionist government, and was to become a trusted ally in defending the state against real or imagined threats from either civic nationalism or militant republicanism. Equally, since the RUC has remained an essentially Protestant and unionist force in terms of religious composition and political outlook it is difficult for many Protestants to differentiate between what republicans regard as a 'legitimate target', and what they see as the killing and injuring of members of *their* community. While the RUC was never to become, like the auxiliary USC, an entirely Protestant force, it has nevertheless remained both in ethos and composition an entirely 'unionist' force.

Conversely, for Catholics and nationalists, the RUC was to serve as a visible and potent reminder of their exclusion from the state and other social institutions (Ruane and Todd, 1996, pp. 196–7). As we have argued, the RUC during the Stormont period was engaged in two interlocking functions. The first concerned countering the threat from militant republicanism, and even when this threat had all but abated by the 1930s, the RUC still engaged in low-level surveillance against Catholics whom they regarded as 'political', that is, those whom they suspected of harbouring nationalist views (Ellison, 1997). The second, involved policing the symbolic world of nationalists to deny expression to minority culture. This was ostensible and overt, in the enforcement of the Flags and Emblems Act to prohibit the display of nationalist symbols, and the Public

Order Act to prohibit nationalist parades and demonstrations. However, it could also be petty and vindictive as with the case of Francis Meenan, who was imprisoned in 1957 without trial for seven months in Crumlin Road prison for replying to an RUC officer's question in Irish (Ruane and Todd, 1996, pp. 182–3).

In ethnically-divided societies such as Northern Ireland, the issue of culture, or perhaps more accurately, that of cultural inequality, can provide a significant arena for conflict. Cultural practices in such contexts become highly politicised, and assume strategic importance as part of a zero-sum scenario, as Ruane and Todd acknowledge: '... the achievements celebrated by one group are frequently those which the other wishes to forget, the traumatic events to which one community returns obsessively may be ignored or regarded as trivial by the other' (1996, p. 200).

Cultural practices and symbols are not neutral phenomena untainted by the political and historical conditions that made their existence possible (Jenkins, 1992; Cairns, 1999) but forms of 'symbolic domination' (cf. Bourdieu, 1991), reflective of material realities, and active constituents in the perpetuation of dominant–subordinate relations. Indeed, as Bourdieu notes, 'symbolic domination' transposes itself into a form of violence that is every bit as insidious as that enacted through more overt techniques. It is, as he suggests, an 'invisible, silent violence', whose power is 'all the more absolute for not having to be stated' (1991, p. 52). While many unionists and Protestants regard the symbolism and trappings of the RUC positively and an important signifier of their identity, for many Catholics the same symbols are an important reminder of their historical exclusion from the Northern Ireland state, and an equally important signifier of the *denial* of their political and cultural identity.

Unfortunately, however, both the RUC hierarchy, and many Unionist politicians, assume a symmetry in the nature of cultural power and its symbolic forms, which is simultaneously atheoretical and ahistorical (Rolston, 1998, pp. 270–72). For example, it would appear that the Chief Constable of the RUC, Ronnie Flanagan, has a rather unreflexive understanding of what constitutes a 'symbol', since he does not regard the widespread display of portraits of the Queen in his police stations as being in conflict with the establishment of a neutral working environment under Northern Ireland's fair employment legislation:

It depends on what you mean by symbols. Certainly there are, in the dining rooms of the RUC, portraits of Her Majesty. I do not think that those can, in any terms be construed as offensive. I do not think that those can, in any terms be construed as offending against a neutral working environment. So those are not what I would describe as symbols. (Northern Ireland Affairs Committee, 1998, p. 33)

This, however, is an argument that McGarry and O'Leary (1999, p. 66) describe as 'preposterous' on the grounds that all other enterprises are obliged to create a neutral working environment under existing legislation. The Chief Constable further argues that issues surrounding the symbolism of the RUC have not featured in research evidence: '... the title of the RUC, the badge and the uniform have not been an issue in research that has been carried out, it would be accepted that the Irish harp, shamrocks and green uniform are as Irish a tradition as one could possibly have'. (Northern Ireland Affairs Committee, 1998, p. 232)

He goes on to consider the role of the flying of the Union flag during the annual Twelfth of July Orange celebrations: '... the flying of the Union flag itself, I cannot see as being offensive. I cannot see that as being at odds with the provision of a neutral working environment' (p. 33). The line of argument expounded by the Chief Constable, and pursued by others, contends that something is either not a symbol at all, as in the case of pictures of the Queen or the Union Jack, or has a unifying function, as in the case of the green uniform or the insignia. Despite these protestations, as will be discussed below, the significance of the symbolic trappings of the RUC is an issue that Catholic respondents to attitudinal surveys feel strongly about.

Similar arguments are gaining currency amongst those commentators sympathetic to the RUC, who are opposed to reform of the force. For example, the PANI consider 'the "Harp and Crown" emblem to be a reasonable and realistic reflection of the two traditions in Northern Ireland,'(PANI, 1998b, p. 53), while David Trimble, writing in the *Sunday Times*, denied that the symbols are political using the rather odd argument that 'The crown is above politics' (12 September 1999). An editorial in the *Daily Telegraph* supporting the opponents of change indulged in a bout of imperial nostalgia complaining plaintively that Patten 'wants to cast away the badge ... which so elegantly combines the British Crown with the Irish Harp' (28 September 1999).

Identity, whether it is class, national or local, is expressed and reinforced through symbols. Within the nation, symbols play a crucial role in condensing socio-economic relations and the symmetry of power from the humble cap-badge of the police constable to the pageantry of a royal wedding. The most potent symbols are those which are seen to stand above internal differences and condense these differences with a lofty finality. Such final instances, such as the law, make profuse use of symbols, often monopolising them for their own use. Symbolic representations of power, place and identity are human constructs and do not, like Athena, spring forth in armour from the head of Zeus. Symbols can be both created from new raw materials, such as political, kinship or economic relations, and from the recasting and appropriation of already existing symbols. National symbols, such as flags, emblems and anthems, once they are in place, can assume an ahistorical and uncontested form as the visual or aural representation of an uncontested reality.

Practically any object, from the humble shamrock (which many might consider a noxious weed) to the majestic Mount Fuji, can be subject to symbolic transformation and inoculated with a complex of meanings, myths and cautions. The purpose of national symbolism is to transcend differences and represent unity, coherence and community. The destruction of symbols can be as historically important as their construction. The tearing-down of the Berlin Wall and the demolition of monuments to communism in eastern Europe are iconic moments of historical change by now embedded in the collective memory. Such moments occur at times of historic change, such as the shooting-out of clocks during the French Revolution and, more prosaically, the removal of the statue of Queen Victoria from the lawn of Leinster House after Irish independence. The use of symbols to represent in a particular way can be challenged, subverted and contested. The harp is probably the symbol most associated with Ireland, yet it expresses not a single uncontested identity and meaning, but one which has a long history of appropriation and reappropriation. The harp on the front cover of the Irish passport has a different symbolic significance and meaning than that on the cap badge of an RUC officer. Under the Flags and Emblems Act, the same officer might have been compelled to remove the flag of the United Irishmen, consisting as it does of a gold harp against a green background – a design startlingly

similar to his own insignia. The fact that many Irish regi-
ments in the British Army display the harp against a green
background is probably the reason why the Irish Army eschews
the use of the harp, not to mention the embarrassing paral-
lels that could be drawn with the insignia of the RIC and the
RUC.

The crowned-harp insignia of the RUC was introduced
after the suppression of the Fenian uprising in 1867, as was
the 'royal' prefix, in gratitude for the central role played by the
police in the defeat of the rebels (Herlihy, 1997, p. 60). Prior
to 1867, the insignia of the Irish Constabulary had been a
crowned shamrock. The symbolic life of the shamrock has been
a chequered one, from being regarded as a vulgar symbol of
the lower orders in the seventeenth century (Sheehy, 1980, p.
10) to its elevation by liberal Protestants in the early nineteenth-
century as the national symbol of Ireland (Hill, 1984, p. 43).
The shamrock was to be incorporated into the official symbolism of the United Kingdom, and on his visit to Ireland in
1821, according to a contemporary newspaper report, George
IV wore a bunch of shamrock. By the time of the Fenian uprising, the shamrock had once again become associated in the
Victorian mind with Irish rebelliousness and the lower orders.
The crowned-harp insignia for the RIC was taken from the
centre of the regalia of the Most Illustrious Order of St. Patrick,
which was inaugurated on St. Patrick's Day 1785, at the height
of the Volunteer agitation (Cullen, 1997, pp. 166–80). The
purpose of the order, and its symbolism, was to integrate the
various factions within Protestant Ireland, Orangeism on one
hand and the Volunteer movement on the other. The British
government was concerned at the aspirations of the Volunteer movement for an independent Irish nation, something
that Catholics were less than happy about, because of the
exclusionary nature of Protestant demands. The government
was equally concerned at the sectarian nature of the Orange
Order and fearful of the effects of the continued exclusion of
Catholics from many areas of life. By the use of typically
'Irish' symbolism, the state hoped to bind Protestants closer
to the Empire, while encouraging a greater regional con-
sciousness and the notion of a particular form of Irish loyalty
to the crown.

Taking the central symbol of the Order of St. Patrick as the
insignia of the RIC was intended to symbolise both the loyalty of the (predominantly Irish and Catholic) RIC to the

Empire and to reappropriate the harp as a symbol which had become increasingly identified with Irish nationalism during the nineteenth century. Ireland's subordinate and loyal place within the United Kingdom was firmly reasserted through the iconography of the RIC insignia. This decision gave a clear signal to nationalists that the harp was subordinate to the crown and countered the increasing use of the harp by nationalists.

Symbols *do* matter. The symbolism of a political movement communicates the nature of the movement, its political agenda, its ideology and the social groups it seeks to mobilise. Symbols also communicate the nature of the society a political movement or party wishes to govern. If a political movement is to embrace political and social change it must be prepared not only to change internally but also express its willingness to change in symbolic form. To attempt to harness sociological change to a redundant system of privilege and authority is the road to disaster, as the case of the British Conservative Party vividly demonstrates (McKibben, 1999). Symbols can themselves become fictions representing no more than the pretence of legitimacy, the pompous façade for a discredited regime unwilling to accept the reality of change (for a discussion of symbolism in Nazi Germany, see Conrad, 1998, pp. 477–99). The obsession of unionists with the trappings of the RUC can perhaps be best grasped in Freudian terms as a displacement activity triggered by the inability to face up to the necessity for far-reaching and fundamental change to the governance of Northern Ireland.

Public Attitudinal Surveys and the Manufacture of Consent

Public attitudinal survey data has an important role to play in the construction of police legitimacy, and police managers have historically used survey data to demonstrate the high regard in which the British police held by the public (Brogden, 1982). The interpretation of survey data consistently demonstrates that the British police are as favourably regarded by the public as occupational groups such as nurses, and institutions such the National Health Service. However, the use of survey data as a means of assessing attitudes to the police needs to be treated with considerable caution since there is a residual core of opinion that never filters into such studies. The opinions of marginalised groups, traditionally defined as 'police property' (Lee, 1981), such as the young, the unemployed, the homeless and minorities of all sorts, are usually excluded, intentionally or otherwise, from survey research.

The conflict in Northern Ireland has generated its own micro-industry in opinion poll surveys, with government departments, private consultancy firms, academic research centres and the mass media surveying attitudes towards every conceivable aspect of social, political and cultural life in Northern Ireland. In the wake of the Patten Report, the issue of cross-community acceptability of the RUC has become an ideological battlefield with attitudinal surveys as the principal ammunition. The British government, the Northern Ireland Office, the Northern Ireland Police Authority and Unionist politicians have all deployed survey data to depict the RUC as a legitimate force that enjoys a broad base of cross-community support. On the other hand, nationalist and republican commentators interpret data – often from the same survey – to depict the RUC as illegitimate, sectarian and politically partial.

It would be impossible to review all the opinion poll data amassed during the last twenty years in connection with the RUC. Even if such an exercise were possible, there are multiple problems concerning the reliability and validity of some surveys (Ellison, 2000; Brogden, 1997). For example, an internal survey conducted by the RUC in 1993 indicated a public satisfaction rate with the force of over 90 per cent. However, on closer inspection it appears that the data is derived from those individuals – or given the managerialist turn in RUC discourse, 'customers'[1] – who have initiated contact with the police in the first instance, and excludes the opinions of those who may have had hostile or adversarial encounters.

Studies that seek to elicit public attitudes towards the RUC fall into four categories: those conducted by the RUC themselves; those conducted by market research organisations for newspapers (for example, the *Belfast Telegraph,* the *Irish News*); those conducted by government agencies (for example, the PANI); and finally those conducted by government departments but which are subsequently assessed by academics, for example, the Northern Ireland Social Attitudes Survey (NISAS).

The following section will provide a thematic overview of main survey evidence conducted in recent years in connection with public attitudes to the RUC. This will be preceded by a discussion of some methodological and other problems inherent in attitudinal surveys generally (Brogden, 1982) which are further compounded in conflict situations such as Northern Ireland (Brogden, 1997; Ellison, 2000; Guelke and Wright, 1992; McGarry and O'Leary, 1999; Weitzer, 1995).

The Under-representation of Certain Forms of Opinion

Brogden (1982) highlights the extent to which surveys aimed at evaluating attitudes to the police tend to overstate 'moderate' opinion. In Northern Ireland, attitudinal surveys evince a similar tendency. For example, two surveys based on the Northern Ireland Social Attitudes Survey data (NISAS), which examined communal attitudes to the RUC (Brewer, 1992) and the security forces generally (Breen, 1995), are characterised by a demonstrable under-representation of 'strong' or 'radical' opinion. Respondents who express a political preference for Sinn Féin (and also the Democratic Unionist Party) are clearly under-represented in contrast with those who express a political preference for the 'moderate' Alliance Party (Guelke and Wright, 1992; Ellison, 2000). In the 1992 NISAS data, the percentage of respondents who indicated a political preference for Sinn Féin is listed at 2.8 per cent, whereas this party has never polled less than 10 per cent of the total vote in Northern Ireland (see Guelke and Smyth, 1992). In fact, during the 1997 Westminster election, Sinn Féin polled 16.1 per cent of the total Northern Ireland vote and approximately 40 per cent of the combined nationalist vote. A similar discrepancy can be seen in the 1995 NISAS sample, wherein the percentage of Sinn Féin respondents is listed at 3.9 per cent.

There is no clear correlation between political support for Sinn Féin and support for Republican paramilitary organisations, since as Guelke and Smyth (1992) point out, support for the IRA military campaign is often extremely problematic and conditional. However, the under-representation of the views of Sinn Féin supporters invariably distorts the data and the interpretations and conclusions that can be derived from it. This is particularly pertinent in the case of policing, since

Sinn Féin supporters are the group *most* likely to hold negative attitudes towards the RUC, and consequently those *most*
likely to call for the disbandment of the force. As a consequence,
some correction of the NISAS data should be undertaken to
more accurately reflect political and constitutional opinion
by voting intention.

The surveys conducted by Northern Ireland Police Authority
(PANI, 1996, 1997, 1998a) have been among the most comprehensive and wide-ranging to be conducted in Northern Ireland
in recent years. While displaying a commendable attention to
detail in many respects, they none the less contain an equivalent distortion, this time on the basis of socio-economic status.
The data deployed by PANI contains an over-representation of
respondents from professional/administrative occupational
categories, and an under-representation of respondents from
'manual' backgrounds, although this is most marked for those
individuals classifying themselves as 'unskilled manual'. In the
1995 survey (PANI, 1996), the proportion of 'unskilled manual'
Catholic respondents represents 58 actual cases out of out of
a total sample of 987 (5.8 per cent). Similarly, in the Protestant sample, the 'unskilled manual' category represents 87 actual
cases out of a total sample of 1571 (5.5 per cent). This occupational category has historically borne the brunt of sectoral
restructuring in Northern Ireland economy and the resulting
high levels of unemployment, with male unemployment in
urban working-class districts of Belfast approaching 70 per cent
(Cebulla and Smyth, 1996).

The discrepancies in the PANI data have the following
effects. First, in terms of surveying 'Catholic' attitudes to the
RUC, the over-representation of Catholics in non-manual
occupational categories – particularly those in the professional/
administrative sector – means that we are essentially analys-
ing the views of 'moderate' SDLP voters, who are more likely
to favour 'reform' than disbandment of the RUC. Thus, it is
reasonable to assume that were the sample adjusted to more
accurately reflect the percentage of respondents in 'manual'
occupational categories, the overall percentage favouring 'disbandment' would also increase, given that this group forms
the bulwark of Sinn Féin support in working-class urban, and
rural small-farming communities. While PANI data provides
incontrovertible evidence – consistent across five surveys –
of an overwhelming level of general Catholic dissatisfaction
with the RUC, the distortions in the sample mean that the

extent of alienation between working-class nationalists and the RUC is obscured (see PANI, 1996, 1997, 1998a). Indeed, in reflecting the views of moderate nationalists, the PANI data provides definitive evidence to counter RUC and unionist suggestions that antipathy to the RUC is confined to a small but vocal minority in the republican movement.

Finally, the distortions in the PANI data raise a number of questions in relation to the RUC's relationship with working-class loyalists. In recent years, the political representatives of fringe loyalist parties have highlighted the often problematic and frequently hostile relationship between the RUC and working-class Protestants, a position which is also given limited expression in survey data (see O'Mahony et al., 1997; McVeigh 1994). Due to the under-representation of respondents in manual-occupational categories, the PANI data might actually underestimate this alienation, and the degree to which loyalists wish to see the RUC reformed or disbanded. This point will be considered later in the chapter but it is sufficient to note here that a variant of this argument has been increasingly adopted by both the RUC and Unionist politicians as evidence of the force's impartiality (that is, that Protestant and Catholic heads are now 'bashed' equally). Leaving aside the somewhat dubious issue of whether the RUC does in fact deal impartially with loyalist and nationalist dissent (Cairns, 1999, pp. 200–17), it is a rather curious barometer of legitimacy that depends on the ability to antagonise both sides of the community in equal measure.

Conducting Opinion Poll Surveys in a Divided Society

The exaggeration of 'moderate' opinion in the NISAS and PANI survey data reflects a general tendency, but one which is undoubtedly exacerbated by the difficulties in conducting survey research in a divided society such as Northern Ireland. Murray (1995, p. 218) estimates that over half the population of Northern Ireland lives in areas that are virtually homogeneous (90 per cent or above) in terms of ethno-religious composition. Indeed, one effect of the conflict has been to reinforce a sense of intra-group solidarity and an inherent suspicion of outsiders (Donnan and McFarlane 1983). For opinion poll researchers, it is notoriously difficult to penetrate these tightly-knit communities, particularly when the aim is to elicit responses to questions that have a controversial or sensitive theme, such as those in connection with policing, security or constitutional matters (McGarry and O'Leary, 1999, pp. 16–17). Indeed, until relatively recently, it would have been extremely difficult for respondents to express open support for Sinn Féin, given the demonisation of the party in sections of the media.

Similarly, those respondents living in staunchly nationalist or republican areas may feel that survey data – in spite of the best assurances and intentions of the researcher – will not be kept confidential, and might, accidentally or otherwise, find its way into the hands of the security forces for low-level intelligence gathering purposes. (This is particularly evident in respect of the allegations of collusion discussed in Chapter Eight.) This was the case during the data-collection phase of the Northern Ireland Omnibus survey (NISRA), when researchers were physically prevented from distributing the questionnaire in a staunchly republican district of Derry. Similarly, one of the authors (Ellison) was advised during the piloting of a questionnaire to examine the participation of local youth and community groups in RUC-sponsored community relations initiatives, that a response from organisations with a predominantly Catholic membership could only be guaranteed if it was stated clearly and unequivocally in a covering letter that the study had no RUC or Northern Ireland Office (NIO) involvement (see Ellison, 2000).

A further problem arises from the tendency to recruit researchers from middle-class backgrounds who may be unwilling to enter areas thought of as 'dangerous' and the unwillingness of those managing the surveys to deal with this issue.

The Language of Surveys

There are problems with the terminology or language used in attitudinal surveys. It is not the case that policing in Northern Ireland – or arguably anywhere else for that matter – exists in an ontological void, untainted by the complex web of social, historical and political factors that give it existence. Thus, the very notion of what policing *is* means something very different to the communities that experience it. In broad terms, this may simply reflect the congruence between social inequalities and traditional police prejudices which range across cleavages of gender, age, social class and race. In Northern Ireland, this problem is compounded by the realities of the political situation, whereby due to the (very real) threat of attack in republican areas, on-the-ground policing has historically been conducted in a much more paramilitaristic fashion than perhaps otherwise would have been the case. This is not to imply that the RUC would be acceptable in republican areas if they were somehow to normalise their role, and indeed there is considerable evidence to the contrary. It is to suggest, however, that republican communities have historically got the *force* without the *service*, and that it is this that governs the reality and experience of policing in such areas.

Opinion polls, by their very nature, treat problematic categories (such as policing) unproblematically. Or expressed another way, particularistic discourses of policing are assumed to have a universal application in attitudinal surveys. Clearly, however, even something as notionally benign as 'community policing' *is* experienced differentially across Northern Ireland. From the tree-lined suburbs of South Belfast, to the economic wasteland of West Belfast, local (or 'community') policing assumes a range of divergent and contradictory meanings. One example will serve to illustrate. A common question in the PANI surveys asks, 'Are you satisfied with the performance of your local police?' This apparently straightforward question could elicit a similar response from someone living in a middle-class suburb *and* in a staunchly republican area, albeit for different reasons. In the former case, the respondent answers in the affirmative because the localised nature of the conflict has meant that in many areas of Northern Ireland the RUC have been able to develop a community-orientated role. As such, the individual may be more than happy with the service provided by the force. On the other hand, the respondent from the republican area may also answer in the affirmative because mistrust of the RUC in such areas makes the relative lack of a routine on-the-ground presence itself a cause for satisfaction. In other words, while the responses are recorded similarly, the meanings and intentions that underpin them are *qualitatively* different and informed by highly discordant notions of what policing is, or is seen to represent. Again, such nuances are rarely teased out in quantitative attitudinal surveys.

Reading the Survey Results: a Heretical View

The interpretation of survey data on the RUC tends to focus on a number of issues regarding their acceptability and the need for reform. The Patten Report did not elaborate on the problems inherent in survey data (Patten Report, 1999, pp. 13–17) but did complement the available data with its own research, which included surveys, focus groups, public and private meetings and written submissions. The report confined itself to summarising the results of both the available evidence and its own research, concluding that 'perceptions and experiences of policing can differ greatly between the two communities' (p. 13). Those opposed to the proposals for reform put forward in the report focused upon an interpretation of the survey evidence that might be seen to undermine the argument for reform. Four main areas were targeted: that there is no public support for reform of the RUC, that the majority of people are satisfied with the performance of the RUC, that there is a large base of 'hidden' support for the RUC and that changing the symbols and emblems of the RUC is not an issue. The remainder of this chapter is devoted to an examination of these issues in the light of survey evidence.

'There is no public support for reforming the RUC'

This argument is patently false and does not square with recent survey evidence. The data in Table 9.1 illustrates that an overwhelming majority of Catholic respondents across five separate PANI surveys believe that the RUC should be 'reformed',

Table 9.1: The Future of the RUC – Catholic

Future of RUC (%)	1995	1996	1997a	1997b	1998
Carry on as now	28	13	11	18	15
Reformed	38	46	52	42	48
Replaced	31	32	29	33	31
Disbanded	1	4	5	2	3
DK/Refusal	2	5	4	4	1

Source: Police Authority for Northern Ireland, 1998b

Note: 1997a and 1997b refer to surveys conducted in February and October respectively.

'replaced' or 'disbanded'. This rose from 70 per cent in 1995, to 86 per cent in the February 1997 survey, falling slightly to 82 per cent in 1998. The pattern across each survey is indisputable and consistent: only a minority of Catholic respondents are in favour allowing the RUC to 'carry on as now', and as McGarry and O'Leary (1999, p. 17) acknowledge, '… these opinions are not merely snapshots but reflections of durable attitudes.'

Admittedly, the percentage of Catholic respondents favouring 'disbandment' of the RUC is low across each year cohort. However, there may be two explanations for this. First, it may be the result of the confusing terminology employed in the survey, since it is not altogether clear (to us anyway) in what way 'replace' differs from 'disband' in any practical sense. Second, as we have already seen, the PANI surveys suffer from an under-representation of working-class Catholic opinion whose political vocabulary, and support for Sinn Féin might lead them to favour the latter term. The evidence from Protestant respondents demonstrates a strikingly divergent picture and illustrates the extent to which views on policing are fractured along lines of inter-group cleavage. An overwhelming majority of those surveyed are in favour allowing the RUC to 'carry on as now' (Table 9.2).

Table 9.2: The Future of the RUC – Protestant

Future of RUC (%)	1995	1996	1997a	1997b	1998
Carry on as now	71	61	68	70	65
Reformed	23	32	26	25	30
Replaced	4	4	4	3	4
Disbanded	0	0	0	0	0
DK/Refusal	1	2	2	2	2

Source: Police Authority for Northern Ireland (1998b)

Note: 1997a and 1997b refer to surveys conducted in February and October respectively.

A minority of respondents in each year cohort favours some element of 'reform' to the RUC. However, since quantitative responses rarely reflect the subtleties in the underlying meanings that people attach to them, it may be that 'reform' for the majority of Protestant respondents simply equates to increasing Catholic representation in such a way that does not involve major structural or institutional changes to the force. Of course, this is not to imply that members of the Protestant community accept the RUC uncritically, and as we have seen, there is some evidence to suggest that the relationship between working-class loyalists and the RUC is problematic (McVeigh, 1994; O'Mahony et al., 1997). None the less, we contend that Protestant criticism of the RUC relates to specific practices such as, for example, the re-routing of controversial Orange marches and demonstrations. Indeed, we are deeply sceptical of the extent to which Protestant support for the RUC as an *institution* has declined (McGarry and O'Leary, 1999; Ellison, 2000). Survey research conducted by Ellison in 1993 and 1995 (see Ellison, 2000) found little evidence to indicate that working-class loyalist alienation from the RUC was a salient issue, with an overwhelming majority of respondents from predominantly (working-class) Protestant youth and community organisations stating that they would like to establish closer links with the force (Table 9.3).[2] Similar findings were discerned by the PANI in their quantitative and focus-group studies, and as they suggest 'working-class Protestant are the strongest of all groups in their expressed preferences for the police service to be allowed to carry on as it is' (PANI, 1998b, p. 36). Interestingly, the data in Table 9.3 corroborates the extent of inter-group polarisation evidenced from the PANI surveys, with an overwhelming majority of working-class Catholic respondents indicating a high level of alienation from the RUC.

Table 9.3: Whether organisation would like closer links with RUC Community Affairs Branch

1993 (%)	Working-class Protestant	Working-class Catholic
Yes	90	16
No	4	84
Don't Know	6	–
1995 (%)	Working-class Protestant	Working-class Catholic
Yes	90	12
No	5	82
Don't Know	5	6

Source: Ellison, 2000

Table 9.4: Proportions of Catholics and Protestants choosing certain words or phrases to describe the RUC during Focus-Group research

Word or Phrase	% of Catholics	% of Protestants
Community-oriented	4	10
Open	2	12
Neutral	0	14
Honest	2	14
Caring	4	12
Kind	4	12
One of us	2	14
Acceptable	0	24
Easy to deal with	4	21
Trustworthy	2	24
Professional	7	21
Representative	4	24
Honourable	0	29
Helpful	2	29
Fair	2	31
Dedicated	7	31
Loyal	27	21
Open to change	29	24
Old-fashioned	44	26
Hard	58	29
Black	71	19
Orange	78	17
Tough	69	45
Bigoted	82	31
Biased	80	43
Bullies	78	45
Protestant	82	41
Aggressive	84	43
Part of the problem	84	45
Well paid	84	88

Source: PANI, 1998b

The extent to which Protestant and Catholic views on the RUC polarise along lines of inter-group cleavage are given further substantiation in the focus-group research conducted by the PANI to supplement the quantitative studies. For instance, Table 9.4, illustrates that Protestant respondents are more likely to use words and phrases such as 'one of us', 'neutral', 'professional' and 'acceptable' to describe the RUC, with Catholic respondents, choosing 'black' (a derogatory term used to describe Protestants), 'orange', 'old-fashioned', 'biased' and 'bigoted'.

'There is a broad spectrum of approval for the RUC's handling of ordinary crime'

The data in Table 9.5 demonstrates that an overwhelming majority of Protestant respondents rate the performance of their local police highly in relation to a range of policing issues. For Catholic respondents, a slight majority in each survey (with the exception of October 1997) also rate the performance of their local police as 'very/fairly good'. What the survey data is reflecting is a degree of consensus between the two communities in Northern Ireland in their desire for a local police service dealing with a range of *quality of life* issues. However, if we aggregate the PANI data from Table 9.1 and Table 9.5, it is clear that there exists an overlap between those Catholic respondents who are generally satisfied with the performance of the RUC, but who *also* express a desire to have the force reformed or restructured. We need to be cautious therefore, about making unilateral generalisations about levels of support for one aspect of the RUC's role, and equating this with more widespread or general patterns of support and acceptability, since there is abundant sociological evidence that the police are viewed within a broader frame of understanding than their interpersonal skills, level of politeness or ability to respond to emergency calls (Ericson and Heggarty, 1997; Brogden, 1999). In other words, the fact that the RUC respond to an emergency call within the allocated ten minutes, or are polite to a speeding motorist, cannot reconcile the fundamental crisis of confidence that exists between the nationalist community and the RUC, and is unlikely to be assuaged in terms of a managerialist emphasis on 'quality of service'. Indeed, this would appear to be supported in the conclusion of the Patten Report, which states:

'For a significant number of Protestants, support for the RUC as an institution may be expressed more strongly than satisfaction with the delivery of a local police service; while for some Catholics the local police service may be satisfactory even if they have misgivings about the wider role of the police or about the RUC as an institution'. (p. 13)

Table 9.5: Performance of local police by community background (1996–98)

Rating (%)	Protestant				Catholic			
	1996	1997a	1997b	1998	1996	1997a	1997b	1998
Very/Fairly good	77	72	78	75	55	44	55	57
Neither good nor bad	10	11	11	15	17	22	17	21
Very/Fairly poor	12	15	9	9	25	32	25	19
DK/Refusal	1	2	1	1	3	1	3	3

Source: Police Authority for Northern Ireland (1998b)

Note: 1997a and 1997b refer to surveys conducted in February and October respectively.

'The RUC has a base of hidden support'

Throughout the conflict, the RUC, PANI and the Northern Ireland Office (NIO) have gone to considerable lengths to highlight the extent to which the RUC have enjoyed a base of 'hidden', or what can be termed 'behind-closed-doors support' (see also Mulcahy, 2000). This extent of this 'hidden' support is often recounted anecdotally, as the following transcript from an RUC officer illustrates:

If you look at it from the perspective of a foot patrol walking along the Falls road I would say that by and large the public would greet them [the RUC] with ambivalence, a reluctant acceptance. But a lot of the same people would deal with them behind closed doors and you get a totally different attitude. They are more wary of others seeing them talking to us. Therefore, we can get on well behind closed doors – and I can understand them being afraid – there are people who are looking and watching us and so on. There is always that cloud of intimidation hanging over people in this area. (cited in Ellison, 1997, p. 202)

The argument that the RUC has a base of 'hidden' support continues to be advanced in opposition to the recommendations of the Patten Report, and for this reason warrants some further discussion here. While the 'hidden' support argument is, in social-scientific terms, empirically unverifiable (that is, because of its very 'hiddenness'), it also contains a logical flaw. The basic proposition is that people (generally nationalists) express public hostility to the RUC, but 'behind closed doors' declare their support. However, in a purely logical sense, the converse proposition is equally true: that nationalists can express public support for the RUC, but in the privacy of their own homes express hostility. Each proposition is as valid as the other, and while we do not intend this to be a facetious point, senior RUC officers and unionist commentators cannot claim validity in the first proposition without also admitting the equal validity of the second.

The reasons why such support should be 'hidden' in the first place deserve some consideration. The need to base a claim to legitimacy in terms of 'hidden' support, is at best suggestive of a level of mistrust, and at worst, a fundamental crisis of confidence, between the nationalist community and the RUC. However, this is rarely acknowledged in official statements, with the preferred explanation being that nationalists are intimidated – by republican paramilitary organisations – from expressing their outright support for the RUC, a factor which is also invoked to explain their reluctance to join the force. Of course, there can be no doubt that intimidation is a factor in dissuading nationalists and Catholics from joining the RUC (McGarry and O'Leary, 1999, p. 17). However, the problem here, and one that McGarry and O'Leary acknowledge, is that senior RUC officers, Unionist politicians, and official commentators, have tended to emphasise it as the *only* factor. However, survey data submitted by the RUC to the Northern Ireland Select Committee indicates that intimidation is only *one* of a number of explanations cited by Catholics for their refusal to join the force. As McGarry and O'Leary suggest:

The survey does show that significant proportions of Catholics pick reasons in addition to (or instead of) republican intimidation when explaining why Catholics do not join the police. Thus 30 per cent list their opposition to the system of government; 22 per cent think that they would be badly treated in the police; while 44 per cent list community 'pressure' as another reason (that is political and social norms as opposed to intimidation). (1999, pp. 14–15)

Similarly, in research conducted with youth and community organisations (Ellison, 1997), 'intimidation' was cited by only a minority of Catholic respondents as a principal reason for not wishing to participate in RUC-sponsored community relations programmes (Table 9.6). Other factors concerning nationalist alienation from the force, 'harassment', and the belief that such schemes were 'PR for the RUC' all ranked more strongly.

Table 9.6: Principal reason for not wishing to participate in RUC-sponsored Community Relations schemes

Reason for non-participation (Catholic)	%
Harassment by RUC in this area	9
Schemes are PR for RUC	20
RUC do not reflect nationalist interests	35
Have never been asked to participate	15
Afraid of paramilitary threat	5
RUC have hidden agenda	9
Community Relations Programmes are a waste of time	5
Other Reason	2

Source: Ellison, 1997

Citing intimidation as the principal factor in dissuading young nationalists to join the RUC also assumes that they would flock to do so in the absence of a (republican) paramilitary threat. However, as McGarry and O'Leary point out: 'Catholics have not joined the RUC in large numbers at any time, even when there was relatively little or no republican violence, and even when there were no effective republican organisations that could have successfully intimidated them. Indeed, as they suggest, 'emphasising "intimidation" as the primary explanation of Catholic and nationalist dispositions towards the RUC is simply not convincing' (1999, p. 16). In support of this, the authors cite figures provided by the human rights organisation, the Pat Finucane Centre, to show that by 1969 the percentage of Catholic officers in the RUC had stabilised at 10 per cent, during a period when the threat from the IRA was virtually non-existent (see Buckland, 1979, pp. 108–110). If this figure is compared to the current one of approximately 7.5 per cent, then the IRA has at most succeeded in intimidating a total of 2.5 per cent of Catholics from joining the RUC (McGarry and O'Leary, 1999, p. 125).

'The cultural symbolism of the RUC is an issue that Catholics do not feel strongly about'

Sir John Wheeler, the Northern Ireland Security Minister under the previous Conservative administration, argued that the issues surrounding the cultural symbolism of the RUC were 'of marginal interest, largely irrelevant to most people' (*Irish Times*, 2 May 1996). However, as McGarry and O'Leary quite rightly ask, 'If these matters are trivial then why is so much time and energy devoted to opposing trivial changes?' (1999, p. 66). As noted above, both the Chief Constable, Sir Ronnie Flanagan, and the Superintendents' Association, have consistently argued that they do not regard the symbolism of the RUC to be a barrier to Catholic recruitment, nor to pose any problems for how nationalists and Catholics view the force.

Certainly, the research evidence on the issue is problematic. The 1995 PANI survey data showed a slight majority of Catholic respondents (51 per cent) to be happy with the name: 'Royal Ulster Constabulary' (PANI, 1996). However, as we noted above the PANI data tends to suffer from an over-representation of 'moderate' opinion, so this figure might need to be interpreted with some caution. None the less, while they do not provide any figures, the PANI acknowledge in their 1998 Report that changing the RUC's name, 'is an issue on which public opinion is sharply divided' (1998b, p. 51). Other research evidence, however, does indicate that the issue of the RUC's symbolism is a salient one for the Catholic community. For example, McGarry and O'Leary cite the Opsahl Commission, who reported that the '"failure" of a "Crown" police to shake off the symbols of the unionist state appeared time and time again as an explanation of Catholics' reluctance to join the RUC' (1999, p. 67). They also cite the results of a survey conducted by the Fortnight Educational Trust, whereby:

... 77 per cent of Catholics thought that it was either 'essential' (59 per cent) or 'desirable' (18 per cent) that the RUC be given a new name, and a mere 3–4 per cent of Catholics found this idea 'unacceptable'. Moreover, 76 per cent of Catholics thought that it was either 'essential' (58 per cent) or 'desirable' (18 per cent) that the police be given new emblems and symbols, while only 4 per cent found this to be unacceptable. (McGarry and O'Leary, 1999, p. 67)

Conclusions

The practice and symbolic form of policing acts as a marker of social relations and cultural values, and serves as a convenient shorthand for a matrix of social and institutional relations and subjectivities within the state (Mulcahy, 1998). It seems logical to accept the proposition that, in order to inspire confidence across the whole community, the new police force of Northern Ireland (whatever it might be called) needs to shed its overwhelming identification with one section of society, and in particular shed its unionist and British cultural and symbolic trappings. Although the modification of the symbolism of the RUC is itself important, measures must also be taken to neutralise an occupational culture which is solidly unionist in nature, since this too is likely to form a significant barrier to Catholic recruitment to, and acceptance of, any new force.

While the occupational culture of the RUC would appear to be little different to that found in other police forces, containing elements of machismo, secrecy, prejudice, cynicism, homophobia, moral conservatism, and so on, it also incorporates a strongly unionist ethos (Brewer and Magee, 1991; Ellison, 1994, 1997; Mulcahy, 1998). In an analysis of the social attitudes of part-time members of the RUC (that is, those in the full- and part-time Reserve), Mapstone suggests that his research results 'reveal a predominantly Protestant part-time force that closely resembles the Protestant population in its social attitudes' (1992, p. 183). This is evidenced in terms of issues surrounding law and order, sentencing policy, community attitudes, social issues, religion, friendship networks and national identity. He also makes the point that Catholic officers in the part-time RUCR (of which there are approximately 3.8 per cent), generally display social attitudes that are 'more in congruence with the wider occupational culture of the RUC' than that of the Catholic community in general' (p. 192). An exception to this is 'support' for the law, which Mapstone suggests is higher among Catholic officers and rather more conditional among their Protestant colleagues. Just over half (52 per cent) of Mapstone's sample of Protestant officers agreed with the contention that the 'law should be obeyed even when it is wrong', with the remainder implying that 'certain laws which necessitate police action being directed at Protestants are wrong' (p. 189). David Miller (1978) has highlighted this well-documented feature of unionism (and loyalism), which he terms the 'conditional loyalty' of Ulster unionists to the British state. In terms of the effect that the occupational culture may have on Catholic recruitment into the RUC, Mapstone argues that 'the organisational culture of the part-time RUC means that Catholic recruitment is limited to those who are prepared to subscribe to a set of values often apparently irreconcilable with those of the Catholic community at large' (1992, p. 192).

An internal and confidential RUC survey (subsequently leaked to the press) assessing the extent of religious and political harassment within the force, indicated that almost two-thirds (63 per cent) of the Catholic sample of officers claimed to have been subjected to religious and political harassment within the organisation. As the report states:

> The most common form of religious/political harassment experienced by both communities was sectarian jokes, banter or sectarian songs, with 258 (92 per cent) Roman Catholic respondents who had been harassed and 221 (64 per cent) Protestant respondents stating that they had experienced this on one or more occasion. Of the other less common forms of harassment reported, more Roman Catholics than Protestants reported experiencing inappropriate displays of flags and emblems, displays of sectarian posters, graffiti, circulation of sectarian notes, letters, and isolation from work.[3]

Recent government reports on policing in Northern Ireland, for example, the Northern Ireland Select Committee's *Composition, Recruitment and Training of the RUC* (1998), make the mistake of regarding the relationship between nationalists and the RUC to be a mirror-image of that which exists between members of minority groups in Britain (particularly the Afro-Caribbean community) and the British police, where the solution to the problem of police racism is seen to lie with enhanced training in the form of racial awareness programmes.

Whatever the efficacy of these programmes in a British context, and there is considerable evidence to suggest that their
effectiveness is limited (Brogden et al., 1988; Brogden and
Shearing, 1993; Bull and Horncastle, 1986), it is clear the crisis of confidence between nationalists and the RUC is unlikely
to be assuaged by similar cultural awareness programmes.

The crisis of confidence between the nationalist community and the RUC is a fundamental one, and far more critical
than that which exists between the British police and members
of ethnic minority groups. The terminology used to describe
the population balance in Northern Ireland by ethno-religious
cleavage – generally depicted in terms of a majority–minority
dichotomy – obscures the fact that in demographic terms the
Catholic/nationalist community is hardly constitutive of a simple minority, representing between 41 per cent and 43 per
cent of the *total* Northern Ireland population (McGarry and
O'Leary, 1995, p. 503). There is no comparison between the
situation in Northern Ireland, where almost half the population is reluctant to engage normatively with the police, and
the situation in Britain or elsewhere within the European
Community.

Indeed, to put the focus of reform on 'attitudes' may inadvertently reinforce the idea (common to police managers) that
the organisational deviance that may arise as a consequence of
such attitudes is an essentially rank-and-file problem confined
to the lower ranks of the organisation, while the organisational
structure itself remains basically sound (and consequently
unexamined). In this context, Steytler (1990) is dismissive of
those accounts of policing that seek to lay the blame for
organisational deviance at the lowest level of the occupation, and which single out the occupational culture of the
rank and file for particular attention. He argues that the beliefs
and values of police officers are not antithetical to political
ideology but reflective of it. In this sense, the occupational
culture of the rank and file perpetuates dominant social structures, and can only be understood in relation to the political
discourse, organisational policy and legal framework within
which the police operate.

10 Epilogue: The Patten Report on the RUC

The Good Friday Agreement, which was intended to form the basis for a political settlement in Northern Ireland, did not directly address the problem of policing but recognised its centrality in general terms:

> The participants recognise that policing is a central issue in any society. They equally recognise that Northern Ireland's history of deep division has made it highly emotive ... They believe that the agreement provides the opportunity for a new beginning to policing in Northern Ireland with a police service capable of attracting and sustaining support from the community as a whole. (Good Friday Agreement, 1998, p. 22)

Under the terms of the agreement, a Commission was set up, under the chairmanship of Chris Patten (one-time government minister in Northern Ireland and last Governor of Hong Kong) to inquire into policing in Northern Ireland and to make recommendations for 'future policing structures and arrangements'. Effectively, the thorny question of policing was kicked into the long grass, as it was perhaps feared that any agreement on policing structures would have been impossible within the context of the protracted and torturous negotiations leading to the signing of the agreement. Indeed, it is a contention of this book that policing goes to the heart of the conflict in Ireland and is a more contentious issue for both nationalists and unionists than for the same groups in the century or so prior to partition, due to the blatantly sectarian nature of the Stormont state and the role of the RUC as direct agents of unionist power. The role of the RUC, particularly after 1974, as the cutting edge of the counter-insurgency campaign against the IRA, has intensified and emotionalised the situation. The majority community views the RUC as the 'thin green line' protecting them from the Armageddon of a united Ireland and the end of their way of life, while the minority tends to see the police as an instrument of state repression. The emotive dimension of attitudes on both sides cannot be over-estimated. The number of policemen and women killed and injured during the last thirty years of conflict, most of whom were Protestants, makes that community deeply suspicious of any attempts, however minor, to tinker with 'their' police. On the nationalist side, particularly in working-class and rural areas, the police enjoy very qualified support and acceptance. It is clear that any reform of policing can only take place in the context of a wider settlement, and that even then, it will be a deeply contentious and divisive issue.

The terms of reference of the Patten Commission were sufficiently general to allow radical recommendations for change, short of disbandment, to be brought forward and contained a mechanism within the terms of reference that 'The commission should consult widely, including with non-governmental expert organisations, and through such focus groups as they consider it appropriate to establish' (Good Friday Agreement, p. 24). This allowed the commission to widen the debate on policing beyond the restrictive and restricted context which had existed hitherto. The commission decided, as the centrepiece of the consultative exercise, to embark upon a series of public meetings to gauge attitudes towards the RUC and policing in general. This decision had interesting implications since, for the first time, attitudes towards the RUC could be assessed in an immediate and localised manner, offering an alternative to the plethora of attitude surveys, the carrying-out and interpretation of which has become both a mini-academic industry and an ideological battlefield.

The Public Meetings

Central to the policy of normalisation and criminalisation is the contention that only a small minority of people were behind the violence and the 'vast majority' of people support the police in their efforts to eradicate terrorism. The selective use of survey results is used to bolster this contention which, until the 'Armalite and ballot box' strategy of Sinn Féin in the early 1980s was made that much easier by the refusal of republicans to participate in the electoral process leaving the argument that Sinn Féin enjoyed little popular support free and uncontested passage. The continued success of Sinn Féin in elections exposed the weakness of this approach and shifted the argument on police acceptability to increasingly arcane attempts to 'prove' that most members of the minority supported the RUC and to explain away the reluctance of Catholics to join the RUC in any numbers as a result of intimidation and coercion.

The core of this argument is a rejection of the divided-society model of Northern Ireland which would postulate that the main faultlines of division lie along cultural or ethnic boundaries rather than class, age or other familiar sociological categories. According to the divided-society approach, the main cleavage on security issues is between the two communities, a cleavage which overrides the divisions within the two ethnic groups.

The approach of the RUC, the Police Authority and unionists is to insist that, for all intents and purposes, Northern Ireland is a normal society which unfortunately has a problem with a tiny minority of terrorists. Giving evidence to the hearings of the House of Commons Northern Ireland Affairs Committee in 1998 both the Chief Constable and the Chairman of the Police Authority made extensive use of surveys to bolster the contention that the people of Northern Ireland had a 'normal' attitude towards policing despite the threat of terrorism and that the low number of Catholics in the RUC was a result of intimidation and coercion from the same terrorists.

The Chief Constable was firm and unambiguous in asserting that the major reason, which overrode all others, why Catholics do not join the RUC was 'the fear of violence that would be offered towards them and indeed towards members of their families' (Northern Ireland Affairs Committee, 1998, p. 31). Although the Chief Constable admitted that there were other 'inhibiting factors' – about which he did not elaborate further – he asserted that these factors had little salience in influencing a decision not to join the RUC. This is a position to which the Chief Constable has tenaciously held, as, for example, in an interview in October 1997: 'When asked about improving the balance of the religious make up of the force, the Chief Constable said the greatest barrier stopping Catholic applications was the threat of violence' (*Belfast Telegraph*, 23 October 1999).

The Chairman of the Police Authority, under more intensive and critical questioning from the Committee, was more ambiguous, if not contradictory in his replies. While admitting

that 'there was no reliable evidence' on which to base a judge-
ment as to why Catholics would not join the police and
admitting that survey evidence was of limited value, the PANI
representatives expounded a discourse which denied the possibility that there might be widespread Catholic disenchantment
with the RUC. This discourse follows a well-established pattern. Central is the introduction of evidence of normality, of a
majority of people going about their business and expressing
concerns about the mundane everyday problems of crime and
policing and showing little interest in the role and practice of
the police as a counter-insurgency force. The chairman of
PANI interpreted the results of the Authority's Community
Consultation Report of 1995 as endorsing an implied state
of normality:

> The main concerns of the people of Northern Ireland in relation to
> policing and crime were that it is the ordinary policing issues which
> exercise their minds most in the total policing scene. All right, we have
> terrorism and we have to have regard to that, but the people in the
> survey were more concerned about burglary, about the traffic in drugs
> and about traffic accidents ... (PANI, 1998a, p. 49)

The chairman of the Police Authority, in responding to further questions from the same MP, swiftly moved to consolidate
the impression of normality and consent: '... with regard to
the perceptions of policing I personally was somewhat sur-
prised at the outcome of some of the surveys in that I felt that
there was a greater support amongst Catholics than some
people would have us believe' (p.49). When it comes to public
pronouncements, the caveats and qualifications tend to disappear. For instance, the chairman, in an interview given in
1998 (soon after the decision was announced to establish the
Patten Commission) stated: 'When asked if they have confidence in the RUC Catholics express a clear desire for reform.
Yet when asked whether they believe the RUC is doing a good
job locally, a clear majority agree' (*Belfast Telegraph*, 29 April
1999).

While making ritual obeisance to the problems inherent in
the use survey data, the PANI representatives then proceed
to interpret the same data to show the RUC in the best possible light. Despite numerous qualifications concerning the
nature of the evidence, the PANI chairman eventually attempted
to explain the lack of Catholics in the RUC with recourse to

the same argument, and almost the same words, as the Chief Constable: '... they [Catholics] were deterred from joining by threats of intimidation, by threats of murder, by threats to their families' (p.56). In a similar vein, the problem of the religious imbalance in the RUC was trivialised and defused by another member of PANI by comparing the situation within the police with that of other large companies: '... the RUC is in a very similar position to very large employers both in the private sector and public sector in Northern Ireland where they have an unbalanced workforce and are trying to find that redress ...' (p. 55). This comparison, which totally ignores the fact that most workforces are not armed or given a panoply of extraordinary powers to arrest, interrogate and even kill their fellow citizens, is a further example of the mindset which uses the results of survey data to bolster a position which refuses to acknowledge adequately the presence of deep divisions and diametrically-opposed attitudes towards the RUC. Attempts by the RUC and the Police Authority to present policing in the best possible light are crucially dependent on the main source of evidence: the results of attitude surveys and the interpretation put upon them. The intense frustration of the nationalist community when faced with the annual PANI reports is an index of the disbelief with which they are greeted in that community.

In the wake of the PANI (1998a) Report, both the SDLP and Sinn Féin voiced their disbelief at the PANI contention that both Catholics and Protestants had a 'generally favourable' view of the performance of the RUC. Sinn Féin highlighted a common criticism of the surveys carried out by PANI, that they did not reflect opinion and attitudes in those communities most exposed to the attentions of the RUC: 'I am quite certain that this survey was not carried out in Ardoyne, Garvaghy Road, Kilwilkie or the Bogside where communities have been on the receiving end of harassment, intimidation and brutality at the hands, feet and batons, and plastic bullets of the RUC.' The SDLP spokesperson felt constrained to comment that 'Their [PANI's] contributions are constantly characterised by both a failure to recognise that the RUC have no credibility among a substantial section of the community in the North and reflect their denial of how deep the problems are.' The response of the PANI chairman was to state that '... he was happy that 51% of those interviewed had expressed confidence in the RUC's ability to provide an effective ordinary day-to-day policing service for all the people of Northern Ireland' (*Irish News*, 20 February 1998).

In the previous chapter, we attempted to elucidate the methodological problems inherent in the use of survey data with regard to policing. The use of such data in societies such as Northern Ireland is particularly difficult since its interpretation depends on the model of society used to construct the survey and to analyse the results. The approach of the Police Authority, the RUC and unionists has been to reject the divided-society model of the North and interpret the conflict as one of a normal society unfortunately beset by a small minority of terrorists or, as the Chief Constable recently put it, as a battle between good and evil. In an interview with the London *Times*, the Chief Constable said that there was ' a real risk of people being taken in by the cleverly constructed myth that what's been going on for the last 30 years is some sort of struggle between two sides of equal validity, when what's actually been going on is a struggle between right and wrong, between good and evil' (13 May 1999).

It is understandable that any large bureaucratic organisation, particularly one vested with extraordinary powers over the citizen should attempt to defend its position and powers within society. Unfortunately, by refusing to acknowledge the nature of society in Northern Ireland and the fact that the practice of policing has been associated with the nature and reality of political power in a divided society, the RUC have made themselves part of the problem. As Chris Patten said in his statement at the launch of the Commission's Report: 'Policing in Northern Ireland has suffered, often with disastrous consequences, from being a political issue and from being associated with the debate about the state itself' (*Irish News*, 10 September 1999). The Patten Report is unambiguous in its acceptance that Northern Ireland is a divided society 'with its own particular history and culture' (p. 3) and that attitudes towards the RUC are conditioned by this fact. In a situation where the very nature of the state has remained the source of political division since 1922, the police do not have a neutral position: 'In one political language they are the custodians of nationhood. In its rhetorical opposite they are the symbols of repression' (Patten Report, 1999, p. 2).

The public meetings held by the Commission drove this point home in a fashion that exposed the ambiguities and methodological evasions of the survey evidence. The Commission held over thirty public meetings attended by about ten thousand people, of whom around a thousand took the floor (Patten Report, 1999, p. 15). It is clear from the Commission's report that one reason for the meetings was to obtain an alternative source of information on policing which would supplement the survey results and perhaps help clear up some of the ambiguities and contradictions of the survey data. The essential difference between the public meetings and the survey data was that while the latter could be filtered through an ideological and methodological sieve, the latter were forums for the expression of unmediated public opinion. Sentiments, especially nationalist sentiments, which were repressed and distorted in the survey results suddenly sprang into sharp relief. If nothing else, the meetings gave clear credence to the divided-society model of the North as expressed through attitudes towards the RUC. Attending back-to-back meetings on the same evening in both nationalist and unionist areas was a sobering experience – it often seemed that there were two police forces in Northern Ireland, one for Protestants and another for Catholics. Although there were some interesting internal divisions within communities – more obvious at meetings in Protestant areas – the factors which united each community were far more persuasive than any internal divisions. Those attending meetings in Protestant areas totally identified with 'our police' and were, in general, opposed to any change. Speaker after speaker denied any wrongdoing on the part of the Unionist administration. One speaker, at the meeting in Craigavon, himself a prominent businessman, talked of never having seen any 'unfair treatment' of Catholics and many agreed with the sentiment expressed by another speaker that 'discrimination is a load of nonsense.' Within this context, it is not surprising that remarks describing the RUC as the 'bulwark against those who would destroy the province' were greeted with applause. The questions of police acceptability and the low numbers of Catholics in the RUC were brushed aside by arguments about IRA intimidation of potential recruits or, more trenchantly, by assertions that Catholics were unwilling to accept the state in any form. For anyone who depended upon the results of surveys and the pronouncements of the Police Authority and the RUC for their information on police acceptability, the meetings in Catholic areas must have been a revelation. The level of Catholic alienation from the RUC was total. Speaker after speaker (from all age groups and social classes) catalogued a litany of abuse, collusion, harassment, insensitivity and threats (often of death) within a context of a refusal of the RUC to engage with the Catholic community on any level other than one of hostility and suspicion. An article in the *Irish Times* on a public meeting in West Belfast captured the tenor of the experiences of the Commission in Catholic areas: 'All the speakers were vehement in their opposition to the RUC, saying it should be disbanded rather than reformed'. Many speakers pointed out the intimate relationship between the RUC and the Stormont state: 'Policing is needed not to bolster the state, but to look after the community, but as the RUC stands it does not represent us' (5 November 1998). At every meeting there were stories of harassment, of children been forced off school buses and made to stand in the rain, of death threats and of constant house searches – one woman from South Armagh stated that her house had been searched eight times in six weeks. At the meetings held in the Armagh/Lurgan area, allegations of collusion were widespread and the names of senior police officers stationed in the area thought to have been involved were openly mentioned.

One speaker in West Belfast said 'The RUC has never been accepted and never will be' expressing a sentiment common to all the meetings in Catholic areas. It is clear from the Patten Report that the Commission adopted a number of broad principles with regard to policing in general and the situation in Northern Ireland in particular. A central principle underlying the report is that policing should be totally removed from the political arena and Patten made specific reference to this at the press conference to launch the report. He stressed that a 'key part' of the report was the 'depoliticisation of policing' and that 'politics would have to be taken out of policing' (*Irish News*, 10 September 1999). This general principle, which could be seen to apply to policing in any democratic society, is underpinned by the acceptance by the Commission of a divided-society model of Northern Ireland and the centrality of the reform of policing to any political solution. If anything, the public meetings must have reinforced the idea that any reform of policing would have to be based upon the principle of consent. The corollary to consent is accountability and this aspect of policing, which comprises the longest section of the report, is central to the Commission's recommendations.

Accountability

The recommendations on police accountability flow from the principle that effective policing can only be based upon consent: 'Policing, to be effective must be based upon consent across the country.' This principle of consent formed no part of either the policy of Unionist governments or the British state since partition and has a particular resonance in Northern Ireland which goes far beyond the question of policing. It is also a principle that applies to all democratic societies and the recommendations that flow from its acceptance are relevant to the nature of policing both in the Republic and other parts of the UK. Consent alone, while essential, must be buttressed by accountability and the report makes it clear that there is a serious problem with the RUC in this regard (p. 22). Accountability is a multi-layered concept. The police should be accountable to the community for providing the type of service required and requested by the community. In addition, the police should be held accountable, by the community, for the implementation of a policing strategy and their everyday actions and activities. All activities of the police as an organisation, down to the actions of individual police officers come within the ambit of the accountability principle. The Commission clearly holds the view that the RUC is not properly accountable: 'So, neither through the Police Authority nor through the government are the people of Northern Ireland – whether unionists or nationalists – able to hold the police of Northern Ireland to proper democratic account in the "subordinate" sense of the term' (p. 23). The Commission would also appear to agree with those people who 'saw the police as an instrument of British government policy rather than a service meeting local priorities' (p. 23). Also rejected is the well-rehearsed RUC excuse for the behaviour of individual officers, the 'bad apple' excuse that has been a component part of police discourse for decades. The Commission recognises that accountability means transparency: 'The presumption should be that everything should be available for public scrutiny unless it is in the public interest – not the police interest – to hold it back' (p. 36). Effectively, the report recommends that the doctrine of operational independence, which has defined the activities of the RUC, should be replaced by operational responsibility. The present situation, whereby the police routinely refuse to account for their actions would be replaced by one where the police would be accountable to a Police Board for every decision made and action taken. The proposed policing Board, which would be democratically constituted, would have extensive powers including the right to appoint and dismiss police officers and civilian staff. The Board would be able to compel senior officers to explain and justify operational decisions and to formally inquire into the conduct of the police if necessary.

Crucially, the Board would have an audit function, both in financial and operational terms. This would allow the Board to check both the cost and effectiveness of particular operations at any time. The recommendations on accountability are a cornerstone of the report and could be seen to apply to other police forces, such as the Garda in the Irish Republic. While the Garda may, broadly speaking, operate with the consent of the population, structures of accountability are conspicuous by their absence. The failure of the Garda to deal with the drugs problem in working-class areas of Dublin, for instance, was initially based upon a failure to listen to the concerns of those communities.

Covert Operations and Demilitarisation

As has been discussed in previous chapters, the involvement of the RUC in covert operations has been a source of contention and controversy for decades. Equally contentious has been the unwillingness of the state, in the form of government and judiciary, to hold the police accountable for its actions as in the case of the shootings in Armagh/Lurgan in 1982. The use of informers and the methods used to recruit informers, which often involve blackmail and coercion, are areas of police practice which came in for severe criticism at the public meetings. One woman, speaking at the public meeting in Derry, said that 'Because of the RUC's recruiting of vulnerable people as informers her family's life had been ruined' (*Irish News*, 2 December 1998). The Patten Report accepts that the RUC Special Branch has operated as a 'force within a force' and recommends that the SB should be amalgamated with the CID and the number of SB officers substantially reduced. At present, the number stands at 850 or about 10 per cent of the police force. The uneasy relationship between CID and Special Branch has been described in earlier chapters as has the way in which the two departments have wrestled for control of the counter-insurgency operation, each benefiting from the mistakes of the other.

The recommendations of the Commission would seem to be aimed at curtailing the autonomy of Special Branch and the abolition of its 'support units', which is probably a euphemism for E4A and other units trained in SAS-type tactics. The recommendation that the Special Branch be integrated into the overall police organisation is backed up by other changes to the way in which covert operations can be carried out. Here the recommendations are threefold: that covert law enforcement techniques should conform to the provisions of the European Convention on Human Rights, that there should be a commissioner to scrutinise covert operations and that there should be a special complaints tribunal to cover such operations (pp. 38–9). If fully implemented, these recommendations would severely restrict the ability of the RUC to operate as a counter-insurgency force by imposing some transparency and accountability on covert operations and effectively dismantling the elitist structure of Special Branch. Such reform of the activities of the RUC in this area should be put in the context of the expanded role being played by the military. Over the last decade or so, various special units within the British Army have taken over the lead role in covert operations from the RUC. The development of a powerful integrated computer system, which according to some commentators, has continued apace despite the IRA cease-fire (Geraghty 1998, pp. 158–64), has helped consolidate the role of the military. Such developments may well reduce the role of Special Branch to that of feeding low-level intelligence to the military who would then collate and assess the information with the use of knowledge-based computer systems. The use of such systems, integrated with overt and covert video cameras, aims to achieve what Geraghty terms an 'open, invisible electronic prison concept' which has implications far beyond Northern Ireland. Although the report does recommend that the proposed commissioner for covert operations should have powers to inspect 'other agencies acting in support of the police' (p. 38), it would be ironic if the military were to use the proposals to make the RUC accountable for its actions to increase its own – largely unaccountable – domination of the field of intelligence and undercover operations.

The control and containment of covert operations are central to the Commission's attempt to transform the RUC from being a quasi-military force into an accountable police service. Running through the report are other recommendations designed to reinforce this change such as the civilianisation of many senior posts within the police and contracting out support services. The Commission sees one objective of civilianisation as 'to help develop a more open culture in a traditionally closed organization' (p. 62) and recommends that up to a thousand posts (out of a recommended complement of 7,500) at all levels of the organisation be civilianised. The Commission also recommends a civilianisation and demilitarisation of police training with the establishment of a new training college with a significant input from outside sources.

Composition

Historically, criticism of the RUC has tended to focus upon the low numbers of Catholic police officers, a criticism that in recent times has been extended to take in the low number of women and members of ethnic and other minorities in the police. Increasing the numbers of Catholics in the police is an essential part of any reform process but, as is recognised by the Commission, cannot be seen in isolation. The RIC was over 80 per cent Catholic by the end of the nineteenth century, but this did not make it any more popular. Without parallel changes to the ethos, culture and structure of the police, changing the religious, ethnic and gender composition of its members will achieve little.

Many of the recommendations of the report address these issues, not least the proposal that the training of the RUC be reorientated towards instilling a culture of human rights among the police. The report notes that in the new curriculum introduced in 1999, scant attention is paid to human rights issues. Of the 700 training sessions for recruits, 40 are drill and 63 firearms training. Two sessions are dedicated to human rights training (p. 19). In an attempt to change the cultural milieu of the police, the report recommends that 'the human rights dimension should be integrated into every module of police training' (p. 11). Changing the culture of the police is perhaps the most difficult task and many of the report's recommendations interlock to achieve the objective of breaking down the 'militaristic and hierarchical' (p. 98) structure of the RUC and putting a human rights-based culture into place.

Conclusions

The Patten Report has implications which go far beyond the borders of Northern Ireland. Whether the report is implemented or not, it presents a blueprint for policing in democratic societies into the twenty-first century. The erosion of the authority and power of the nation state, and the development of global institutional and economic structures have weakened traditional sources of power and authority and loosened the bonds between state and citizen. The increasing importance of recognising diversity and the breakdown of cultural homogeneity indicate that governments are faced with the stark choice of developing new technologies of control, based upon electronic surveillance and the use of artificial intelligence, or to devolve democratic accountability to the local level. The Patten solution to the crucial problem of policing is based upon accountability and consent, not authoritarianism and control. In attempting to deal with the complications of an ethnically-divided society, the report is part of a wider effort to find a political settlement to what is fast becoming a European problem, the governance of diversity. One solution to this problem is to adopt the US model and transform the criminal justice system into an industry for the incarceration of ethnic minorities and those who cannot be absorbed into the culture of individualistic consumerism. The Patten recommendations offer a radically different view of policing and, if they can work in Northern Ireland, many will have cause to be grateful.

Notes

Chapter 1

1 The term 'hougher' came from the practice of maiming cattle or sheep by cutting their hamstrings. The peak years of the disturbances were 1711–12 and many of the characteristics of later agrarian disturbances were evident: the use of disguises, the issuing of proclamations and threats and an obsession with secrecy.

2 In a similar fashion the then Prime Minister, Mrs Thatcher, rushed to the defence of the locally recruited and predominantly Protestant *Ulster Defence Regiment* when it came under attack for collusion with loyalist death squads in 1989. The regiment was effectively abolished a few years later.

3 Daniel O'Connell emerged as the leader of constitutional nationalism in the first decades of the nineteenth century. The achievement of Catholic emancipation in 1829 allowed O'Connell to dominate Irish politics until his death in 1847.

4 *Hansard*, House of Commons, 1831, 5, Col. 1183

5 *Hansard*, House of Commons, 1829, 24, Col. 390.

6 *Hansard*, House of Commons, 1831, 4, Col. 389.

Chapter 2

1 Following the Anglo-Irish Treaty the RIC had itself asked to be disbanded when Collins made it plain that the IRA would not countenance the force (Farrell, 1983, p. 325, footnote 1)

2 See Hezlet (1972) for what McGarry and O'Leary term an 'unintentionally risible *apologia*' for the USC (1999, p. 126, footnote 7).

3 Collins and Craig met twice in the first two months of 1922. Mutual mistrust, the pressure of events and the inability of both leaders to deal with the inherent contradictions of their own position proved insurmountable obstacles to any agreement.

4 *Hansard,* House of Commons, Northern Ireland Parliament, *Official Report of Debates,* Vol. II, Col. 12, 1922

5 Craig cited in *Hansard,* ibid., Col. 603–4.

6 Farrell in his book about the RUC and USC lists this as the *Fermanagh Vigilance Force.* However, Viscount Brookeborough in an interview with the editor of the Enniskillen-based, *Impartial Reporter* (June 1970) refers to it as the *Citizen's Defence Force* (see Dane 1970).

7 *Hansard,* House of Commons, Northern Ireland Parliament, *Official Report of Debates,* Col. 12, 1922

8 Article 5 of the Anglo-Irish Treaty meant that the new Free State government was liable for a proportion of the British national debt. Kevin O'Higgins, the Irish Minister for Justice on the Boundary Commission argued that rebuilding the Irish economy after the devastation of the War of Independence plus financing part of the British national debt would cripple the economy even further. He suggested that if Britain could waive Article 5, the Irish government would relax its attitude to partition.

Chapter 3

1 The accession of Terence O'Neill to the Unionist leadership in 1963 brought with it some modernising tendencies which were reflected in a more interventionist approach by the Stormont government (see McGarry and O'Leary, 1995). It should be noted that the Catholic Church hierarchy in Northern Ireland were also vehemently opposed to state intervention. They were relatively content with the Unionist government's position since it left them with control over (Catholic) education and schools (O'Dowd, 1980a, p. 15–16).

2 The Welfare State reforms were introduced only reluctantly by the Unionist leadership who voted against their introduction at Westminster. Economic decline and a high level of Protestant unemployment during the interwar period forced the Unionist government to implement the reforms in Northern Ireland (see Bew, 1995). However, much of the legislation was introduced in Northern Ireland much later than in Britain. For example, the 1944 *Education Act,* was only introduced to Northern Ireland in 1947. In any case, and in spite of the welfare state reforms, local

authorities still retained considerable autonomy from central government direction, retaining control of housing, for example. This was later to become one of the principal grievances of the Civil Rights campaigners in the late 1960s.

3 See for instance the *Constabulary Gazette* for the period. This was established in 1933 to represent the interests of the Royal Ulster Constabulary and Ulster Special Constabulary.

4 Northern Ireland Parliamentary Debates, *Hansard*, House of Commons, Vol. 32, Col. 492, 1948. Warnock represented the extreme right wing of the Unionist Party during the 1950s; however, as an MP during the Civil Rights period, he privately showed great sympathy for the demands of the CRM and wrote to O'Neill calling for immediate change (*Irish Times*, 1 and 2 January 1999).

5 During the post-war period, the Catholic Church was the most cohesive and influential organisation on the nationalist side. It had broad control over education, welfare and health. The provisions of the welfare state threatened this control and the Catholic Church in Ireland fought a long rearguard action to maintain its control. It retains control over education, but even here its grip is loosening.

6 An index of Unionist unease is illustrated by the fact that the Unionist MPs at Westminster voted against welfare state legislation. The Stormont parliament had little option but to accept Britain's largesse (albeit with a considerable time-lag), otherwise it would have invoked the ire of its own working-class supporters as well as perhaps sending them into the arms of the Northern Ireland Labour Party.

Chapter 4

1 The idea of a blocked political system being responsible for political action has been explored for both Italy and Germany in the 1960s (see Della Porta, 1995).

2 The concept of 'political opportunity structure' (POS) was developed by Tarrow (1992). The POS defines the field of constraints and limitations that constructs the actions available to the actors involved. The opportunity structure affects a movement's decision to organise, the results of collective action and the institutional response such as reform or a slide into political violence.

3 'Injustice frame' is a term from social movement theory: grievances are 'framed' in a particular way by the movement as a means of mobilisation. In this case, a source of injustice is put into a framework of analysis, action and a proposed solution.

4 Such symbolic events – the ambush at Burntollet, the killing of Sammy Devenny and later the shooting of 13 unarmed civilians in Derry by British paratroopers – act as important focal points for mobilisation. Although the killings took place in 1972 the events still have great symbolic significance. The pressure to hold an impartial inquiry has been relentless and the British government recently acceded to demands for a fresh inquiry. Della Porta (1995) points to the importance in Germany of the killing of Benno Ohnesorg and the 'Battle of Valle Giulia' in Rome for the future course of events in those countries.

5 The ruling Unionist Party was divided between those tending towards some measure of reform and those arguing for the maintenance of Protestant and Unionist power. The latter were to form the nucleus of the Democratic Unionist Party (DUP) led by Ian Paisley, while the former were to fragment with some joining the middle-of-the-road Alliance Party.

6 Even the arch-conservative Edmond Warnock argued for change, warning O'Neill that to prosecute the Civil Rights marchers would be disastrous and show sympathy for the marchers: 'If ever a community had a right to demonstrate against the denial of civil rights, Derry is the finest example' (*Irish Times*, 1 and 2 January 1999).

7 Dermot Healy's fine novel, *A Goat's Song*, uses this incident as a hinge to develop the character of the fictional RUC man, Constable Adams.

8 *United Kingdom Parliamentary Debates*, Hansard, *House of Commons*, Vol. 28, p. 170, 23 June 1814.

9 This was called the Ulster Defence Regiment and was recruited heavily from the ranks of the disbanded USC. It was never particularly popular with the nationalist community in Northern Ireland being heavily infiltrated by loyalist paramilitaries and its membership quickly gaining a reputation for sectarianism and brutality. Indeed a number of UDR soldiers were charged with membership of loyalist paramilitary organisations under the terms of the 1988 Stevens inquiry. Also, in 1989 two members of the UDR

were convicted of the sectarian murder of a Catholic and sentenced to life imprisonment. The Ulster Defence Regiment was disbanded in 1991 and replaced by the Royal Irish Regiment.

Chapter 5

1 These specialist units come under the direct control of RUC Special Branch, known as 'E' Department. 'E' Department is divided into five sections: RUC E1 – administration; RUC E2 – legal affairs; RUC E3 – intelligence; RUC E4 – operations; RUC E5 – military liaison. The operational arm of Special Branch, E4A, was heavily implicated in the shootings in the late 1970s and early 1980s that gave rise to the Stalker Inquiry. E4A is one of four covert surveillance and 'executive action' groups that operate in Northern Ireland, the others being the SAS Ulster Division, 14 Intelligence and Security, and the Field Research Unit/Forward Reconnaissance Unit of the British Army.

2 An Assistant Chief Constable cited at the trial of a number of RUC officers involved in controversial shooting incidents in the early 1980s (see Stalker, 1988).

Chapter 6

1 Twenty-one members of the security forces were prosecuted for killings using firearms while on duty in the North between 1969–91. Nineteen were found not guilty, one was convicted of manslaughter and given a suspended sentence. One was convicted of murder and released after 27 months. He was subsequently reinstated in the British Army (Amnesty International, 1994).

2 There has been little research into the background of judges in the North. The now-defunct *Belfast Bulletin* is the only publication of which we are aware to examine the issue (see *Belfast Bulletin*, No. 10, Spring, 1982).

Chapter 7

1 The remarks of Judge Gibson did not go unchallenged. The Irish Taoiseach, Garrett Fitzgerald, said that they were 'entirely unacceptable; unworthy of any judicial authority' and Cardinal Ó Fiaich said the remarks were 'inexplicable and inexcusable' (Jennings, 1988b, pp. 116–7). Judge Gibson and his wife were killed by an IRA landmine close to the border in 1987.

2 No charges were to follow the death of Pearse Jordan, Gerald Maginn and Patrick Finucane (see CAJ, 1992).

Chapter 8

1 The Report is available on the Internet: www.unhcr.ch/ Huridocda/ For more information on human rights in Northern Ireland see: Amnesty international: www.amnesty. org International Commission of Jurists: www.geneva.ch/ ICJ.htm Human Rights Watch: www.hrw.org International Federation of Human Rights: www.fidh.imaginet.fr

Chapter 9

1 See, for example, the *Report of Her Majesty's Inspectorate of Constabulary,* Primary Inspection, HMSO: December 1996, p. 15.

2 One hundred and thirty one youth and community groups across Northern Ireland returned questionnaires in 1993, and 118 in 1995. The response rate for the 1993 survey was 70.4 per cent and for the 1995 survey, 68.6 per cent.

3 'Survey of Religious and Political Harassment and Discrimination in the Royal Ulster Constabulary', December 1997. A copy of this document marked 'confidential' can be found at the Pat Finucane Centre website: http:/www.serve.com/ pfc/survey

Bibliography

Altheide, D.L. and Johnson, J.M. (1980), *Bureaucratic Propaganda*, London: Allyn and Bacon.

Anderson, B. (1983), *Imagined Communities*, London: Verso.

Anderson, D.M. (1991), Policing, Prosecution and the Law in Colonial Kenya', in D.M. Anderson and D. Killingray (eds), *Policing the Empire*, Manchester: Manchester University Press.

Anderson, D.M. and Killingray, D. (eds), (1992), *Policing and Decolonisation*, Manchester: Manchester University Press.

Anderson, D.M. and Killingray, D. (eds), (1991), *Policing the Empire*, Manchester: Manchester University Press.

Amnesty International (1994), *Political Killings in Northern Ireland*, London: Amnesty International.

Amnesty International (1978), *Report of a Mission to Northern Ireland*, London: Amnesty International.

Asmal, K. (1985), *Shoot to Kill*, Cork: Mercier Press.

Bardon, J. (1992), A *History of Ulster*, Belfast: Blackstaff Press.

Barritt, D. and Carter, C. (1972) *The Northern Ireland Problem: A Study in Group Relations*, Oxford: Oxford University Press.

Bartlett, T. (1983), 'An end to the "Moral Economy": The Irish Militia. Disturbances of 1792', *Past and Present*, No. 99, May, pp. 41–64.

Barzilay, D. (1981), *The British Army in Ulster, Vol. 4*, London: Century Books.

Beckett, I. and Pilmott, J. (1985) (eds), *Armed Forces and Modern Counter-Insurgency*, London: Croom Helm.

Beckett, J.C. (1972), *The Ulster Debate*, London: The Bodley Head.

Bennett Report (1979), *Report of the Committee of Inquiry into Police Interrogation Procedures in Northern Ireland*, Cmnd. 7497, London: HMSO.

Bew, P. (1995), *Northern Ireland, 1921–1994: Political Forces and Social Classes*, London: Serif.

BIRW (British – Irish Rights Watch), (1992), *Intimidation of Defence Lawyers in Northern Ireland*, London: BIRW.

BIRW (British – Irish Rights Watch), (1995), *Supplementary Report to the United Nations Special Rapporteur on the Independence of Judges and Lawyers*, London: BIRW.

Bishop, P. and Mallie, E. (1987), *The Provisional IRA,* London: Heinemann.

Bloch, J. and Fitzgerald, P. (1983), *British Intelligence and Covert Action: Africa, Middle East and Europe since 1945,* Dingle: Brandon.

Bourdieu, P. (1991), *Language and Symbolic Power,* Cambridge: Polity Press (in association with Blackwell).

Bowden, T. (1978), 'Guarding the State: The Police Response to Crisis Politics in Europe', *British Journal of Law and Society,* Vol. 5, Part 1, pp. 69–88.

Boyle, K. and Hadden, T. (1994), *Northern Ireland: The Choice,* London: Penguin.

Boyle, K. and Hadden, T. (1980), *Ten Years on in Northern Ireland: The Legal Control of Political Violence,* London: The Cobden Trust.

Boyle, K., Hadden, T. and Hillyard, P. (1975), *Law and the State: The Case of Northern Ireland,* London: Martin Robinson.

Breen, R. (1995), 'Beliefs about the treatment of Catholics and Protestants by the Security Forces', in R. Breen, P. Devine, and G. Robinson, (eds), *Social Attitudes in Northern Ireland: The Fourth Report,* Belfast: Appletree Press.

Breen, R., Devine, P. and Robinson, G. (eds), (1995), *Social Attitudes in Northern Ireland: The Fourth Report,* Belfast: Appletree Press.

Brewer, J.D. (1993) 'The history and development of policing in Northern Ireland', in M. Mathews, P. Heymann, and A. Mathews, (eds), *Policing the Conflict in South Africa,* Gainesville, FL: University Press of Florida.

Brewer, J.D. (1992), 'The Public and the Police', in P. Stringer and G. Robinson (eds), *Social Attitudes in Northern Ireland – 1990–91,* Belfast: Blackstaff Press.

Brewer, J.D. (1990), *The Royal Irish Constabulary: an oral history,* Belfast: Institute of Irish Studies, Queen's University.

Brewer, J.D. (1989), 'Max Weber and the Royal Irish Constabulary: a note on class and status', *British Journal of Sociology,* 40, pp. 82–96.

Brewer, J.D. and Magee, K. (1991), *Inside the RUC,* Oxford: Clarendon Press.

Brewer, J.D et al. (eds) (1988), *The Police, Public Order and the State,* London: Macmillan Press.

Broeker, G. (1970), *Rural Disorder and Police Reform in Ireland 1812–36,* London: Routledge and Kegan Paul.

Brogden, M. (1999), 'Community Policing as Cherry Pie', in R.I. Mawby (ed.), *Policing Across the World: Issues for the 21st Century*, London: UCL Press.

Brogden, M., (1997), 'Burning Churches and Victim Surveys', paper presented to the British Criminology Society Conference, Queen's University, Belfast, July.

Brogden, M. (1987), 'An Act to Colonise the Internal Lands of the Island: Empire and Origins of the Professional Police', *International Journal of the Sociology of Law*, 15, pp. 179–208.

Brogden, M. (1982), *The Police: Autonomy and Consent*, London: Academic Press.

Brogden, M. and Shearing, C. (1993), *Policing for a New South Africa*, London: Routledge.

Brogden, M., Jefferson, T. and Walklate, S. (1988), *Introducing Policework*, London: Unwin Hyman.

Broznat, M. (1981), *The Hitler State*, London: Longman Publishing.

Buckland, P. (1979), A *Factory of Grievances: Devolved Government in Northern Ireland 1921–39*. Dublin: Gill and Macmillan.

Bull, I. and Horncastle, P. (1986), *Police Recruit Training in Human Awareness: An Independent Evaluation*, London: Police Foundation.

Cain, M. (1991), 'Some go Backward, Some go Forward: Police Work in Comparative Perspective', *British Journal of Criminology*, Symposium, pp. 319–26.

Cain, M. (1979), 'Trends in the Sociology of Policework', *International Journal of Sociology of Law*, Vol. 7, Part 2, pp. 143–67.

Cain, M. (1973), *Society and the Policeman's Role*, London: Routledge & Kegan Paul.

Cain Web Service (n.d.), *An Appalling Vista:* www.cain.vist.ac.uk

Cairns, D. (1999), 'Sectarianism in Popular Culture', unpublished D.Phil. thesis, University of Ulster.

CAJ (Committee for the Administration of Justice) (1992), *Inquests and Disputed Killings in Northern Ireland*, Belfast: CAJ.

CAJ (Committee for the Administration of Justice) (1990), *Plastic Bullets and the Law*, Belfast: CAJ.

Cameron Report (1969) *Disturbances in Northern Ireland, Report of the Commission appointed by the Governor of Northern Ireland*, Cmnd. 532, Belfast: HMSO.

Cebulla, A. and Smyth, J. (1996), 'Disadvantage and New Prosperity in Restructured Belfast', *Capital and Class*, No. 60.

Clancy, P., Drudy, S., Lynch, K. and O'Dowd, L. (eds) 1986, *Ireland: A Sociological Profile*, Dublin: Institute of Public Administration.

Clark, C. and Donnelly, J. (1983) (eds), *Irish Peasants: Violence and Political Unrest 1780–1914*, Dublin: Gill and Macmillan.

Cohen, S. and Scull, A. (eds) (1983), *Social Control and the State*, Oxford: Robertson.

Compton Report (1971) *Report of the enquiry into allegations against the security forces of physical brutality in Northern Ireland arising out of events on the 9 August 1971*, Cmnd. 4823, Belfast: HMSO.

Connolly, S.J. (1992), *Religion, Law and Power: The Making of Protestant Ireland, 1660–1760*, Oxford: Clarendon Press.

Conrad, P. (1998), *Modern Times, Modern Places: Life and Art in the Twentieth Century*, London: Thames and Hudson.

Coogan, T.P. (1995), *The IRA*, rev. edn, London: HarperCollins.

Coulter, C. (1999), *Contemporary Northern Irish Society*, London: Pluto.

Critchley, T.A. (1978), *The History of the Police in England and Wales*, London: Constable.

Crossman, V. (1996), *Politics, Law and Order in 19th Century Ireland*, Dublin: Gill and Macmillan.

Cullen, F. (1997), *Visual Politics: The Representation of Ireland 1750–1930*, Cork: Cork University Press.

Curtis, L. (1984), *Ireland: the Propaganda War*, London: Pluto Press.

Dandeker, C. (1990), *Surveillance, Power and Modernity*, Oxford: Polity Press.

Dane, M. (1970) *The Fermanagh 'B' Specials*, Enniskillen: William Trimble Ltd, Publishers.

Della Porta, D. (1995), *Social Movements, Political Violence and the State*, Cambridge: Cambridge University Press.

Dewar, M. (1985), *The British Army in Northern Ireland*, London: Arms and Armour Press.

Diplock Report (1972), *Report of the Commission to Consider Legal Procedures to Deal With Terrorist Activity in Northern Ireland*, Cmnd. 5185, London: HMSO.

Donnan, H. and McFarlane, G. (1986), 'You get on better with your own: Social Continuity and Change in Rural Northern Ireland', in P. Clancy, S. Drudy, K. Lynch and L. O'Dowd (eds), ibid.

Donzelot, J. (1980), *The Policing of Families*, London: Hutchinson.

Dooley, B. (1998), *Black and Green: the Fight for Civil Rights in Northern Ireland and Black America*, London: Pluto Press.

Elliott, M. (1989), *Wolfe Tone: Prophet of Irish Independence*, New Haven: Yale University Press.

Ellison, G. (2000), 'Reflecting All Shades of Opinion: Public Attitudinal Surveys and the Construction of Police Legitimacy in Northern Ireland', *British Journal of Criminology*, 40, 1, Winter, pp. 88–110.

Ellison, G. (1997), *'Professionalism in the Royal Ulster Constabulary: an examination of the institutional discourse'*. Unpublished D.Phil. thesis, University of Ulster.

Ellison, G. (1994), 'The RUC: Drink, Dames and Debt', *The Irish Reporter*, No. 14, Second Quarter.

Ellison, G. and Martin, G. 'Policing Collective Action and Social Movement Theory', *British Journal of Sociology* (forthcoming).

Ellison G. and Smyth, J. (1996), 'Bad Apples or Rotten Barrel? Policing in Northern Ireland' in O. Marenin (ed.), *Policing Change, Changing Police*, New York: Garland Publishing.

Emsley, C. (1997), *Crime and Society in England 1759–1900*, London: Longman.

Emsley, C. (1996), *The English Police*, London: Longman.

Ericson, R.V. and Haggerty, K.D. (1997), *Policing the Risk Society*, Oxford: Clarendon.

Evelagh, R. (1978), *Peacekeeping in a Democratic Society*, London: C. Hurst & Company Publishers.

Faligot, R. (1983), *Britain's Military Strategy in Ireland: the Kitson Experiment*, Dingle: Brandon.

Farrell, M. (1986), *Emergency Legislation: The Apparatus of Repression*, Derry: Field Day pamphlet No. 11.

Farrell, M. (1983), *Arming the Protestants*, London: Pluto.

Farrell, M. (1980), *The Orange State*, London: Pluto.

Finnane, M. (1991), 'The varieties of policing: colonial Queensland, 1860–1900', in D.M. Anderson and D. Killingray (eds), *Policing the Empire*, ibid.

Fisk, R. (1975), *'The Point of No Return': The strike which broke the British in Ulster*, London: Andre Deutsch.

Foster, R. (1988), *Modern Ireland 1600–1972*, London: Allen Lane.

Foucault, M. (1979), *Discipline and Punish: The Birth of the Prison*, London: Penguin.

Gallagher, F. (1957), *The Indivisible Island*, London: Gollancz.

Gamson, W. (1992), *The Social Psychology of Collective Action* in A. Morris, and C. Mueller (eds)

Garland, D. (1990), *Punishment and Modern Society*, Oxford: Oxford University Press.

Gash, N. (1961), *The Life of Sir Robert Peel to 1830*, London: Longman.

Gatrell, V.A.C. (1980), 'The Decline of Theft and Violence in Victorian and Edwardian England' in Gatrell, V.A.C, Lenman, B. and Parker, G. (eds), *Crime and the Law: The Social History of Crime in Western Europe since 1500*, London: Europe Publications.

Geraghty, T. (1998), *The Irish War*, London: HarperCollins.

Giddens, A. (1981), *A Contemporary Critique of Historical Materialism*, London: Macmillan.

Gifford, T. (1984), *Supergrasses: the Use of Accomplice Evidence in Northern Ireland*, London: Cobden Trust.

Goldstein, R. (1983), *Political Repression in Nineteenth Century Europe*, London: Croom Helm.

Good Friday Agreement (1998), Belfast: HMSO.

Greer, S. (1988), 'The Supergrass System', in A. Jennings (ed.), *Justice Under Fire*, London: Pluto.

Greer, S. and White, A. (1986), *Abolishing the Diplock Courts: The Case for Restoring Jury Trial to Scheduled Offences in Northern Ireland*, London: Cobden Trust.

Grimshaw, R. and Jefferson, T. (1987), *Interpreting Policework*, London: Allen and Unwin.

Guelke, A. and Smyth, J. (1992), 'The Ballot Bomb: Terrorism and the Electoral Process in Northern Ireland', *Terrorism and Political Violence*, Vol 4, No 2, Summer, pp. 103–124.

Guelke, A. and Wright, F. (1992), 'On a British Withdrawal From Northern Ireland', in P. Stringer, and G. Robinson, (eds), *Social Attitudes in Northern Ireland*, Belfast: Blackstaff Press.

Hall, P. (1999), *Cities and Civilisation*, London: Phoenix.

Harris, M. (1993), *The Catholic Church and the Foundation of the Northern Irish State*, Cork: Cork University Press.

Hawkins, C. (1991), 'The "Irish Model" and the Empire: A case for reassessment', in D.M. Anderson, and D. Killingray, (eds), *Policing and Decolonisation*, ibid.

Hay, D. (ed.) (1975), *Albion's Fatal Tree*, London: Allen Lane.

Healy, D. (1994), *A Goat's Song*, London, Harvill.

Held, D. et al. (1999), *Global Transformation: Politics, Economics and Culture*, Oxford: Polity Press.

Herlihy, J. (1997), *The Royal Irish Constabulary: A Short History and Genealogical Guide*, Dublin: Four Courts Press.

Hermon, J. (1997), *Holding the Line*, Dublin: Gill and Macmillan.

Hezlet, A. (1972), *The 'B' Specials: A History of the Ulster Special Constabulary*, London: Pan Books.

Hill, J. (1984), 'National Festivals, the State and Protestant Ascendency in Ireland 1790–1829', *Irish Historical Studies*, No. 24, pp. 30–51.

Hillyard, P. (1988), 'Political and Social Dimensions of Emergency Law in Northern Ireland', in P. Jennings (ed.), *Justice Under Fire*, ibid.

Hillyard, P. (1987), 'The Normalisation of Special Powers: From Northern Ireland to Britain', in Scraton, P. (ed.), *Law, Order and the Authoritarian State*, Milton Keynes: Open University Press.

Hillyard, P. (1983), 'Law and Order', in J. Darby (ed.), *Northern Ireland: The Background to the Conflict*, Belfast: Appletree Press.

Hollingsworth, M. and Fielding, N. (1999), *Defending the Realm: MI5 and the Slayer Affair*, London: Andre Deutsch.

Honneth, A. (1995), *The Struggle for Recognition: The Moral Grammar of Social Conflicts*, Cambridge: Polity Press.

Huggins, M.D. (1991), *Vigilantism and the State in Latin America: Essays on Extra-Legal Violence*, Westport CT: Greenwood Press.

Human Rights Watch / Helsinki (1997), *To Serve without Favour: Policing, Human Rights and Accountability in Northern Ireland*, New York: Human Rights Watch.

Human Rights Watch / Helsinki (1992), *Human Rights in Northern Ireland*, London: Human Rights Watch.

Human Rights Watch (1994), *Brazil – Final Justice: Police and Death Squad Homicides in Brazil*, New York: Human Rights Watch.

Hunt Report (1969), *Report of the Advisory Committee on Police in Northern Ireland*, Cmnd. 535, Belfast: HMSO.

Ignatieff, M. (1983), 'State, Civil Society and Total Institutions: A Critique of Recent Social Histories of Punishment' in S. Cohen and A. Scull (eds), *Social Control and the State*, Oxford: Robertson.

Ignatieff, M. (1978), *A Just Measure of Pain: The Penitentiary in the Industrial Revolution 1750–1850*, New York: Pantheon.

Irish Information Partnership (1990), *Irish Information Agenda*, London: Irish Information Partnership.

Jack, I. (1989), 'Gibraltar', *Granta*, 25, London.

Jenkins, R. (1992), *Pierre Bourdieu*, London: Routledge.

Jennings, A. (1988a), 'Bullets Above the Law', in A. Jennings, (ed.), *Justice Under Fire*, London: Pluto.

Jennings, A. (ed.) (1988b), *Justice Under Fire*, London: Pluto.

Jennings, A. (1988c), 'Shoot to Kill: The Final Courts of Justice', in A. Jennings (ed.), *Justice Under Fire*, London: Pluto.

Kitchin, H. (1989), *The Gibraltar Report*, London: NCCL.

Kitson, F. (1971), *Low Intensity Operations*, London: Faber and Faber.

Kitson, F. (1960), *Gangs and Counter Gangs*, London: Barrie and Rockliff.

LCHR (Lawyers Committee for Human Rights) (1996), *At the Crossroads: Human Rights and the Northern Ireland Peace Process*, London, LCHR.

Lecky, W. (1972), *A History of Ireland in the Eighteenth Century*, Chicago: Chicago University Press.

Lee, J. (1989), *Ireland 1912–1982: Politics and Society*, Cambridge: Cambridge University Press.

Lee, J.A. (1981), 'Some Structural Aspects of Police Deviance in Relations with Minority Groups', in C.D. Shearing (ed.), *Organisational Police Deviance*, Toronto: Butterworth and Co.

Leersen, J. (1996), *Remembrance and Imagination*, Cork: Cork University Press.

Lewis, G. Cornewall (1836), *Local Disturbances in Ireland*, London: B. Fellows.

Limpkin, C. (1972), *The Battle of the Bogside*, Middlesex: Penguin.

Lindbaugh, P. (1975), *The London Hanged: Crime and Civil Society in the Eighteenth Century*, London: Allen Lane.

Loader, I. (1997), 'Policing and the Social: Questions of Symbolic Power', *British Journal of Sociology*, Vol. 48, Issue 1, March, pp. 1–18.

LSEW (Law Society of England and Wales) (1995), *Northern Ireland: An Emergency Ended?* Report of the International Human Rights Working Party, London: Law Society.

Macpherson, C. (1964), *The Political Theory of Possessive Individualism*, Oxford: Oxford University Press.

Manning, P. (1978), 'The Police: Mandate, Strategies and Appearances' in P. Manning, and J. Van Maanen, (eds), *Policing: A View from the Street*, Santa Monica, CA: Goodyear.

Mapstone, R. (1992), 'The Attitudes of Police in a Divided Society', *British Journal of Criminology*, Vol. 32, No. 2, Spring, pp. 183–92.

Marenin, O. (1996a), 'Policing Change, Changing Police: Some Thematic Questions', in O. Marenin (ed.), *Policing Change, Changing Police: International Perspectives*, New York: Garland.

Marenin, O. (1996b), 'Changing Police, Policing Change: Towards More Questions', in O. Marenin (ed.), *Policing Change, Changing Police: International Perspectives*, New York: Garland.

Mark, R. (1977), *Policing a Perplexed Society*, London: Allen and Unwin.

McAughtry, S. (1993), *A Belfast Boyhood and Hard Times: a series of Short Stories*, Bangor: NI Adult Literacy Liaison Group.

McAughtry, S. (1978), *Play it Again Sam*, Belfast: Blackstaff.

McCann, E. (1993), *War and an Irish Town*, London: Pluto.

McGarry, J. and O'Leary, B. (1999), *Policing Northern Ireland: Proposals for a New Start*, Belfast: Blackstaff Press.

McGarry, J. and O'Leary, B. (1995), *Explaining Northern Ireland*, Oxford: Blackwell.

McKibben, R. (1999), 'The Government at mid-term', *London Review of Books*, Vol. 21, No. 19, 30 September.

McVeigh, R. (1994), 'It's Part of Life Here: The security forces and harassment in Northern Ireland', Belfast: Committee on the Administration of Justice.

Melucci, A. (1996), *Challenging Codes: Collective Action in the Information Age*, Cambridge: Cambridge University Press.

Miller, D. (1978), *Queen's Rebels: Ulster Loyalism in Historical Perspective*, Dublin: Gill and Macmillan.

Morris, A. and Mueller, C. (1992) *Frontiers in Social Movement Theory*, New Haven, CT: Yale University Press.

Muenger, E.A. (1991), *The British Military Dilemma in Ireland: Occupational Politics 1886–1914*, Dublin: Gill and Macmillan.

Mulcahy, A. (2000), 'Policing History: The Official Discourse and Organisational Memory of the Royal Ulster Constabulary', *British Journal of Criminology*, 40, 1, Winter, pp. 68–87.

Mulcahy, A. (1999), 'Visions of Normality: Peace and the Reconstruction of Policing in Northern Ireland', *Social and Legal Studies*, Vol. 8, No. 2, June, pp. 277–95.

Mulcahy, A. (1998), 'The Dynamics of the Police Legitimation Process in Northern Ireland', unpublished PhD thesis, Arizona State University.

Murray, D. (1995), 'Culture, religion and violence in Northern Ireland', in S. Dunn, (ed.), *Facets of the Conflict in Northern Ireland*, London: St Martin's Press.

National Council of Civil Liberties (1936), *Report of a Commission of Inquiry appointed to examine the purpose and effect of the Civil Authorities (Special Powers) Acts, 1922 and 1933*, London (reprinted London, 1972).

Newman, K. (1980a), Keynote Address at Cranfield Institute of Technology: Conference on Strategies Against Crime in Europe.

Newman, K. (1980b), 'Terrorism Versus Democracy', talk to Messina Conference, October 1980.

Newman, K. (1980c), 'Training Policemen', *Constabulary Gazette*, April, pp. 33–37.

Newman, K. (1979), Address by Sir Kenneth Newman to Guild of British Newspaper Editors: 'The Nature of Violence in Northern Ireland', *Constabulary Gazette*, 23 November, pp. 9–10.

Newman, K. (1978a), 'Violence in Northern Ireland', *Constabulary Gazette*, March, pp. 7–10.

Newman, K. (1978b), 'Prevention in Extremis: The Preventative Role of the Police in Northern Ireland', *The Cranfield Papers*, London: Peel Press.

NICRA (n.d, 1978?) *We Shall Overcome: the History of the Struggle for Civil Rights in NI 1968–1978*, Belfast: NICRA.

NISRA (annually), Northern Ireland Omnibus survey, Northern Ireland Statistics and Research Agency, Belfast: NIO.

Northern Ireland Affairs Committee, House of Commons (1998), *Composition, Recruitment and Training of the RUC*, Minutes of Evidence, London.

Ó Ceallaig, T. (1966) 'Peel and Police Reform in Ireland', *Studia Hibernicia*, 6 1966.

O'Connor, F. (1993), *In Search of a State: Catholics in Northern Ireland*, Belfast: Blackstaff Press.

Ó Dochartaigh, N. (1997), *From Civil Rights to Armalites: Derry and the Birth of the Irish Troubles*, Cork: Cork University Press.

O'Dowd, L. (1980a), 'Shaping and Reshaping the Orange State: An Introductory Analysis', in L. O'Dowd, et al., (eds), *Northern Ireland: Between Civil Rights and Civil War*, London: CSE Books.

O'Dowd, L. (1980b), 'Regional Policy', in L. O'Dowd, et al., (eds), *Northern Ireland: Between Civil Rights and Civil War*, London: CSE Books.

O'Dowd, L., Rolston, B. and Tomlinson, M. (eds) (1980), *Northern Ireland: Between Civil Rights and Civil War*, London: CSE Books.

O'Farrell, P. (1975), *England and Ireland since 1800*, Oxford: Oxford University Press.

O'Mahony, D., McEvoy, K., Geary, R., Morison, J. and Brogden, M. (1997), *The Northern Ireland Communities Crime Survey*, Institute of Criminology and Criminal Justice / School of Law, Belfast: Queen's University.

Palmer, S. (1988), *Police and Protest in 19th Century Britain and Ireland*, Cambridge: Cambridge University Press.

PANI (Police Authority for Northern Ireland) (1998a), 'Reflecting All Shades of Opinion', Belfast: PANI.

PANI (Police Authority for Northern Ireland) (1998b), 'Policing: A New Beginning', submission by the Police Authority of Northern Ireland to the Independent Commission on Policing', Belfast: PANI.

PANI (Police Authority for Northern Ireland) (1997), 'Listening to the Community, Working with the RUC', Belfast: PANI.

PANI (Police Authority for Northern Ireland) (1996), 'Everyone's Police, A Partnership for Change: A Report on a Community Consultation undertaken by the Police Authority for Northern Ireland in 1995', Belfast: PANI.

Parker, C. (1891), *Sir Robert Peel*, London: John Murray.

Pat Finucane Centre (1999), *Rosemary Nelson: the Life and Death of a Human Rights Defender*, Derry: Pat Finucane Centre.

Patten Report (1999) *Report of the Independent Commission on Policing in Northern Ireland*, Belfast: HMSO.

Phillips, D. (1983), 'A Just Measure of Crime' in S. Cohen and A. Scull (eds), *Social Control and the State*, ibid.

Purdie, B. (1990), *Politics in the Streets. The Origins of the Civil Rights Movement in Northern Ireland*, Belfast: Blackstaff.

Ramsey, A. (1928), *Sir Robert Peel*, London: Constable.

Reith, C. (1938), *The Police Idea*, Oxford: Oxford University Press.

Roberts, P. (1983), 'Caravats and Shanavests: Whiteboyism and Faction Fighting in East Munster 1802–11', in S. Clark, and J. Donnelly, (eds), *Irish Peasants: Violence and Political Unrest 1780–1914*, Dublin: Gill and Macmillan.

Robson, W.A. (1939), *The Government and Misgovernment of London*, London: Allen and Unwin.

Rock, P. (1983), *Law, Order and Power in Late 17th and Early 19th Century England* in S. Cohen, and A. Scull, (eds), *Social Control and the State*, ibid.

Rolston, B. (1998) 'What's Wrong with Multiculturalism?', in Miller, D. (ed.) *Rethinking Northern Ireland*, London: Longman.

Rolston, B. (1983), 'Reformism and Sectarianism: The State of the Union after civil rights', in J. Darby, (ed.), *Northern Ireland: The Background to the Conflict*, ibid.

Rolston, B. (1980), 'Community Politics', in L. O'Dowd, B. Rolston, and M. Tomlinson, (eds), *Northern Ireland: Between Civil Rights and Civil War*, London: CSE Books.

Ruane, J. and Todd, J. (1996), *The Dynamics of Conflict in Northern Ireland*, Cambridge: Cambridge University Press.

Ryder, C. (1989), *The Royal Ulster Constabulary: A Force Under Fire*, London: Methuen.

Saville Inquiry (n.d.), www.bloody-Sunday-inquiry.org.uk

Scarman Report (1972) *Violence and Civil Disturbance in Northern Ireland in 1969, Report of the Tribunal of Inquiry*, Cmnd. 566, Belfast: HMSO.

Scorer, C. and Hewitt, P. (1981), *The Prevention of Terrorism Act: The Case for Repeal*, London: National Council for Civil Liberties.

Sheehy, J. (1980), *The Rediscovery of Ireland's Past: The Celtic Revival 1830–1930*, London: Thames and Hudson.

Smyth, C. (1989), *Ireland's Physical Force Tradition Today*, Lurgan: Ulster Society.

Smyth, J. (1995) 'Manning the Ramparts: Ireland and the Agenda of the Roman Catholic Church', *History of European Ideas*, Vol. 20, Nos 4–6, pp. 681–87.

Smyth, J. (1988), 'Stretching the Boundaries: The Control of Dissent in Northern Ireland', *Terrorism*, Vol. 11, pp. 289–308.

Smyth, J. and Cairns, D. (2000), 'Dividing Loyalties: Local Identities in a Global Economy', in E. Slater, and M. Peillon, (eds), *Memories of the Present: Ireland 1997–1998*, Dublin: Institute of Public Administration.

Smyth, J. and Cebulla, A. (1995), 'Belfast – Industrial Collapse and Post-Fordist Overdetermination', in P. Shirlow, (ed.), *Development Ireland*, London: Pluto.

Spitzer, S. (1983), 'The Rationalisation of Crime Control in Capitalist Society' in S. Cohen, and A. Scull, (eds), *Social Control and the State*, ibid.

Stalker, J. (1988), *Stalker*, London: Harrap.

Stanley, W.D. (1996), *Protection Racket State: Elite Politics, Military Extortion and Civil War in El Salvador*, Philadelphia: Temple University Press.

Steytler, N. (1990), 'Policing Political Opponents: Death Squads and Cop Culture', in D. Hansson, and D. van Zyl Smit, (eds), *Towards Justice?* Cape Town: Oxford University Press.

Storch, R. (1975), 'The Plague of the Blue Locusts: Police Reform and Popular Resistance', *International Review of Social History*, No. 20, 1975.

Storch, R. (1976), 'The Policeman as domestic missionary', *Journal of Social History*, IX: 4, Summer.

Tarrow, S. (1992), 'Mentalities, Political Cultures and Collective Action Frames', in A. Morris, and C. Mueller, (eds), *Frontiers in Social Movement Theory*, New Haven CT: Yale University Press.

Taylor, P. (1980), *Beating the Terrorists?* Harmondsworth: Penguin.

Thompson, E. P. (1980), *Writing by Candlelight*, London: Merlin.

Thompson, E. P. (1975), *Property, Authority and Criminal Law* in Hay, D. (ed.), *Albion's Fatal Tree*, London: Allen Lane.

Thompson, E. P. (1965), *Whigs and Hunters,* London: Allen Lane.

Thompson, E. P. (1963), *The Making of the English Working Class,* New York: Pantheon.

Tomlinson, M. (1980a), 'Housing, the State and the Politics of Segregation', in L. O'Dowd, et al. (eds), *Northern Ireland: Between Civil Rights and Civil War,* ibid.

Tomlinson, M. (1980b), 'Reforming Repression', in L. O'Dowd, *et al.* (eds), *Northern Ireland: Between Civil Rights and Civil War,* ibid.

Townshend, C. (1983), *Political Violence in Ireland: Government and Resistance since 1848,* Oxford: Oxford University Press.

Ulster Year Book (1956–57), Belfast: HMSO.

UNCHR (United Nations Commission on Human Rights) (March 1998), *Report of the Special Rapporteur on the Independence of Judges and Lawyers,* Geneva: United Nations. Internet: www.unhcr.ch/Huridocda/

Urban, M. (1992), *Big Boys' Rules: The SAS and the Secret Struggle Against the IRA,* London: Faber and Faber.

Ulster Society (1986), *Ulster: An Ethnic Nation,* Papers delivered to a seminar held by the Ulster Society, Lurgan: Ulster Society.

Waddington, P.A.J. (1999), 'Armed and Unarmed Policing' in R.I. Mawby, (ed.), *Policing Across the World,* London: UCL Press.

Walker, C. (1990), 'Police and Community in Northern Ireland', *Northern Ireland Legal Quarterly,* Vol. 41, No. 1, pp. 105–142.

Walsh, D. (1988a), 'Arrest and Interrogation', in A. Jennings, (ed.), *Justice Under Fire,* ibid.

Walsh, D. (1983), *The Use and Abuse of Emergency Legislation in Northern Ireland,* The Cobden Trust.

Weitzer, R. (1995), *Policing Under Fire: Ethnic Conflict and Police-Community Relations in Northern Ireland,* Albany: State University of New York Press.

Williams, A. (1979), *The Police of Paris, 1718–1789,* Baton Rouge, LA: Louisiana State University Press.

Wilson, T. (ed.) (1955), *Ulster Under Home Rule,* Oxford: Oxford University Press.

Workers Research Unit (1982), *The Law in Northern Ireland,* Belfast: Spring.

Zald, M.N. (1996), 'Culture, Ideology and strategic framing', in D. McAdam, J.D. McCarthy, and M.N. Zald, (eds) *Comparative Perspectives on Social Movements,* Cambridge: Cambridge University Press.

Index